Ilze Ruse
(Why) Do Neighbours Cooperate?

Ilze Ruse

(Why) Do Neighbours Cooperate?
Institutionalised Coalitions
and Bargaining Power
in EU Council Negotiations

Budrich UniPress Ltd.
Opladen • Berlin • Toronto 2013

All rights reserved. No part of this publication may be reproduced, stored in or introduced into a retrieval system, or transmitted, in any form, or by any means (electronic, mechanical, photocopying, recording or otherwise) without the prior written permission of Barbara Budrich Publishers. Any person who does any unauthorized act in relation to this publication may be liable to criminal prosecution and civil claims for damages.

You must not circulate this book in any other binding or cover and you must impose this same condition on any acquirer.

A CIP catalogue record for this book is available from
Die Deutsche Bibliothek (The German Library)

© 2013 by Budrich UniPress Ltd. Opladen , Berlin & Toronto
www.budrich-unipress.eu

ISBN 978-3-86388-029-3
eISBN 978-3-86388-184-9

Das Werk einschließlich aller seiner Teile ist urheberrechtlich geschützt. Jede Verwertung außerhalb der engen Grenzen des Urheberrechtsgesetzes ist ohne Zustimmung des Verlages unzulässig und strafbar. Das gilt insbesondere für Vervielfältigungen, Übersetzungen, Mikroverfilmungen und die Einspeicherung und Verarbeitung in elektronischen Systemen.

Die Deutsche Bibliothek – CIP-Einheitsaufnahme
Ein Titeldatensatz für die Publikation ist bei Der Deutschen Bibliothek erhältlich.

Budrich UniPress Ltd.
Stauffenbergstr. 7. D-51379 Leverkusen Opladen, Germany

86 Delma Drive. Toronto, ON M8W 4P6 Canada
www.budrich-unipress.eu

Jacket illustration by Bettina Lehfeldt, Kleinmachnow, Germany
Editing: Ute Reusch, Berlin, Germany
Druck : Books on Demand, Norderstedt
Printed in Europe

Abstract

Negotiations in the Council of the European Union do not only take place within formal decision-making structures. Member states strive to find allies and coordinate their positions prior to formal negotiation meetings. They either create *ad hoc* coalitions to pool voting power or cooperate within more durable institutionalised coalitions that traditionally exist on the basis of geographical proximity or among like-minded member states as task-specific coalitions on particular issues. Institutionalised coalitions give their members a bargaining advantage even if they cannot generate enough voting weight to achieve voting thresholds. The author argues that cooperation within institutionalised coalitions enhances the bargaining power of its participants through three mechanisms: the exchange of information, which counterbalances the asymmetries in information distribution in the pre-negotiation stage; the exchange of expertise that allows the member states to share resources and provide common lines of argument for their positions; and the "rhetorical action" that lends more strength to normative justifications. This argument differs from existing research that suggests that durable coalitions can influence the preferences of participating member states. The argument is tested by drawing on a study of the role of Nordic-Baltic and task-specific coalitions in negotiations on climate policy, the Stockholm Programme and the Baltic Sea Strategy. The evidence, largely gained through elite interviews, confirms the argument by showing that institutionalised coalitions provide their members with better information and expertise, and allow them to jointly frame arguments in favour of their positions, thus generating a bargaining advantage for them. The study also highlights the limitations of regional cooperation within the EU that stem from the heterogeneity of policy preferences.

Ilze Rūse took her Dr.phil in 2011 at the Centre of European Union Studies at Salzburg University. She is a docent at the Riga Graduate School of Law and teaches European Politics at the EuroCollege at University of Tartu. Prior to her academic career, Ilze Rūse dealt with EU issues on a practical level as a diplomat.

Acknowledgements

This book is a revised version of my doctoral dissertation completed at the Salzburg Centre of European Union Studies (SCEUS) at Salzburg University (2008–2011). Many institutions and individuals have contributed to this result; however, Prof. Andreas Dür (Salzburg University) deserves particular credit for supervising my doctoral thesis throughout the research process and for offering valuable comments prior to the publishing of this book. This publication also benefited from the advice of Prof. Peter Nedergaard (University of Copenhagen). Financial support for the doctoral research project was provided by the Salzburg Centre of European Union Studies, which is headed by Prof. Puntscher-Riekmann. Thanks to this research grant, I was able to carry out the empirical part of the research project in the Nordic and Baltic countries. I am grateful to all the interviewees who generously shared their experience in Stockholm, Helsinki, Denmark, Riga and Tallinn. I owe special thanks to Riga Graduate School of Law for the financial support to have this book published by *Barbara Budrich Publishers*.

Contents

Abstract 5
Acknowledgements 7
List of tables and figures 11
    Tables 11
    Figures 11
INTRODUCTION 13
CHAPTER 1 6

1.1	Bargaining power in EU negotiations...	6
1.1.1	Power determinants: structural, issue-specific and behavioural bargaining power	24
1.1.2	Power pooling through coalition-building: a view from the rational choice perspective	38

CHAPTER 2 43

2.1	Typology of coalitions in EU negotiations: ad hoc and institutionalised coalitions	43
2.1.1	Patterns of coalitions in Council negotiations	45
2.1.2	How stable are they?	50
2.2	Explaining the effects of institutionalised coalitions on bargaining power	52
2.2.1	On the notion of institutionalisation: shared goals, structures and interaction intensity	55
2.2.2	Explaining the effects of institutionalisation: a theoretical framework	59
2.3	Brining preferences in	70
2.4	Rational choice institutionalism and alternative theoretical explanations	79

CHAPTER 3 85

3.1	Institutionalised coalitions in the EU...	85
3.2	Territorially constituted coalitions...	87
3.2.1	The Benelux group	89
3.2.2	Nordic-Baltic cooperation: evaluating the regional potential	96
3.3	Task-specific coalitions: beyond the territorial framework	110
3.4	Do neighbours cooperate? Evidence from EU negotiations cases	120

CHAPTER 4 .... **123**
4.1   The Baltic Sea Strategy 123
4.2   EU negotiations on climate change 136
4.3   The Stockholm Programme 154

CONCLUSIONS **165**

REFERENCES **175**
    Policy documents 187
    Council documents 189
    Media and internet sources 190
    Speeches 194

ANNEX **195**
List of interviews 195

List of tables and figures

Tables

Table 1	Research on the determinants of bargaining power	24
Table 2:	Typology of coalitions according to stability and degree of institutionalisation	51
Table 3:	Research design	78
Table 4:	Explaining the distinction between institutionalised coalitions	81
Table 5:	A list of some task-specific coalitions in Council decision-making	107
Table 6:	A list of government input during the drafting of the Baltic Sea strategy by the Commission	114
Table 7:	Discussion agenda on the Baltic Sea strategy in the Council	116
Table 8:	Informal consultation work on the Baltic Sea Strategy	117
Table 9:	Agenda of the climate negotiations	131
Table 10:	Comparing the wording in the text of the proposal and the outcome	138

Figures

Figure 1:	Model of measuring bargaining power with A and B positioned on one side of SQ	37
Figure 2:	Model of measuring bargaining power with SQ positioned between A and B	37
Figure 3:	Zone of agreement	72
Figure 4:	Three-level cooperation	76
Figure 5:	Institutionalised territorial coalitions in the EU: NB6, V4, Benelux and Mediterranean	88
Figure 6:	Causality mechanism through which the degree of institutionalisation causes the variation in bargaining power	122
Figure 7:	The Baltic Sea region: NB6+2	123
Figure 8:	Effects of NB6+2 coordination on the bargaining outcome of the overall deal on the Baltic Sea Strategy	134
Figure 9:	The effects of the institutionalised task-specific coalition on the bargaining power regarding the emission targets of the EU internal negotiations on the climate change	149
Figure 10:	Effects of Quadro group cooperation on bargaining power	164

INTRODUCTION

In the run-up to EU enlargement in 2004, the Austrian government proposed developing a "Benelux-like alliance" for Central and Eastern Europe. The initiative, the brainchild of the Austrian Minister of Foreign Affairs, was aimed at establishing "a community of interests which would become an alliance in the EU" (EurActiv, 14 Feb. 2001). At the same time, evaluating the existing Benelux cooperation, a Dutch politician called the Benelux cooperation a "fossil from the 1940s" (in Jobse 2010:6). How can we explain this puzzle? What is the value added (if there is any) of cooperation within institutionalised coalitions in the context of EU decision-making? Can these formats be perceived as permanent coalitions and, if so, how do they exist? If we assume that along with the increasing tendencies towards transgovernmentalism (Wallace 2010:84) the significance of sub-groups in the EU decision-making is increasing, then what are the effects of institutionalised coalitions on bargaining power in EU negotiations?

Territorial alliances in the EU have been around since the six founding countries established the European Steel and Coal Community. The history of regional partnerships in the context of European integration dates back to 1958, with the Benelux cooperation and the creation of the German-French partnership. The dynamics of cooperation within sub-groups and the efficiency of coalitions have changed over time, depending on the increase of the number of EU member states, as well as on the geopolitical and regional changes. Scholars' views on the "rise or fall" of these country groupings differ. A recent study by Blavoukos and Pagoulatos (2011:576) demonstrates that the Mediterranean group is undergoing "erosion" compared to the period before enlargement, whereas Schild (2010:1371) acknowledges a further increasing potential of the German-French partnership to launch common political initiatives and contribute to the search for European compromises in situations of deadlock in Council negotiations. The latter has increased in significance in relation to driving the political decision-making on the Eurozone crisis and has been labelled the "Merkozy effect" (The Economist, 15 Oct. 2011). Similarly, research on the Visegrad group provides evidence that the Visegrad intergovernmental alliance is still active (Klemenčič 2011:1).

This book does not pose the question of whether or not territorial coalitions exist. It assumes that they do. The aim of this study is to evaluate the effects of their intergovernmental cooperation on bargaining power, thus answering the question "*why* do neighbours cooperate?"

In this book I generate the hypothesis that institutionalised coalitions give their members a bargaining advantage even if they cannot generate enough votes to achieve voting thresholds. My argument is that cooperation within institutionalised coalitions enhances the bargaining power of its participants through three mechanisms: the exchange of information, which counterbalances the asymmetries in information distribution in the pre-negotiation stage; the exchange of expertise that allows the member states to share resources and provide common lines of argument for their positions; and the "rhetorical action" that lends more strength to normative justifications. The argument is tested empirically by focusing on a study of the role of Nordic-Baltic and task-specific coalitions in negotiations on climate policy, the Stockholm Programme and the Baltic Sea Strategy.

Policy decisions in the EU are the outcomes of intensive processes of negotiation and bargaining. Negotiations in the EU are typically multilateral and comprise a complex set of actors (Elgström and Jönsson 2004). In the Council alone, agreement has to be reached among 27 actors, with each of the 27 member states entering negotiations with different policy preferences. The heterogeneity of the policy preferences across the EU has, in particular, increased since enlargement. With a larger number of negotiation participants and greater differences in their socio-economic preferences, it has become more difficult to agree on common EU policies (Majone 2009:200, Thomson 2011:4). The EU as a political process can exist and undergo further integration if a "certain quality and quantity of outcomes are assured" (Meerts and Cede 2004:229). Despite controversies among the member states, they still manage to agree on common policies and drive forward the EU integration process.

It is widely acknowledged that informal interaction, consultation and intergovernmental coordination have increasingly become part of the negotiation process in the EU in general and among the member states in the EU Council of Ministers ("Council") in particular. One could compare the decision-making process to an iceberg, with the majority of interaction taking place below the surface (informal negotiations) and a considerably smaller visible share (formal negotiations) above the surface. Pre-agreement beyond the formal decision-making scope is facilitated by informal cooperation prior to meetings (Meerts and Cede 2004), with the aim of these interactions being to informally exchange views before formal negotiations begin, thus increasing the bargaining power of participants through joint action. The agreements reached at the pre-negotiation stage can create a common understanding among parties that serves as the basis for final agreement in the formal negotiation stage (Stein 1989, Blavoukos and Pagoulatos 2008). The question that is thus of key importance to negotiation outcomes is "Who cooperates with whom, and why?" We cannot see the full picture by looking only at formal decision-making, as "formal rules do not necessarily reflect the actual distribution of power in a political system accurately" (Thomson 2011:9).

Coalition-building in terms of coordinated action by reaching jointly agreed goals has been widely acknowledged by the existing scholarship as strategic behaviour of power pooling (Elgström *et al.* 2001). One can even say that coalitional behaviour is an inevitable part of EU decision-making (Klemenčič 2005). When voting by unanimity, each actor has the formal power to block a decision by veto. Yet, only 30 per cent of all Council decisions are taken by applying the unanimity voting rule (Wallace *et al.* 2010:95). Member states therefore have to consider various strategies to increase their bargaining power under the qualified majority voting (QMV) rule, where they can be easily overruled (Cede 2004:37). By selecting *ad hoc* peers, member states aim to achieve blocking minorities or winning majorities by aggregating votes (Winkler 1998, Hosli 1999, Reynaud *et al.* 2008, Hosli *et al.* 2009). Such coalitions are short-term cooperation arrangements with a low degree of institutionalisation. According to the choice of peers, *ad hoc* coalitions are "coincidental". Coalition structures tend to be complex and unpredictable. These *ad hoc* coalitions are dissolved after agreement is reached on the dossier.

Apart from *ad hoc* coalitions, scholars distinguish more consistent alignments of actors or "solid coalitions" (Blavoukos and Pagoulatos 2011:570) with a considerable degree of institutionalisation measured in terms of established cooperation structure, interaction frequency, durability and advanced internal coordination. Under the increased application of the QMV rule and following enlargement, "the functional demand for more stable coalitions" has increased (Naurin 2008:12). Such more persistent coalitions are created with the intention of solving joint problems and achieving cooperative gains (Powell 1999:219) and may operate either on the basis of common geographical proximity, or they interact repeatedly, striving to attain common preferences regarding the negotiation outcomes on particular policy issues.[1] More durable inter-governmental territorial cooperation[2] has been labelled in the literature as country "partnerships", "alignments", "blocs", "alliances" or "groupings" (Hosli 1999; Panke 2008, Thomson 2009, Tallberg 2010a, Blavoukos and Pagoulatos 2011, Klemenčič 2011).

Though the existing literature acknowledges the existence of more persistent coalitions in the Council, the effects of such institutionalised coalitions on the bargaining power of its members are largely unexplored. The issue of power-pooling through institutionalised cooperation during the preparatory phase of negotiations is virtually missing from explanations of bargaining power determinants. Drawing on coalition theory, one could assume that the member states strive to aggregate their voting power in order to achieve the blocking minority by building coalitions (Winkler 1998, Hosli *et*

---

1 This study labels preference proximity-based, persistent institutionalised coalitions as "task-specific coalitions" (see 3.3.).
2 The author uses the term "institutionalised coalition", emphasising governments' deliberate choice to engage in structured cooperative action with stable peers. The focus is thus on the process at the pre-negotiation stage, not the voting outcome in the end-game.

al. 2009). This explanation, however, cannot be applied to justify the formation of institutionalised (e.g. territorially constituted) coalitions, since their aggregated votes are often insufficient to achieve the blocking threshold.

How can we then explain the existence of institutionalised coalitions in Council negotiations? Fifty years after the establishment of the Benelux cooperation, ministers and prime ministers continue to organise the "Benelux breakfast" before European Council meetings and there is no evidence that the alliance is disappearing. One might expect institutions to be established because member states strive to overcome collective action problems (Stacey and Rittberger 2003:864), to reduce the transaction costs of bargaining (Tallberg 2010b:635) or to deal with information uncertainty (Moravcsik 1997:522). If these meetings did not serve the common beneficiary goal of fulfilling the expected function, the practice of consulting and exchanging views prior to EU meetings would be abolished. What is the value added of territorial institutionalised coalitions? Naurin and Wallace (2008:8) have said that "geography is obviously only a proxy for some underlying concept". By drawing on the empirical analysis of territorially constituted coalitions, this book tackles the following question: To what extent and under what conditions can the institutionalised coalitions that do not make up a blocking minority enhance member states' bargaining power?

This study argues that the institutional conditions facilitate effective coordination within "informal networks" (Börzel 2010:194). In contrast to *ad hoc* arrangements, the institutionalised coalitions can take advantage of the established inter-action framework and operate within an environment of repeated interaction that enables more informal exchange in the pre-negotiation stage. Further, it is argued that expertise-pooling in institutionalised coalitions gives more strength to normative justifications that may lead to normative entrapment of other member states outside the group (Schimmelfennig 2001, Grobe 2010).

By developing this argument, the book contributes to the existing literature in several ways. First, by approaching the coalitions as a process, it reveals additional aspects of the persistent coalition patterns that have often been neglected by scholars focusing on voting outcomes (Hosli 1996, Winkler 1998). Second, the approach differs from that which explains persistent coalitions using constructivist theoretical tools. The author assumes that institutionalised coalitions, even the territorial ones, are perceived by their members as strategic power-pooling instruments. Drawing on rational choice explanations, the study explains how member states solve the shortcomings and collective problems (Stacey and Rittberger 2003:864) of asymmetries in information distribution at the pre-negotiation stage and how they use the institutional conditions for power-pooling purposes in Council negotiations.

In assessing the effects on the bargaining outcome of inter-state cooperation in the pre-negotiations stage, the study takes account of policy preferences, stressing their impact on the member states' coalition behaviour. Viewing member states' policy preferences as the background variables, the findings imply that coalitions in the EU, even the highly institutionalised ones, do not change member states' preferences.

CHAPTER 1

1.1 Bargaining power in EU negotiations

Harold Lasswell became famous not only for his contribution to political science in the United States but also for the following definition of politics: "Politics is who gets what, where, and how." His definition captures the notion of power and the means by which the different actors distribute the gains within a political system. We can rightly apply this interpretation of "politics" to EU decision-making, where the issue of the redistributive conflict forms the core of policy-making. With a large number of decision-makers and uneven distribution of power based on population size and economic strength, disagreement in Council negotiations is part of day-to-day business. Yet, despite the controversies, the member states "usually find ways of resolving their disagreements" (Thomson 2011:4). This chapter focuses on bargaining power in the EU Council. It starts by introducing the power definition, explaining the concept of bargaining power, and goes on to outline different power determinants that the member states have at their disposal when negotiating on legislative proposals. Finally, the chapter takes a closer look at power-pooling through coalition-building, and links the dependent and independent variables of this study.

What does bargaining mean in the context of EU decision-making? In order to answer this question it is useful to first take a closer look at the legislative process within the EU. Proposals, once drafted by the Commission, are passed for decision-making to the legislative institutions of the EU, i.e. the Council of Ministers and the European Parliament. Depending on the policy area, decisions are taken by the legislators either as part of the ordinary legislative procedure (formerly "co-decision"), or by special legislative procedure. The main legislative body is the Council, which comprises the member states' governments. Being a complex body, the Council may operate on the expert level in Council working groups, on the Permanent Representative Committee (COREPER) level, i.e. involving senior diplomats, or among national ministers representing the relevant policy area. Accordingly, the Council is divided into Council configurations, for example Agriculture, Environment, Foreign Affairs, etc. When member states negotiate on different legislative proposals, they meet within different Council formats. Proposals may be passed up and down the structural hierarchy of the Council until conflicts are resolved and agreement is reached. In most policy areas the Council agrees by qualified majority voting (QMV). Exceptions are made for highly sensitive policy areas where unanimity is still required. However, practitioners and scholars point out that in practice agreement is reached by consensus (Merts and Cede 2004, Hayes-Renshaw and Wallace 2006). It should be noted that the politically salient legislative proposals and political initiatives are adopted by the European Council, which is a separate forum of the heads of states, and usually decides by unanimity. When highly controversial issues cannot be resolved on the level of the Council of Ministers, they are forwarded to the European Council for agreement on the highest political level.

This brief overview of the operation of the Council of Ministers and the European Council shows that the Council is a "permanent negotiation institute" or a "negotiation marathon" (in Jönsson and Elgström 2004:2). However, EU negotiations differ from multilateral negotiations in international organisations because of the hybrid structure of the EU itself. Since the EU is not an international organisation but a partnership of sovereign member states (that have partly authorised the supranational institutions, e.g. the Commission to propose laws and to monitor their transposition into national law), EU negotiations are "institutionalised" in terms of actors, and include the elements of "hard bargaining" in terms of conflict dimensions. The two concepts of "negotiation" and "bargaining" in the EU are often merged, showing that in practice they are often difficult to separate.

According to the definition of negotiation, a negotiation is a sequence of actions in which two or more parties address demands, arguments, exchange offers, make concessions, raise threats or otherwise influence each other to reach an agreement (Filzmoser and Vetschera 2008:421, Odell 2010:620). The definition refers to two important determinants, namely – *time*, emphasising the sequence of negotiation steps, and *actors*, focusing on different choices that negotiation parties have at their disposal to achieve their goals. Strictly speaking, "negotiation" is understood to be a problem-solving process in which the negotiation parties "are left to themselves to combine their conflicting points of view into a single decision" (Zartman 1977:622). By contrast, bargaining is characterised as comprising more conflicting elements and includes different power-pooling strategies, which result in some parties gaining better outcomes than others. Bargaining situations often contain an "exchange of verbal or non-verbal communication" and are compared to "bazaar-like haggling" (Jönsson and Elgström 2004:3). What makes the situation more complex is the fact that apart from formal bargaining, which dominates negotiations in the EU Council, informal bargaining at the pre-negotiation stage has gained increasing importance. Interestingly, a recent study by Thomson (2011:166) proves empirically that "the process through which inputs are transformed into outputs is defined by informal bargaining rather than formal decision-making procedures." Moreover, on account of its structure the decision-making hierarchy means that the negotiation process will involve a large number of government officials who try to reach agreement on the working group or COREPER level. The controversial issues do not come as a "surprise" for the ministers. "Only legislation that has been 'pre-cooked' successfully at previous bargaining states enters the arena of the ministers" (Veen 2011:21).

Negotiation theory suggests that international negotiations go through a series of phases: the pre-negotiation phase, the formal negotiation phase and the post-negotiation phase (Zartman and Berman 1982). Each of the phases has an important role in determining the outcome and they are strictly interlinked. Bearce *et al.* 2009 depict the negotiation process as a continuum along the time axis, where t_0 = the pre-negotiation phase, t_1 = the negotiation and bargaining phase and t_2 = the enforcement phase. Drawing on this three-step process, they argue that at t_0 actors must first recognise the problem and arrive at a common understanding of the possible solutions before they proceed to negotiations. Similarly, Stein (1989:232) expresses the importance of the pre-negotiation phase in the following way: "(the) pre-negotiation process is about 'getting to the table'. It is important because it defines the boundaries, shapes agenda, and affects the outcome of the negotiations". During the pre-negotiation phase the negotiation parties identify the problems to be addressed (Meunier 2000:112), the governments "sketch out their negotiation positions" (Dür and Mateo 2004:5) against the background of their socio-economic preferences, explore the costs and benefits of a possible negotiation outcome and gauge whether they will be able to reach their preferred outcome unilaterally. Further, they undergo an investigation process that permits them to sound out other parties (Odell 2010) and to evaluate their relationships (Stein 1989:232). Coalition-building is a consequent step when the governments actively cooperate with the selected peers (Saam and Sumpter 2009:362).

According to Schiff (2007:388), the task of the pre-negotiation stage is to trigger perceptions of the parties about the possible outcome of negotiations. In international negotiations, this preparatory process may last from some days to several months (Zartman and Berman 1982); in the context of EU decision-making, the pre-negotiation phase may overlap with the period in which a legislative proposal is prepared and submitted to the legislative bodies, for instance the Council and the Parliament, for adoption. When submitted to the Council, the proposal undergoes scrutiny by the member states; the process that is often preceded by informal consultation activities amongst member states. It is *then* that the real informal bargaining process starts, though this is not visible from the outside. In EU negotiations, the negotiation outcome is not revealed to the general public until the final stage of the negotiation process is reached, i.e. through voting. Voting results are documented in the Monthly Summary of Council Acts and are available to the public; the rest of the negotiation process, including the pre-negotiation phase, remains strictly confidential and "invisible" to an external observer. It is acknowledged that the voting records do not necessarily illustrate governments' real policy preferences. By voting "against", governments may "signal" to their constituencies (Heisenberg 2005:73). Likewise, there may be a series of underlying political and practical considerations why governments, for instance, make concessions instead of voting against the proposal. Most frequently such a shift in a government's position is related to normative concerns or reputation precautions. Thus, the government's behaviour at the voting stage may not be directly continued at the bargaining stage.

Veen (2011:117) suggests that the real power games take place during the bargaining stage. Accordingly, the strategies governments choose in EU decision-making are outlined at the outset of the proposal and exposed during the bargaining stage. One might expect more cooperative bargaining during the pre-negotiation phase. Whether a member state opts for hard bargaining tactics may depend on its size, i.e. large member states chose harder bargaining strategies than smaller ones (Dür and Mateo 2010a:565). Furthermore, depending on the preference intensity and importance governments attribute to the issue, they may opt for "hard bargaining" tactics to pursue their self-interest. Research by Moravcsik (1997) builds upon the intergovernmental tradition of EU decision-making and emphasises the role of governmental preferences. Moravcsik links the theory of preference formation by domestic constituencies to a theory of interstate bargaining. For liberal intergovernmentalists the member states' success in EU decision-making largely depends on their power based on size. According to a study on the Amsterdam Treaty negotiations, large member states are more powerful (Moravcsik and Nikolaïdis 1999). However, we should not overestimate size advantage and address also other power resources. What are the main power determinants that predict "who gets what"? How is bargaining power distributed across the EU?

In EU decision-making the outcome that each country achieves in negotiations is often linked to the country's influence, bargaining power or even to luck. Indeed, the latter may sound paradoxical but is a feasible option both practically and theoretically. In his study "Is it Better to be Powerful or Lucky?" Brian Barry (1980:339) argues that "we can say that for any member [...] the outcome will correspond to his preferences some proportion of the time if he does nothing. [...] Call the proportion of adventitious success his luck". In practice that would mean that in the absence of intervention on the part of actors, the negotiation outcome will happen to be similar to a member state's "policy demand" (Thomson 2011:18). Yet, the bulk of the literature that evaluates negotiation outcomes assumes that it is not luck but a result of governments' bargaining power that matters when it comes to moving the negotiation outcome closer to actors' preferences (Clark et al. 2000, Slapin 2006, Tallberg 2008, Bailer 2010). It is more likely that governments influence the outcome in one or other way, rather than just ensuring that it coincides with a member state's policy demand. In spite of the central significance of the bargaining power concept for political science in general and for EU decision-making in particular, knowledge of the mechanisms of exerting power is still quite limited.

The difficulties surrounding the concept of power lie in its "elusive" nature (Keohane 1989:9) and, consequently, in defining and measuring it. Because no agreement can be reached on terminology, Baldwin (1989:2) characterises the analysis of power as "intellectual chaos". While numerous attempts have been made to pinpoint the nature of "power" and its sources, the most basic interpretation is that power is the ability to control one's environment and to shape the behaviour and conduct of others within that environment. In the EU context power can be seen as (1) affecting others' behaviour in decision-making, i.e. 'A' getting 'B' to do something that 'B' would not otherwise do; (2) the ability to prevent things from happening, for example "non-decisions"; and (3) control over the political agenda. The first dimension applies to the concept of power by using the theoretical tools of international relations (IR), where power is most often approached as the ability to control others. This reasoning is captured by Dahl's (1961:9) definition: "'A' has power over 'B' to the extent that he can get 'B' to do something that 'B' would not otherwise do".

The problem in applying Dahl's definition in a negotiation environment is twofold: Firstly, it does not provide for multilateral relationships as a usual condition of international negotiations; secondly, it does not "distinguish clearly enough between the outcome and process which leads to it" (Clark *et al.* 2000:71). The problem with multilateral relationships has been explained by Baldwin (1989:146), who argues that in a political system interaction can be equated with interdependence. Since interdependence may be distributed asymmetrically, power, accordingly, derives from these patterns of asymmetrical interdependence. "The actors continually alternate the roles of power holder and power subject in the total course of their interaction" (ibid.). This has several practical effects, such as reciprocity or incentives for a cooperative exchange.

Negotiation theorists who deal with power concepts in the relational sense approach power in international negotiations in the same way as within any other international interaction (Habeeb 1988). By focusing on the causal relation that the power variable brings to the negotiation environment, Habeeb (1988:10) argues that all political phenomena in negotiations can be boiled down to three basic types: keeping power, increasing power and/or demonstrating power. All three dimensions are a part of EU decision-making and will be addressed in the following sections.

The literature on EU decision-making predominantly draws on Weber's definition of power. This is also the point of departure for this study. In the Weberian tradition power is seen as the ability to overcome the resistance of others (Bailer 2003, Schneider *et al.* 2010). Hindes (in Schneider *et al.* 2010) further elaborated on Weber's power concept and defines power as the "quantitative capacity that may be put to work for a variety of purposes". To this end, power is defined as an ability or capacity that is better suited to explaining the complex relationships of multilateral interactions. The strength of the latter definition of power, when it comes to the negotiation environment, lies in focusing on the determinants of the outcomes not on the outcome itself, i.e. the factors that determine the ability of one player to get another player to alter their behaviour (Clark *et al.* 2000). Moreover, Weber's definition also "implies that the focus of power is on influencing social or collective actions" (Thomson 2011:167). Baldwin (1989:112) has rightly pointed out that it is difficult to treat power as an "asymmetrical human relationship". This is particularly important in the context of Council negotiations, when power is approached in terms of exchange.

In research on EU decision-making power is often approached from an inter-institutional perspective by comparing the influence of the Commission, the Council and the European Parliament. When dealt within the Council, the power concept is most often addressed in terms of the bargaining power of an individual actor. To this end, Tallberg (2008:687) provides a definition of bargaining power as the capacity of a member state to achieve a distributional outcome that as closely as possible reflects the preferences of the member state. This approach most accurately fits the meaning of bargaining power as used in this study, because it focuses on the ability of a member state to achieve a specific outcome. It also specifies the deliberate action of actors in striving to achieve their ideal points, thus excluding the possible effect of "luck" on the congruence between outcomes and preferred preferences (Thomson 2011:203). Drawing on the definition of bargaining power, the different determinants of bargaining power will be introduced in the next section and the means by which theses determinants can be applied to EU decision-making will be outlined.

1.1.1 Power determinants: structural, issue-specific and behavioural bargaining power

Negotiations take place within the context of the distribution of power as dictated by states' assets, for example, population, financial capacity, economic strength, government capacity, military forces. This group of power determinants indicate the structural power. Apart from the aforementioned power resources, the literature on bargaining power suggests that power determinants should be extended beyond the structural power to include behavioural aspects such as skills, information asymmetries, coalition-building, communication networking (Clark *et al.* 2000, Naurin and Lindahl 2007,

Bailer 2010), as well as issue-related power determinants (Bal 2004, Merts and Cede 2004). Discussion of which determinants should be considered as prevailing has contributed to the development of three strands in the literature in relation to bargaining power.

Based on various interpretations of power determinants, the existing scholarship on power can roughly be divided into three groups: (1) studies focusing on the resources of structural power; (2) studies exploring issue-specific power; and (3) research on behavioural power. The first group focuses on the influence of large compared to small member states, voting weight and the impact of economic and market strength on bargaining outcome.

The structural determinants of bargaining power are often associated with resources (Goldmann and Sjöstedt 1979, Keohane 1989, Hopmann 1996, Tallberg 2008). "Power resources are defined as means by which one actor can influence the behaviour of other actors" (Baldwin 1989:207). Bailer (2010:744) defines these resources as "state related", and, while easy to measure, they are difficult to change. Furthermore, structural determinants are normally perceived as "given" and cannot be deliberately altered by a member state. That does not, however, mean that a structural advantage is always translated into a bargaining advantage. As Tallberg (2008:690) illustrates in his study on bargaining power in the Council, Italy is a large member state in terms of structural power although it has not fully managed to become an influential player in Council bargaining.

In sum, possession of power resources gives a country the potential for aggregate structural power. In other words, aggregate structural power comprises the total of all structural power resources. Introducing his concept of aggregate structural power, Habeeb (1988:27) distinguishes between several sub-categories: economic, military and demographic power resources. When applied to EU decision-making, this list can be adjusted. Military resources tend to be less valid in the context of the Council, whereas aggregate structural power should include the stability of the political system and administrative capacity (Tallberg 2008:689).

Economic strength is considered as a power resource according to the position in market and within international economic networks (Bailer 2010:745). There is a direct link between economic system and underlying preferences, as acknowledged by Moravcsik (1997). According to his argument the preferences of national governments in the process of European integration have mainly reflected the concrete economic interests of the member states (Moravcsik and Schimmelfennig 2009:70). If that is true, economic situation largely determines negotiation parties' power. This assumption is also supported by the findings of Tallberg (2008:689) that illustrate that "GDP is among the most important factors explaining the bargaining power of the EU member states".

Bailer (2003) shows that economic power variables can explain the positioning of member states; indeed, two main factors influence their positions in negotiations: economic interdependence (Keohane and Nye 1998) and domestic factors (Moravcsik 1993). The link between structural variables, i.e. economic resources and positions, clearly appears in liberal intergovernmentalism theory: according to the three levels of EU decision making, preference formation, inter-state bargaining and institutional delegation, "state preferences are based on economic interests" (Moravcsik 2010:8). On some issues this correlation is particularly strong. For example, in EU budget negotiations a country's economic power is an important asset (Schneider 2011:15). It is worth noting that economic resources are easier to convert into another resource than political power (Baldwin 1989:138). Member states' economic strength is a well-known and quite a stable indicator, hence knowledge of a country's economic resources creates power perceptions concerning who is more powerful. Wolfe and McGinn (2005:17) demonstrated, from a social psychology perspective, that structural variables help to predict outcomes in advance.

When referred to structural power, one most naturally links it to size, which has, arguably, received the most attention in explanations of bargaining power. Several studies dealing with EU negotiations find a linear relationship between size and negotiation success (Moravcsik 1998, Golub 1999, Arregui and Thomson 2009). In their explicit study of the negotiations prior to the adoption of the Treaty of Amsterdam, Moravcik and Nikolaïdis (1999) examine the preferences of large states and find good support for the structural power hypothesis. Analysing the negotiating positions of France, Germany and the UK at the Intergovernmental Conference (IGC) on the Treaty of Amsterdam negotiations in the field of migration policy, social and employment policies and the Common Foreign and Security Policy (CFSP), they argue that the preferences of large states prevail in the outcomes of the negotiations. Yet, there are other studies on the Treaty of Amsterdam negotiations that do not observe the effects of size and economic strength on the outcomes (Slapin 2006:51). Furthermore, several scholars argue that small states may counterbalance their structural disadvantages. In other words, "weak states do not always suffer" (Tallberg 2007:17). Suggested strategies include: exerting influence via arguing (Risse 2000, Novak 2010, Grobe 2010), the use of intergovernmental coordination (Panke 2010) or influence through charismatic political leaders (Tallberg 2008). Some studies find empirical evidence to suggest that larger member states are often outvoted by small ones (Mattila and Lane 2001, Arregui 2008). This should not be considered as an anomaly but rather as the deliberate use of alternative means of gaining bargaining power. For instance, Schure and Verdun (2008:460) argue that small states rely on help from the Commission. Accordingly, small states prefer to adopt open-ended legislation, i.e. incomplete contracts, in which discretion is delegated to the Commission. A recent study by Schneider (2011:6) hypothesises that weak states gain more leverage in extraordinary bargaining situations. Drawing on the examples of EU enlargement, the study demonstrates that, whereas "routine bargaining" is usually unfavourable for economically weak states, they can "exploit the extraordinary institutional environment during enlargement to increase their own benefits" (ibid.).

In addition to the power that is attributed to the large member states in EU decision-making, the involvement of supranational actors plays a decisive role (Cini 2011). The European Commission, which sets the annual and multi-annual political agenda and has the power of initiative, is a supranational body that the member states have to take into consideration. Holding a position that is close to the Commission's proposal can indicate that a member state has been able to influence the agenda (Bailer 2003:5), which certainly gives a bargaining advantage. Extending the ordinary legislative procedure (formerly the co-decision procedure) to the broad scope of policy areas after the adoption of the Lisbon Treaty implies an increase in inter-institutional power for the European Parliament. The Council can approve the Commission's legislative proposal only with the agreement of the European Parliament. As regards dossiers to which the European Parliament gives its consent, it has to give its opinion and has formal rights to object. The aforementioned procedural provisions (defined in the treaties) give the EU institutions formal institutional power. Actors in the legislative system, including the EU Council, have to interact with each other if they want to apply their power resources strategically. Moreover, based on the European Parliament's strong position in relation to the Council and Commission, the member states "attribute at least equal power to the Commission and European Parliament as the Council" (Thomson 2011:171).

This explains the constant informal consultation process that takes place between the member states and the EU institutions. The rational choice approach assumes that political actors are "acting purposefully" and that they do not possess "perfect information" about other actors' preferences (Thomson 2011:14). Since information gives leverage, the rational member states exchange information with the Commission about their preferred outcomes and interact with the European Parliament in order to find out about the political groups' preferences.

The proposition that bargaining power is based on member states' size reflects underlying indicators, such as geography, territory and demography. Population is the most common indicator of size and is officially recognised in evaluating the distribution of power in the EU (Dür and Mateo 2010a:565). Population rate gives the member states influence in terms of their actual power because the demographic criterion serves to calculate votes in QMV systems. The current QMV voting system is based on the provisions agreed in the Treaty of Nice. The number of votes was adjusted following the enlargement of 2004 and 2007 and aimed to distribute votes proportionally across the 27 member states. Under the current system, for a proposal to be passed it requires 255 votes out of the total of 345. Further conditions are the number of the member states and the share of the total population they represent. Some recent studies, however, demonstrate that the relationship between population, size and the number of votes in the QMV system is not linear. Arguing in favour of less populous states, Schneider (2011:5) notes that some small states are "over-represented" according to their votes in relation to population share. The leverage of countries like Malta, Cyprus and Luxemburg depends on the scarcity of these over-represented states. Similarly, Widgrén (2009) argues that the current distribution of votes favours some member states because the calculation of votes does not accurately reflect population differences. Widgrén's study demonstrates that the large states, for example Germany and France, have fifteen times the size of population than Finland, yet, under the provisions of the Treaty of Nice, large states have only three to four times more votes. Indeed, the six largest EU member states: Germany, France, the UK, Italy, Spain and Poland have the largest number of votes in the QMV system in the Council (29 votes for Germany, France, the UK and Italy and 27 votes for Spain and Poland). This observation explains Polish and Spanish efforts during negotiations on the Lisbon Treaty to maintain their favourable proportion of power on the basis of population. Both being medium-size countries, they have enjoyed 27 votes according to the current system, compared to Germany with double the population number and 29 votes.

Under the Treaty of Lisbon the voting system will change, introducing a double majority system. The current voting rules are in force until 31 October 2014, with a possibility of further transitional rules until 31 March 2017. According to new voting provisions as defined in Art. 16(4) of the Treaty of the Functioning of the European Union (TFEU), a decision is passed when "at least 55 per cent of members of the Council, comprising at least 15 of them and representing member states comprising at least 65 per cent of population of Union" (Craig 2010:43). Some studies have modelled the possible effects of voting changes and predicted the increased power of large states under the new voting system (Plechanonova 2008:10). Yet, a recent study by Thomson (2011:161) does not foresee any major changes in terms of decision outcome.

Comprehensive and systematic research has been undertaken on the voting power issue (Bailer 2010:747) and it can be roughly classified into three groups: literature on factors that influence voting behaviour; attempts to evaluate voting rules according to specific criteria, i.e. population size; and voting power as leverage in negotiations (Nedergaard 2007:696). The point of departure for scholars working on this issue is that power stems from the voting rule (Winkler 1998, Roozendaal et al. 2008, Bailer 2003, 2010). Most studies that focus on bargaining power by measuring voting power, approach it through the theoretical lens of realism. According to realist accounts, bargaining power in the Council is derived preliminary from aggregate structural power resources. Aggregate power comprises the overall capacities of a state or actor and includes different aspects of structural power. Aggregate resources can be added up and seen as a national "power score" of the negotiation actor (Tallberg 2008:689), with governments usually strategically selecting the most appropriate available power resources in order to maximise their utility (Hopmann 1996). Differences in aggregate structural power certainly matter because of uneven power distribution and, hence, power asymmetries (Clark et al. 2000, Schure and Verdun 2008). Aggregate power resources serve as the foundation for negotiation tactics. Using Council data from 1994 to 2002, Heisenberg (2005:66) finds that the propensity to vote against or to abstain is correlated with size and aggregate power. Studying negotiations on the EU's Financial Perspective, Dür and Mateo (2010a:565) found that countries with more power resources relied more on hard bargaining tactics. Tallberg (2008:689) provides explanations for the dominance of large member states in Council negotiations. He argues that the superior position of states with more structural power can be explained by the credibility of their threats and promises. He also acknowledges the importance of the stability of the political system as one of the components of aggregate power. This possibly explains the above-mentioned paradox in the case of Italy, which, despite its structural power weight, is not able to fully exert influence in Council negotiations.

It would, however, be oversimplifying to presume that aggregate structural power determines the outcome of negotiations. This would lead to assumptions that the negotiation environment in the Council is dominated by threats and promises that are exerted on the weaker negotiation parties. Wagner (1988:462) warned that "asymmetric economic interdependence does not imply that one bargainer will be able to exercise political influence on another". By drawing on an empirical case of relations between oil-importing and oil-exporting countries, his argument draws on political concessions, unexploited bargaining gains and issue linkages as factors that are *complementary* to the purely structural view of power resources and economic interdependence. He illustrates that through their market power alone the Arab states would not be as influential as they are in their dialogue with the United States. The above-mentioned study indicates that aggregate structural power has its limitations in explaining the outcomes of international negotiations (Clark et al. 2000) because it is far from clear how different power determinants are interrelated (Goldmann 1979) and because it says nothing about the interaction between the actors themselves (Habeeb 1988:25). In line with this reasoning, contrary to the conventional knowledge of power distribution effects, Slapin (2006:72) has found that large member states do not possess bargaining advantage only because of their size. He claims that "size is neither necessary nor a sufficient condition of power". There is an additional aspect in regard to aggregate power distribution that has to be taken into consideration when evaluating the outcomes. Aggregate structural power includes available and potential power resources. Baldwin (1989:139) calls the latter "a paradox of unrealized power" or "would-be power". This means that power is applied through its realisation process. As indicated in Weber's definition, power is an attribute not something that is always put into effect (in Thomson 2011:168). Thus, to be powerful an actor has to decide to use its power resources. If that decision is not taken, one can only should of potential power. Potential power implies non-realised power that negotiation actors do not actively put into effect. Actors may not even be aware of their power resources or their real interests (Lukes 1974) and, thus, become objects that can be manipulated by others.

The aforementioned limitations in characterising power determinants show that aggregate structural power can be useful in providing an "overall picture" of an actor's place in the system, but it is less suitable for analysing the role of power in international negotiations. However, when focusing on aggregate power alone, a whole list of other significant power determinants can easily be overlooked. It would be wise to follow Habeeb's (1988:29) suggestion that aggregate structural power should be regarded as a *foundation* for behavioural power. His argument refers to the inter-relation between different power resources, i.e. structural power may be "translated" into behavioural power in international negotiations. These aspects are discussed further in this chapter.

Another limitation to the application of aggregate structural power relates to bargaining outcomes on specific issues (Panke 2010, Bailer 2010, Odell 2010). For example, aggregate power hypotheses fail to explain situations in which member states with structural disadvantages still prevail in negotiations. Alternative and complementary tools for dealing with negotiation situations can, therefore, be provided by relying on explanations of issue-specific power. Issue-specific power deals with states' positions in relation to another state's bargaining positions on a specific issue (Tallberg 2008). Two aspects are important in this regard: (1) the nature of the issue, and (2) domestic constraints. The nature of the issue has been addressed by Habeeb (1988), Tallberg (2008) and Bailer (2004), who demonstrates that bargaining power depends on the commitment of a state, its stake in the issue and its willingness to spend resources. Issues can by their very nature be inherently fixed-sum or can have integrative potential (Odell 2010:622). Fixed-sum issues imply a higher conflict potential because the gains are difficult to distribute without one of the parties taking the loser's position. A typical fixed-sum negotiation situation would be EU negotiations on the multiannual financial framework in which the member states attempt to agree on sharing a fixed amount of funding. Accordingly, fixed-sum issues would provoke more distributive bargaining strategies (McKibben 2010). By contrast, those issues that by nature have integrative potential would imply more cooperative bargaining tactics because negotiation actors opt for integrative bargaining strategies. Bargaining power may also be attributed to those countries with sceptical national parliaments (Hug and König 2002).

In Council negotiations member states may take advantage of the nature of particular issues and generate issue-specific power. It is important to point out that issue-specific power is not directly related to the size of the member state. Small states may have additional leverage in some dossiers because they "specialise" in particular issues. For instance, despite its size, Luxembourg is often perceived as a powerful player in regard to monetary policy issues. In contrast, large states may have restricted influence on some particular issues, as Tallberg (2008:693) demonstrates in regard to Germany's influence within the Common Foreign and Security Policy (CFSP). Specialisation on particular issues or "prioritisation of issues" is one of the small states' strategies in power-counterbalancing (Panke 2010). Practical observations regarding member states' power strategies in the Council show that Luxembourg, one of the least populous states of the EU, applies a "pick-and-choose" approach, focusing on prioritised issues and that it "will attend working group only when 'interesting dossiers' are on agenda" (Bal 2004:137).

Secondly, issue-specific power may stem from domestic constraints. Scholars dealing with issue-specific power often draw on the theoretical model of Putnam in explaining these effects. Putnam (1988:432) triggered a scholarly debate on the so-called two-level game theory, which originally draws on Thomas Schelling's idea of the "paradox of weakness". Schelling (1960) commented on issue-specific power in terms of domestic constraints, arguing that negotiation actors can use domestic constraints to their advantage at the international negotiation table. Schelling addresses the paradoxical idea that bargaining strength can derive from a *position of weakness*. Nevertheless, this is plausible only under certain conditions. According to his model, the strategic use of information plays an important role. In the bargaining situation, actors do not know each other's reservation price, allowing for the possibility for manipulation (Schelling 1960). Putnam's two-level game elaborates on Schelling's theory by emphasising the strategic interaction between the domestic and international levels during international negotiations. At the national level, domestic groups pursue their interests by pressuring governments to adopt favourable policies; on the international level state representatives negotiate and interact with their foreign counterparts in an attempt to maximise their ability to satisfy domestic pressures while minimising the adverse consequences of foreign developments. Putnam's two-level game provides that the agreement lies within each actor's "win set", i.e. within alternatives that each actor prefers to a "no-agreement outcome". Thus domestic politics indirectly affects the "odds of agreement" and the distribution of gain in an international agreement (Odell 2010:626).

The implications of "two-level games" are largely acknowledged by scholars analysing bargaining power in the EU (Clark *et al.* 2000, Bailer 2003, 2010, Schneider *et al.* 2010). Bargaining power can stem either from domestic ratification constraints or the role of domestic actors, for example social partners, stakeholders or federal governance structures (Bailer 2010). A study on EU trade negotiations demonstrates that Denmark has "disproportionate bargaining power" in EU negotiations because of its unique system of parliamentary oversight (Dluhosch and Ziegler 2008:2). The Danish parliament has to approve the government's positions before they are presented in the EU, which allows the government to refer to their domestic (parliamentary) constraints and to ask for a "parliamentary reservation". By delaying overall agreement in the Council, the Danish delegation becomes a powerful player the Council presidency has to take account of. The same applies to all member states whose national parliaments are highly involved in national EU policy coordination.

The conventional application of the two-level game would predict that the domestic constituencies affect the outcomes on the international level. Yet, the opposite is also true. For instance, as demonstrated in a study on the negotiation tactics of central bankers, in some cases public officials may use international agreements as a "way of escaping domestic politics" (Kapstein 1992:287). This may explain domestic interest groups' fears of a "democratic deficit", as domestic regulators may forge agreements with their colleagues in other countries.

Hug and König (2002:25) have found empirical evidence to suggest that domestic constraints grant bargaining power in European Council negotiations. By drawing on the ICG negotiations on the Amsterdam Treaty, they demonstrate that domestic ratification constraints, determined by institutionally-defined ratification hurdles and the preferences of actors, influence the outcome of the bargaining process. Despite the seemingly smooth ratification process of the Amsterdam Treaty, they show that those countries preferring the *status quo* in particular issues were able to shift the bargaining outcome towards their ideal point because of the constraints created through the process of ratification by national parliaments. According to the two-level game, domestic constituencies have an important role to play. A study on the political leadership in the European Council Tallberg (2008) found that the heads of state who domestically are under political 'control', have a "stronger standing" in the Council.

However, scholars fail to agree on the conditions under which domestic constraints lead to increased bargaining power. Clark *et al.* (2000:74) refer to the difficulties of compliance within the Nash Bargaining Model.[3] The model predicts that the member states that need the agreement the most will offer concessions and side payments to those that need it less (Lehtonen 2009:40). Bailer refers to Moravcsik (1998), demonstrating that domestic interests that are too strong can make negotiators willing to make concessions because they would prefer to achieve something rather than nothing at all (Bailer 2010:747). Another hypothesis suggests that actors may derive an advantage in negotiations by choosing to take extreme positions or to make extreme opening offers for negotiations (Fischer and Ury 1981, Teply 2005, Shell 1999). The success of the strategy of extreme positions is dependent on the voting rule in the Council: where QMV is applied it is extremely likely that the state presenting an extreme position will simply be ignored (Bailer 2003).

The discussion on power resources reveals a common tendency that dominates the research of international relations in general, i.e. asymmetries in power distribution. In Council negotiations power is distributed unevenly across the member states. The distinction most commonly follows the 'large - small' divide. However, some studies attribute even greater importance to the factors that stem from actors' interdependence. Interdependence in general is one of the core concepts in international relations and implies the mutual dependence of international actors. Because of the asymmetries in the political system, interdependence itself can be asymmetrical, i.e. it can reflect a situation in which one party in a relationship is more dependent than the other. The idea of asymmetric interdependence as a source of power was elaborated by Keohane and Nye (1998:11). They claimed that because of asymmetrical interdependence one should not focus on power as an isolated concept but rather as a means of translating a potential into effects through political bargaining. The rationale behind this argument can also be applied to EU negotiations. This approach draws on intergovernmentalist explanations of power distribution derived from asymmetric interdependence, i.e. actors' dependence on an agreement on the one hand and the interests of the other parties on the other. The paradigm of asymmetric interdependence rests on patterns of preferences, the domestic situation and preference intensity. The configuration of state preferences influences state behaviour at the international level, either by provoking conflict or proposing cooperation. Accordingly, each state seeks to achieve its preferences under the constraints imposed by the preferences of other states (Moravcsik 1997:521).

Clark *et al.* (2000) demonstrate that even in the absence of asymmetries in structural power, a variation in distributional outcomes can be observed. Focusing on EU-US trade relations, they analyse complementary factors in power asymmetries, i.e. domestic variables and information asymmetries.

---

3   In 1950 Nash formulated a model according to which two actors must cooperate during negotiations in order to gain mutual benefit. The model has been adjusted for application to EU decision-making (see e.g. Achen 2006, Bailer and Schneider 2006, Thomson 2011).

Hopmann (1996) addressed asymmetry among negotiation partners that stems from differences in administrative capacity, resources and expertise in framing policy positions, and pointed out that expert advice and extensive government bureaucracy may also enhance a country's position, especially in negotiations involving highly technical issues (ibid.:56). During the preparatory phase of negotiations, expert power is achieved by the ability to provide knowledge and solutions based on scientific expertise in a specific policy field on a specific dossier.

How can the negotiation actors overcome asymmetries in power distribution? The first step is to acknowledge that the power of an actor is determined by a variety of power resources (aside from structural power alone). Following the suggestion of Keohane (1989:59), one should consider structural and institutional power only as capabilities that have an impact on outcomes through their "translation" into behavioural power. Some scholars argue that behavioural power, such as negotiation skills, can help influence policy outcomes more than structural power resources (Bailer 2004). Clark et al. (2000:73) go even further, claiming that "structural factors are neither necessary, nor sufficient, […], or even misleading in attempts to predict the distribution of bargaining outcomes".

The concept of behavioural power as introduced by Habeeb (1988) and further elaborated by Bailer (2003, 2004, 2010) opens up a new perspective for explanations of power determinants in international negotiations. Taking into account the multidimensional nature of exerting power, states do not usually apply the full range of power resources, but select a few preferred power dimensions (Hopmann 1996). Parties that successfully select their strategic power source alternatives have been shown to achieve larger gains in negotiation outcomes (in Wolf and McGinn 2005). Behavioural power is more a question of applying alternative resources apart from aggregate power in terms of bargaining skills (Bailer 2003), dealing with information asymmetries (Saam and Sumpter 2009), aggregating interests into a single voice (Meunier 2000) or using intergovernmental coordination (Panke 2010). Information asymmetries are crucial elements in negotiations in general and in EU negotiations in particular because of the complex setting of intergovernmental and supranational actors taking part. The degree of information that negotiators have at their disposal about others' preferences (Hopmann 1996:27, Bailer 2003:7) or the positions of domestic ratification constraints (Slapin 2006:55) frames negotiation tactics and may confer power (Bailer 2010:746).

Studies on negotiation theory have revealed that negotiation skills matter when it comes to success in bargaining (Zartman 1977). Moreover, negotiation theory distinguishes between the communicational aspects of bargaining and even pays attention to psychological characteristics (Bailer 2010:746). As the means of communication, behavioural power stems from negotiation skills (threats, promises, rewards and/or concessions). Experienced and trained negotiators can effectively apply tactics, for instance a strong opening offer at the outset of negotiations, threats and concessions, issue linkage etc. to obtain a "better deal". Practitioners point out that the small states can counterbalance their size disadvantage by having a skilful negotiation team, which is often the case with Luxembourg or Sweden (Merts and Cede 2004). Successful communication and good networking with other negotiation parties are one aspect of negotiation skills. By introducing the term "network capital", Naurin and Lindahl (2007) have emphasised the "micro-level" of communication among negotiation actors in terms of interpersonal trust and reciprocity. Linking psychological studies with negotiation theories, Odell (2010:624) draws attention to the potential power of argumentation and persuasion in negotiations.

Both negotiation theoreticians and scholars dealing with research on EU bargaining (Fisher and Ury 1981, Dür and Mateo 2010a) highlight the importance of BATNA (best alternative to the negotiated agreement). In practice that means that the negotiation party with an "outside option" other than the stated position has a stronger standing in negotiations. The main argument here is that parties that are prepared to break down negotiations by using BATNA gain more bargaining power.

The aforementioned skills frame the potential that may translate an actor's assets (e.g. structural power) into bargaining success (Keohane 1989, Bailer 2003). It is important to point out that power resources, in particular behavioural power, should be regarded as a *process*. Contrary to one early interpretation of power as a constant variable, studies of bargaining power assume that its value can change over time (Zartman and Berman 1982). Behavioural power is an attribute that can be changed and enhanced during negotiations. This is largely used by the smaller member states since they cannot easily increase their structural power resources.

Table 1 provides an overview of various power determinants as discussed in the above.

One of the major difficulties that research on power encounters is how to measure it. Power has been characterised as "an essentially messy concept" (Barry 1980:349) and therefore difficult to measure. Reflecting the power concept metaphorically, it is the weight each actor brings to the side it supports. "To estimate the actors' power we need to know how much of a disparity between the weight of the supporters and the weight of opponents he can reverse by taking part in the decision on a measure" (Barry 1980:349). Existing scholarship applies different approaches to the determinants of bargaining power. Structural power is often measured in terms of member states' size, population, economic growth indicators and by the Shapley value for voting power (Hopmann 1996, Winkler 1998, Thomson 2009:655). In international trade studies, an actor's power may be measured in terms of control (Dür

2008:653), while studies dealing with influence and success operationalise power as an actor's self-estimation and decisiveness (Barry 1980:348).

Table 1: Research on the determinants of bargaining power

Power determinants		Authors
Structural power	Territory Size Economic strength	Moravcsik 1998 Slapin 2006 Panke 2010 Shure and Verdun 2008 Bailer 2004 Tallberg 2008
Issue-specific power	Voting power Population	Roozendaal *et al.* 2008 Dür and Mateo 2010a
	Aggregate power	Tallberg 2009
	Administrative capacity	Habeeb 1998
	Stability of the political system	Tallberg 2008, 2009
	BATNA (best alternative to negotiated agreement)	Dür and Mateo 2010a Odell 2010
	Preference intensity	Bailer 2004
	Commitment	Habeeb 1988
	Domestic constraints	Shelling 1960 Putnam 1988 Moravcsik 1993 Bailer 2006
Behavioural power	Negotiation skills (threats, concessions)	Bailer 2010 Zartman 1977
	Negotiation strategy (hard, soft)	Dür and Mateo 2010a,b Odell 2010
	Extreme positions	Bailer 2003
	Experience	Meerts and Cede 2004
	Information	Saam and Sumpter 2009
	Power-pooling, coalitions	Elgström *et al.* 2001 Tallberg 2008

Source: Literature review.

This study focuses on evaluating bargaining outcomes compared to actors' expectations and uses the approach of Bailer (2003), Thomson (2006, 2011) and Tallberg (2008), in which bargaining power is operationalised as an actor's ability to shift negotiation outcomes towards its own ideal point. In the study at hand, bargaining power is measured as the difference between the distance to outcome and the distance to reversion point. The reversion point is the point where negotiations end up if member states fail to reach agreement. The reversion point is often treated as a *status quo* (SQ) point (Achen 2006). Figures 1 and 2 show how bargaining power (BP) is illustrated in graphs. The preferences of bargaining actors A and B are indicated on the axis, together with the SQ point and the negotiation outcome. Actor B here can represent a coalition, i.e. the aggregation of closely located preferences. Actor B's bargaining power is measured as the difference (a–b), where 'a' is the distance from B to SQ and 'b' is the distance from B to the outcome: see (a–b) on the graph. Bargaining power of the opposition to the coalition (here A) is measured in the same way: as the difference (c–d), where 'c' is the distance from A to SQ and 'd' is the distance from A to outcome: see (c–d) on the graph. Accordingly, BP(A) < BP(B). The arrow (dotted lines) shows the bargaining advantage of the actor B (the dotted line encompasses closely located preferences of coalition members). It should be noted that the design of the study does not envisage reflecting *all* policy preferences in negotiations. They may possibly be more coalitions than only 'B'. The model focuses on the particular coalitions (NB6 or a task-specific group) and evaluates bargaining power in relation to the opposing actor/coalition 'A'.

Figure 1: Model of measuring bargaining power with A and B positioned on one side of SQ

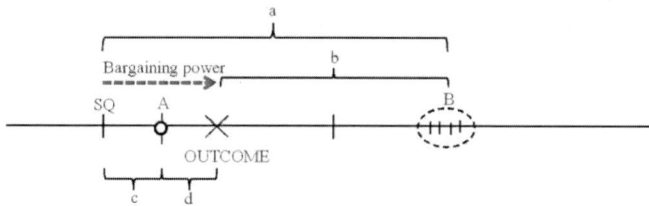

Source: based on the study's methodological approach.

In cases where preferences and negotiation positions are contested, the SQ is situated on the axis between the preferences (see Fig. 2) of the negotiation actors A and B (that is most often the case in Council negotiations).

Figure 2: Model of measuring bargaining power with SQ positioned between A and B

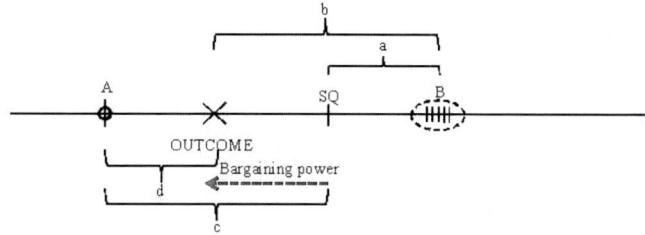

Source: based on the study's methodological approach.

Here the bargaining power of A is equal to (c–d), i.e. shifted towards the ideal point of A; while the bargaining power of B is equal to (a–b), shifted away from the preferred outcome of the actor (coalition) B. In this case BP(A) > BP(B).

1.1.2 Power pooling through coalition-building: a view from the rational choice perspective

Despite broad coverage of different power determinants, coalition-building as a power-pooling strategy has so far attracted insufficient attention in scholarly literature. Coalitions and alliances have been viewed from different angles, i.e. as organisational processes, group behaviour, cooperation and conflict dimensions, and as outcome-oriented actions. However, few scholars have approached coalition-building as a power-pooling process, viewing it beyond the logics of voting power aggregation. Existing studies on coalition-building evaluate the motives behind peer selection (Sam and Sumpter 2009), explaining the influence of small states on the basis of territorial partnerships and intergovernmental coordination (Panke 2010) or comparing coalitions during the bargaining and voting stages on the basis of the policy space or issue level (Veen 2011).

Those who have identified persistent coalitions on the basis of geographical proximity (Naurin and Lindahl 2007) have usually favoured social constructivism explanations, putting the emphasis on the "logic of appropriateness" (March and Olsen 2009). Supporters of social constructivism accounts would expect member states' interaction in persistent coalitions to contribute to the convergence of their preferences. This section summarises the literature on coalitions as power-pooling mechanisms and outlines the gap in the literature that this study aims to fill.

International relations literature has applied three main categories in addressing coalition issues: formation, stability and the impact on the outcomes. The discussion of coalition formation is directly linked to cooperation patterns, i.e. who cooperates with whom and what goals are to be achieved. According to coalition theory, a coalition emerges as soon as more than two actors are involved (Dupont 1994:153). In this sense, coalitions are the concept of multilateral, as opposed to bilateral, negotiations. Different scholars provide different definitions, depending on a coalition's composition, duration and the perceived aims. Dupont (1994) defines coalitions as "cooperative efforts for the attainment of short-range, issue-specific objectives". Another definition focuses on the functions of coalitions "to reduce the complexity of the negotiation situation" (Zartman and Berman 1982) by reducing the number of actors and thus facilitating the bargaining process. In the EU context, coalitions are defined as a "set of actors that coordinate their behaviour in order to reach the goals they have agreed upon" (Elgström *et al.* 2001:113) (the latter definition being applied by this study). Finally, Odell focuses on common preferences and defines coalitions as a "set of parties that explicitly coordinate among themselves and defend the same position" (2010:624). All the above-mentioned definitions share the assumption that, within a shorter or longer space of time, actors share common objectives and engage in joint action to achieve a commonly defined goal. By doing so, the coalition members improve their bargaining situation compared to the outcome that would have been gained individually. Thus, the relevance of coalition-building behaviour very much depends on the goals of cooperation. Social psychology and game-theoretical models offer different models of how to deal with the bargaining actors' motivation to align.

Two answers to the issue of coalition-building goals are proposed in the literature: actors either strive for *power maximisation* to create minimum winning coalitions (Reynaud *et al.* 2008, Hosli 1999, 2009, Winkler 1998) or to *influence the outcome* by demonstrating common objectives and support for common preferences or a particular policy. In both cases, the rationale is to improve the actors' influence by acting collectively. Accordingly, coalition-building can be seen as a "strategy of pooling bargaining power, rather than an independent source of power" (Tallberg 2008:687). Power-pooling is one of several "strategies of the weak" that can be used to mitigate the disadvantages in power distribution (Keohane 1971). By acting strategically, countries can aggregate power resources and achieve outcomes that are more favourable than what they could have secured individually. By pursuing coalition-building tactics, framing coalitions or joining an existing coalition, negotiation actors can increase the level of commitment by combining several individual commitments or can increase control by combining resources (Dupont 1994).

Power-based coalitions are supported by rational choice theories that predict that actors will strive to maximise their utility. In international organisations, a coalition's impact varies with the prevailing decision norm, i.e. "when decisions are made by voting, a coalition reaching the required minimum share of votes wins" (Odell 2010:624). Analysts observe that member states tend to align when QMV is applied (Winkler 1998, Hosli 1999, Selck 2005, Novak, 2010). Under the QMV rule, member states seek coalition partners either to block the decision or to promote the issue (Elgström *et al.* 2001). Schure and Verdun (2008:475) evaluate the impact of the Lisbon Treaty provisions and find that the trend towards "power-pooling" is increasing.

Most quantitative studies on voting power measurements apply the Shapley value and the Banzhaf index. These methods permit the distribution of voting power in the Council to be determined quite accurately (Winkler 1998, Widgrén 2009, Bailer 2010, Schneider *et al.* 2010). They allow the expected power of member states in the decision-making process to be calculated. The Shapely value describes the relative distribution of voting power as a percentage and can be interpreted as a measure of member states' chances of casting a vote that is decisive for the decision-making process (Winkler 1998:395). In this regard, the studies distinguish between coalition-neutral voting power, i.e. a value that coincides with the distribution of votes, and coalition-sensitive voting power that may cause considerable reaction in terms of outcome due to small changes in circumstances (ibid.:391). Banzhaf introduced a voting index that draws on game theory (Ploeg 2008:12) and is based on counting only those coalitions for which the country is pivotal, i.e. turns a coalition into a winning coalition.

Following this logic, one might expect actors to align with large countries, i.e. following the philosophy of "most important first" (Tallberg and Johansson 2008:1225). Odell (2010:625) shows that a coalition is more powerful if it includes powerful players; the coalition between France and Germany serves as an example of the power-based approach (Hosli 1999:375). This assumption, however, is contested by Selck's study (2006) that examined the coalition behaviour of large countries: the United Kingdom, France, Germany and Italy on their preference basis and was unable to support the often-cited Franco-German axis. Selck finds that Germany's interests are closer to the United Kingdom's, and that France's positions correlate more often with Italian positions. Accordingly, the question of "who cooperates with whom and why" is still unanswered.

Saam and Sumpter (2009:370) investigated why an EU government should select another government as a coalition partner. They suggest that member states frame coalitions based on the proximity of actors' positions, or by selecting other countries with the same "stake in the issue". Accordingly, governments are guided by power-pooling considerations. Interestingly, this study also includes a pattern of peer-selection on "neighbourhood grounds". Their findings on the empirical evaluation of IGC negotiations in 1996 are quite surprising, i.e. governments prefer to coordinate their positions with "those governments which they have already contracted during *ex ante* cooperation". In contrast to purely voting power-based consideration, this result demonstrates the significance of the stability of intergovernmental networks that are formed prior to formal meetings.

Pre-meeting communication amongst member states usually takes place in smaller groups, which enhances effective channels of interaction and in-group conditions that facilitate mutual exchange. In practice, pre-meeting exchanges often take place as bilateral or multilateral group consultations. In Council negotiations the consultations are viewed as "channels of access to information" that take place prior or beyond the formal negotiation process (Fouilleux *et al.* 2005:615). Moreover, consultations may merge with negotiations, i.e. the differences between them are no longer distinct. Drawing on the study of EU coordination in the UN, Degrand-Guillaud (2009:428) notes: "to simplify, there are two types of meetings: international negotiations and informal consultations". Likewise, consultations may be held amongst government officials on the expert or political level or amongst the interested parties on the non-governmental level. The aim of these informal contacts is to exchange views in an informal way before formal negotiations start. Fouilleux *et al.* (2005) observed that consultations usually start before the first working group meeting in the Council. Parties participating in the consultations may to some extent reach agreement. "Consultations in fact *mean* negotiations" (ibid.:616). In other words, the dividing lines between consultations, pre-negotiations and negotiations are very thin. In order to increase pre-negotiation efficiency, actors may agree to establish special preparatory groups. These formats aim to identify member states' preferences at a lower negotiator level and thus to "reduce the distributional part of bargaining to choice among several well-specified options" (Dür and Mateo 2004:5), as in the case of IGC negotiations. There is strikingly frequent evidence of such preparatory groups operating outside the formal decision-making procedures at the pre-negotiation phase even within other international organisations, such as the OSCE (Organization for Security and Co-operation in Europe) and the UN (United Nations) in terms of informal preparatory EU coordination meetings (Cameron 2005, Delreux 2009, Degrand-Guillaud 2009).

The aforementioned examples illustrate that the power maximising hypothesis, with the goal of achieving a blocking threshold, is, apparently, not the only explanation for widely practiced intergovernmental coordination prior to negotiations. There is enough evidence of stable coalitions in EU decision-making (Tallberg 2010a, Schild 2010, Blavoukos and Pagoulatos 2011, Klemenčič 2011) that operate as sub-groups of intergovernmental cooperation and demonstrate a considerable degree of institutionalisation. Yet, there are no systematic studies that attempt to explain their formation and effects. Among the existing literature on coalitions, insights into the effects of institutionalised coalitions on bargaining power are surprisingly scarce, with weaknesses being grouped into several categories.

First, there are gaps in the application of theoretical tools in explaining durable coalitions in the EU. Drawing on culture, geography, history and language as the explanatory factors of coalition-building, scholars often explain territorial coalitions by relying on social constructivist tools, i.e. the role of social norms that may constitute the identity of actors and create common "rules of the game" (Beyers and Dierickx 1998, Elgström *et al.* 2001, Naurin and Lindahl 2008, Lewis 2005, 2010). This approach would thus lead to the assumption that, as the result of interaction, the member states shift their preferences. This study, by contrast, aims to explain the effects of institutionalised coalitions on bargaining power by using rational choice theoretical tools. The argument here is that, by engaging in institutionalised cooperation, member states take advantage of the institutional preconditions while acting rationally (see 2.2.).

Second, the existing literature exposes considerable gaps in the empirical testing of the effects of durable coalitions. Though there are some studies on territorial partnerships (Kaeding and Selck 2005, Naurin 2008, Panke 2010, Schild 2010, Klemenčič 2011), the findings are contradictory. Some scholars do not recognise the advantage of institutionalised cooperation and predict the decline of territorial partnerships (Hosli 1996), whereas others acknowledge the potential of geographical alliances (Schild 2010, Klemenčič 2011). Apart from territorial coalitions, the research on more durable like-minded groups in Council negotiations can be compared to a "black box". There are no systematic studies on stable like-minded groups in EU decision-making processes. The reason for the scarcity of empirical findings in this field is possibly related to the difficulties in accessing data in the highly restrictive pre-negotiation stage.

Finally, existing research on coalition-building often treats coalitions as end-game products. Those studies that evaluate coalitions as power-pooling mechanisms mainly focus on the voting outcomes in terms of the distribution of votes and the ability to influence the outcome in decision-making (Winkler 1998, Hosli 1999, Reynaud *et al.* 2008, Hosli *et al.* 2009, Schneider *et al.* 2010). Explanations of bargaining power nearly all fail to include the issue of power-pooling through institutionalised cooperation within territorial coalitions or institutionalised task-specific coalitions during the preparatory phase of negotiations. Drawing on coalition theory, one could assume that, by building coalitions, member states strive to aggregate their structural power, for example voting power, in order to achieve a blocking minority (Winkler 1998, Hosli *et al.* 2009). This logic, however, cannot explain the effects of stable territorial coalitions, since their aggregated number of votes is usually insufficient to achieve the blocking minority thresholds.

The aim of this book is to complement the understanding of the informal inter-governmental cooperation processes that take place prior to formal negotiations in the Council and to fill the gap in the literature by shedding light on the effects of institutionalised coalitions.

CHAPTER 2

2.1 Typology of coalitions in EU negotiations: ad hoc and institutionalised coalitions

The question of "who cooperates with whom" and under what conditions (Naurin 2008:2) is essential when it comes to understanding coalition behaviour. Although some authors argue that there is a "lack of structure in the positions of actors" in the Council (Thomson 2009:757), the majority share the view that in a collective decision-making environment governments tend to align. Indeed, because of the large number of actors in Council negotiations and due to the conflicting preferences of individual member states, building alliances between the member states belongs to day-to-day business in Brussels (Elgström et al. 2001, Merts and Cede 2004, Reynaud et al. 2008, Hosli et al. 2009). The member states' alignments differ in terms of stability and in terms of the determinants behind coalition-building behaviour.

Sometimes when member states' preferences are polarised and represent two conflicting negotiation positions opposing "blocs" may emerge. This has become particularly evident since EU enlargement because of the increased heterogeneity of the member states' policy preferences. In his recent study Thomson (2012:611) refers to fact that the "actors' positions largely reflect their economic interests". This leads to the assumption that the member states' positions can be explained "by the extent to which they share similar underlying economic and political attributes" (Thomson 2011:39). Consequently, we might expect there to be "more structure" to interaction amongst the member states (Naurin and Lindahl 2008:64) than has been predicted in the past.

Despite numerous studies on coalition-building in the Council, our knowledge on this issue is still far from complete (Veen 2011:114). Guided by conventional coalition theory, one might expect coalitions to form when actors' overall policy preferences conflict. In such cases countries that prefer a different policy alternative will strive to identify like-minded peers and will thus pool their power in two or more 'blocs'. Strictly speaking, the informally constructed coalitions reduce the complexity of multilateral negotiations. In other words, it is easier to reach agreement among fewer negotiation actors. This assumption stems from coalition-building theory (Zartman 1982) and fully applies to the 27-member state EU framework. The member states themselves would, however, deny that this rationale underlies their coalition-building behaviour. This study demonstrates that the determinants of coalition-building are more complex than that.

According to Elgström *et.al* (2001:112), coalition-building in the Council can be seen in the light of classical coalition theory, which suggests that states look for partners either for power-pooling reasons by creating minimum winning coalitions or they strive to influence policy and therefore select peers with similar preferences. Another aspect that can be borrowed from classical theory deals with the secretive nature of negotiations. International negotiations in general and Council deliberations in particular are surrounded by a veil of secrecy. Coalitions in the EU are also the consequence of the restricted nature of Council decision-making, where agreements are concluded behind closed doors, in corridors and at dinner tables (Heisenberg 2008:263). Hence, two sets of negotiations emerge in EU decision-making: those among the EU-27, which are held within the formal Council framework following prescribed procedures, and those taking place inside the sub-group, where information is shared exclusively with the "insiders" of the coalition. In practice, that means that the member states forming a coalition first negotiate on common preferences (it is unlikely that several actors will have exactly the same preferences). Then, in the second stage, they bargain with the other coalition (Elgström *et al.* 2001). When applied to the EU decision-making framework, the distinction between two layers of negotiations, i.e. "intra-coalitional" and a coalition versus its "opponents" is highly relevant because it helps to explain the ways in which a bargaining advantage is gained.

One sociological aspect is the number of actors within a negotiation group. Social psychologists acknowledge the differences that exist in decision-making ways when comparing small and large groups. Actors interacting in smaller groups demonstrate more cooperative spirit, whereas large groups show more conflict potential.

Our understanding of coalitions is based on the definition we apply. Traditionally, coalitions have been approached by evaluating the relative voting power of the member states in the Council (Widgrén 1994, Hosli 1996, Raunio and Wiberg 1998). This approach has two problems: When evaluating voting power indices scholars do not pay enough attention to political interaction among the member states. Moreover, voting power indices can be measured practically by the voting outcome, thus neglecting the important role played by the negotiation (and pre-negotiation) process.

An accurate definition should, thus, also capture the "interaction" between negotiation actors throughout the negotiation process. I draw here on the definition by Rasch (1997 in Elgström *et al.* 2001:113), who states that a coalition is a "set of actors that coordinate their behaviour in order to reach goals that they have agreed upon". This definition outlines two important aspects that are relevant for this study:

(1) First, coalition-building is a *deliberate* and intended behaviour of governments in improving their utility in Council decision-making. In

searching for like-minded peers, the governments are guided by political rationale and they calculate their gains in advance. This is contrasted with the voting outcome approach, which may find coalitions of countries that happen to have voted in the same way without having coordinated their behaviour.

(2) Second, the definition of coalition-building also emphasises governments' goal-oriented cooperation during the preparatory phase of decision-making. To this end, the framework encompasses coalition formation towards the pre-negotiation stage, which is practically excluded from conventional studies on coalition-building that mainly focus on the bargaining and voting stages (see also Veen 2011:114).

In practice, the member states seek to identify like-minded allies before negotiations start. Interaction and coordination are essential features of the EU negotiation system in general (Cede 2004:13). Day-to-day interactions take place at all levels of the government hierarchy throughout the negotiation process. By engaging in collective strategies, governments coordinate their positions and act collectively in order to enhance their power compared to individual action (Klemenčič 2005). Hence, a great deal of agreement is settled during the pre-negotiation stage. The advantage of the institutional setting is that cooperation can be more effective because governments may rely on existing pre-established structures, networks and even routines, which facilitate exchange at the initial stage. Pre-meeting coordination usually involves informal civil servant consultations between the capitals, or in Brussels by the officials of the permanent representations. It has become a tradition that prime ministers and ministers meet in sub-groups (i.e. beyond the EU-27) during informal breakfast meetings in the run-up to European Council and Council meetings.

2.1.1 Patterns of coalitions in Council negotiations

Several attempts have been made to map the determinants of coalition-building behaviour. Kaeding and Selck (2005) offer a systematic approach by proposing four explanatory factors for coalition formation: power-based, interest-based, ideology-based and culture-based. The first two coalition patterns follow rational choice logics because governments aim to maximise their utility by aggregating votes (and consequently power). The latter two explanations stem from constructivist theoretical accounts, as the member states, when selecting their cooperation partners, are guided by social norms and, thus, follow the "rules of the game".

This study draws on the aforementioned approach and analyses coalition-building behaviour with the help of rational choice. However, it also slightly modifies the classification by merging interest-based and power-based coalitions[4] into one classification group and by framing an additional pattern, i.e. territorially constituted coalitions. The latter mirrors considerations of geographical affinity that have been observed in several studies (Naurin and Lindahl 2007, Klemenčič 2005, 2011, Blavoukos and Pagoulatos 2011). Hosli (1996:259) has claimed that some coalitions may be "more likely" than others. She argues that geographical alliances exist, though she also points out that the traditional territorial alliances, like the Benelux countries or the Franco-German alliance, may have lost their significance. This debate will be further elaborated in the following sections.

As regards the determinants of coalition formation, this study distinguishes between four coalition patterns: interest-based, culture and identity-based, territorially constituted, and ideological affinity-based.

Interest-based coalitions have been confirmed by extensive research in both qualitative (Dudley and Richardson 1999, Tallberg and Johansson 2008) and quantitative studies (Hosli 1999, Mattila 2009). Member states' behaviour is here supported by rational choice explanations, with coalition-building motivation drawing primarily from the proximity of actors. It should be pointed out, for reasons of clarity, that actors' stated positions (or negotiation positions) usually reflect their policy preferences (or policy positions). As Thomson (2012:610) argues in a recent study on a dataset of EU decision-making, "policy positions are represented on the issues". In other words, member states' preferences on the national level are "translated" into their stated positions in EU negotiations (see 2.3. for clarifications on terminology). Accordingly, the formation of interest-based coalitions is related to the two-level process between the domestic and international domain (Moravcsik 1993, Selck 2006). In negotiations on controversial issues, where the negotiation partners' policy preferences differ, interest-based coalitions reflect policy-distance considerations on the issue at hand (Kaeding and Selk 2005:274). Since governments in EU negotiations are perceived as the "advocates of the interests of their nation-states" (Zimmer *et al.* 2005:407), coalitions are "likely to form between governments with similar policy goals" (Hix 2005:87). In other words, governments try to upload these national interests at the EU level by attracting like-minded peers on each particular issue.

Kaeding and Selck (2005:274) argue that interest-based coalitions are not stable; they exist on a short-term basis and are dissolved after the decision is taken and agreement is reached. Accordingly, interest-based coalitions can by their very nature be seen as *ad hoc* aggregations of member states. (However,

---

4   Since interest-based coalitions are characterised as "issue-specific", this study approaches them as "power-based" because member states' main rationale is to pool power by achieving the blocking minority on the issue at hand.

this study proposes a concept of more durable interest-based coalitions, i.e. 'task-specific' groupings, which are explained in 3.3.)

The heterogeneity of policy preferences has contributed to the dimensions of conflicts in Council negotiations (Zimmer *et al.* 2005, Hosli and Arnold 2007). In practical terms, that means that on controversial issues the distance between the policy positions of individual member states is large, hence the cleavages between policy alternatives (Thomson 2012:610). Such cleavages most often emerge in distributional bargaining situations, for example during negotiations on the EU's Financial Perspective where clear conflict dimensions can be identified between net contributors and net recipients. A group of six net contributors: Germany, Austria, France, the Netherlands, Sweden and the UK is often perceived as an interest-based coalition. The main policy preference of this group is to keep the increase in the EU's budget below 1 per cent of the EU's gross domestic product (GDP), whereas net recipients advocate spending more. Apart from the issue of cutting the budget pie into slices, there are also widely acknowledged conflicts of interest in the field of social and environment policy (Hosli 1996:260).

The **culture- and identity-based coalition pattern** is another way of explaining coalition formation using more normative accounts. These explanations have been developed by scholars who support a social constructivist approach and focus on culture, history and language (even nationality) as the driving forces behind coalition formation (Faure 2002, Naurin and Lindahl 2008). Alliances that were formed within the group of founding members of the European Community in the 1950s were largely based on common history. In his study on the Franco-German partnership in the EU, Schild (2011) points out that the alliance between France and Germany has deep historical roots and over time has turned into "regularized intergovernmentalism". The Franco-German alliance, which has recently experienced a come-back through the historic decisions by the Council on how to rescue Europe from the financial crisis (The Economist, 10 Dec. 2011), can only partly be characterised as a historically-affiliated alliance. Much of its relevance draws on power and leadership considerations, as rightly argued by Schild (2011:1387).

A more accurate reading of culture- and identity-based explanations is provided by those scholars who focus on macro-regions, like interaction between the officials in the Nordic or Mediterranean regions. Here we can distinguish between identity-based considerations and a common history. Typically, these coalition patterns are approached on the micro-level, i.e. by analysing the behaviour of individuals who prefer to cooperate with people from the same region, often neighbours. It has been observed that common cultural affinity enhances communication. In their explanations of this phenomenon, Naurin and Lindahl (2007) emphasise inter-personal trust in communication. They argue that this trust stems from deep-rooted identity and similar ways of approaching things. There is even a "habit" of cooperating with neighbours, regardless of preferences on the narrow issue. Through such repeated interaction, durable coalitions often establish an institutionalised mechanism for their in-group cooperation. Blavoukos and Pagoulatos (2011:562) hypothesise that institutional conditions enhance bargaining continuity because bargaining deals may be revised in future rounds. Accordingly, these "future prospects cement exiting coalitions to safeguard a favourable bargain". Kaeding and Selk (2005:276) point out that culture-based coalitions tend to be rather fixed.

Apart from culture in the meaning of identity, some scholars point to the normative aspect of culture. In the light of negotiation theory, "culture is the set of behaviour patterns, beliefs, norms and values that is (implicitly) shared by a social group" (Dür and Mateo 2010b:685). Thus, culture can be seen as "a way of doing things" or the determinant according to which actors choose negotiation strategies. This aspect of culture has been captured by constructivist scholars. The role of social norms that may constitute the identity of actors and create common rules of the game were captured in Lewis' studies (2003, 2005, 2010). Lewis focused empirically on member states' interaction in the context of COREPER[5] and observed a shift in behaviour in the group of Brussels-based Justice and Home Affairs counsellors. Because of the tightly knit *esprit de corps* among them, the member states' Brussels-based officials were more open to mutually cooperative deals. This approach was further augmented by Naurin and Lindahl (2007) in terms of network capital and personal inter-linkages among the negotiation actors in Council working groups.

Territorially constituted coalitions. Drawing on a survey of Swedish officials in EU Committees, Elgström *et al.* (2001) found support for the culture- and identity-based hypothesis before enlargement in 2004 and argued that coalition patterns follow the North-South divide. Other authors who have recently evaluated the distribution of conflict dimensions of member states' positions in the EU similarly acknowledge a North-South divide (Hosli and Arnold 2007, Thomson 2009,) that, after enlargement, has been further extended to a North-South-East pattern (Mattila 2009, Veen 2011) or a centre-periphery pattern (Plechanonova 2011). Apart from its focus on the geographical dimension, this literature reveals a pattern of coalitions that is more persistent and durable. In other words, neighbouring member states (or countries in the same geographical region) have more close intergovernmental ties and coordinate positions with their intra-coalition partners more often than

---

5   The meetings of member states' permanent representatives that are held in Brussels following Council working group discussions.

with those outside the geographical region. The logic behind the territorially constituted coalition pattern is rather complex. As Naurin and Wallace (2008:8) rightly point out, "geography is obviously only a proxy for some underlying concept". The fact that the member states can be found next to each other on a map is insufficient reason for their coalition behaviour. Several underlying conditions have to be taken into account. Geographical proximity is often associated with common culture and values. Neighbouring countries may share a common history and sometimes their languages share linguistic roots. They often undertake common initiatives and coordinate cross-border projects because there is a well-established cooperation network and an institutional framework for such cooperation. The question remains "why do neighbours cooperate?" One could hypothesise that neighbours may establish common preferences on account of their strong tradition of consulting each other.

Even though some authors claim that territorial coalitions are based on similarity of preferences by maintaining that "policy preferences of Nordic EU members are to a large extent similar" (Selck and Kuipers 2005:167), this study shares the view of Elgström *et al.* (2001), Tallberg (2008) and Thomson (2009), who consider that preference distribution docs not follow geographical lines of division and may stretch across regions from issue to issue. Instead, one can speak of the "long-term common interests" (Elgström *et al.* 2001:116), common values and shared identities that produce more fixed coalitions on the basis of geographical proximity. In this respect, it may be helpful to apply the model developed by Veen (2011:125) that proposes three levels of analysis when approaching coalition behaviour, i.e. political space, policy domain and policy issues. The stability of coalitions decreases the narrower the issue level. This analytical framework will be further elaborated in 2.3.

Given similar socio-economic conditions, governments representing the same region tend to form coalitions according to political space, i.e. as indicated by Elgström *et al.* (2001:116) they aggregate their voice on common values and long-term interests. This leads to the formation of distinct clusters: Northern, Central Eastern European countries etc. (Veen 2011:126). At the domain level coalitions that follow specific issue areas (Winkler 1998, Zimmer 2005) are known as "like-minded" in Council negotiations because the member states favour the same policy outcomes. Most prominent examples are interest aggregation in the financial policy domain across net payers and net recipients. Finally, on the issue level governments often follow rational considerations and select peers according to preference proximity. The stability of alignments is much lower on the issue level than on the policy space level (Veen 2011:126). In general, however, it should be noted that territorially constituted coalitions are more stable than interest-based or ideology-based coalitions. The fact that territorially constituted coalitions are more fixed has to do with the degree of institutionalisation. Due to their common historical background and shared values, the actors in these coalitions have over time established an institutional framework that enhances cooperation. Hence, the more stable the coalition is, the more embedded it is in an institutional structure. The opposite could also be said to be the case, namely that institutionalisation strengthens coalitions. This correlation is analysed more explicitly in 2.2.1.

Ideology-based coalitions. The fourth distinction in coalition behaviour emphasises the role of party ideology. Yet, the link between ideological affiliation and coalition-building behaviour is not straightforward. Some authors support an ideology-based hypothesis (Hagemann and Hoyland 2008, Hix 1999), while others (Tallberg and Johansson 2008, Mattila 2004, Hosli and Arnold 2007) do not find empirically convincing evidence for such an argument. Supporters of the ideology hypothesis argue that the Council's decision-making is not "politically innocent" (Hagemann and Hoyland 2008:1216). Consequently, theories of comparative politics predict that member states align on the basis of party ideology considerations. Ideology is seen by these authors as a powerful explanatory factor behind member states' coalition-building behaviour. According to the partisan hypothesis, one would expect actors' alignments to reflect ideological proximities and differences in ideological preferences, i.e. government representatives representing the same ideological affiliation would form alignments in EU negotiations. Member states' cooperation and cleavages are assumed to follow the left-right dimension (Hix 1999) and to derive from such ideological considerations. Hoghe and Marks (2001) confirm the left-right dimension, ranging from social democracy to market liberalism (in Hosli and Arnold 2007).

Ideology-based coalitions are perceived to be stable over time as long as the particular party stays in office. Drawing on a quantitative analysis of voting patterns between 1999 and 2007, Hagemann and Hoyland (2008) find empirical support for an ideology-based hypothesis of coalition-building. They also observe left-right cleavages in decision-making that can, in particular, be detected with respect to socio-economic issues, since party groups tend to present similar preferences on social policy dossiers.

2.1.2 How stable are they?

The section on coalition-building determinants demonstrated that coalition stability varies depending on coalition type. In general, coalitions are treated as "unstable", resulting in a variety of preferences (Hopmann 1996:251). Given similar preferences on particular issues, governments frame coalitions on an *ad hoc* basis (Hayes-Renshaw and Wallace 2006). Accordingly, *ad hoc* coalitions can be regarded as issue-based power-pooling attempts by member states that coordinate their action in order to achieve short-term goals. These coalitions are not fixed in terms of participants (peers) and their composition changes from issue to issue. When choosing peers for *ad hoc* coalitions, member states' behaviour is largely guided by preference-based reasoning, i.e. following an interest-based proxy. Thus, cooperation between states is not supported by any existing durable procedural or structural framework. In other words, *ad hoc* coalitions are not "institutionalised".

However, in contrast to *ad hoc* formations, studies drawing on the identity or cultural affinity determinants of coalition-building, also acknowledge more stable and persistent alignments. These studies exhibit a pattern of territorially constituted coalitions (Beyers and Dierickx 1998, Elgström *et.al.* 2001, Zimmer *et.al.* 2005) and indicate that neighbouring countries or those representing the same macro-region in the EU tend to align. The question is: How do these more persistent coalitions operate? How stable are they? What is the rationale behind the territorial constituted coalition formation?

Table 2: Typology of coalitions according to stability and degree of institutionalisation

	Ad hoc coalitions	Institutionalised coalitions (e.g. territorially constituted)
Peers	Comprising *ad hoc* peers	Constant peers
Stability	Short-term, unstable alignments	Quite stable alignments
Rationale	Maximise utility by aggregating voting power	Maximise utility by overcoming information asymmetries; through exchange, information distribution, and rhetorical action. Voting power has a secondary role to play (this requirement is not necessarily always met)

Source: Data retrieved from literature review.

Building upon Naurin's question (2007:2) of "who cooperates with whom?", Table 2 provides an overview of coalition typology based on two distinct coalition types (*ad hoc* and institutionalised coalitions). The distinction between *ad hoc* and institutionalised coalitions is central to the study at hand. It explains the difference in outcome in terms of coalition members' bargaining power with the help of the notion of "institutionalisation". Formed with a task of reaching short-term objectives, *ad hoc* coalitions are not embedded in an institutionalised environment of interaction. There are neither any underlying structures nor has any prior "agreement" to cooperate been reached. Hence, intra-coalition consultations and coordination in the case of *ad hoc* coalitions lack any persistent operational framework. Institutionalised coalitions, by contrast, have underlying structures of cooperation, shared long-term goals and interaction frequency, which may sometimes be perceived as routine cooperation. In extreme cases, this "routine cooperation" may be supported by a formal agreement, like the Benelux cooperation. Most commonly, territorially constituted coalitions are highly informal and their institutionalisation follows an "unwritten agreement". The distinction between *ad hoc* and institutionalised coalitions is further elaborated in 2.1.

At this stage it is worth mentioning that the logic of coalition-building varies across both coalition types. By framing short-term alignments among like-minded peers, member states seek to maximise their utility by aggregating voting power. An obvious rationale here is to aggregate enough votes to achieve the necessary threshold by which coalition members could block a decision. In the case of institutionalised coalitions, by inter-acting with constant peers, member states strive to achieve other advantages apart from voting power alone. These benefits may stem from the mutual exchange of information, the pooling of expertise or framing of a stronger argument on behalf of the coalition.

2.2 Explaining the effects of institutionalised coalitions on bargaining power

In his study on the role of leaders in Council decision-making, Tallberg (2010a) generates a hypothesis that states are likely to delegate process powers to formal leaders. The rationale of such strategies stems from the assumption that in multilateral bargaining situations asymmetrical access to information places states in an unequal situation, i.e. gains are distributed unevenly among the negotiation actors because multilateral bargaining is subject to the collective action problem. In such situations leaders are supposed to influence the outcomes in the preferred direction. Interestingly, a link can be identified between the leadership and cooperation, namely the evidence from states' cooperation in advance of EU Council meetings shows that the most institutionalised cooperation format within territorially constituted coalitions is the so-called "prime ministers' breakfast". Such highly informal "prime ministers' breakfast meetings" have been held among the Benelux heads of state since the 1980s, now involve high-level consultations of the prime ministers of Visegrad countries, and are regularly held in the run-up to Council meetings among the Nordic-Baltic (NB6) prime ministers.

To explain the effects of such regular interaction within territorially constituted sub-groups, we have to take a closer look at the institutional origins of these formations and to explain the effects of the aforementioned regular exchange of views. The logic behind these breakfast meetings can be summarised as follows: First, member states in EU negotiations work out the means by which they can improve their bargaining advantage, and, second, the territorially constituted coalition offers the benefits of intra-coalition exchange in terms of sharing information, pooling expertise and framing stronger arguments without being too costly. There is a trace of the rational choice perspective in these two aspects that, according to this study, drives the heads of state of the territorially constituted coalitions to take an earlier flight to Brussels. Moreover, approached in a broader sense, this pattern of "interaction with neighbours" is repeated in consultations between the civil servants of line ministries, spreads to the expert networks and, consequently, comprises multiple levels of the legislative process in the EU.

This section provides theoretical explanations for the question of "why neighbours cooperate". It starts by clarifying the notion of institutionalised cooperation and goes on to develop a theoretical framework for explaining its effects on bargaining power in Council negotiations. Theoretically, the study addresses two competing explanations of the more stable and durable coalitions in EU decision-making that, viewed through an institutionalism theory lens, can open up additional interpretations of the institutional context within bargaining situations. I argue that the effects of durable and stable coalitions in the Council can be explained with the help of institutional conditions, i.e. an institutionalised environment within which the interaction between coalition partners takes place. As a result, this study applies rational choice theoretical explanations, an approach that is innovative; previous studies have usually linked the institutional conditions to normative considerations and, consequently, find constructivist accounts to be more appropriate.

Decision-making in the EU is largely shaped by the institutional arenas that structure the decision-making process. In the case of Council decision-making one can rightly apply agree with Tallberg (2010b:635) that "institutions matter". Council negotiations are based on rules and procedures both relating to voting, interaction with EU institutions and member states in Council working groups, meetings of COREPER and meetings of ministers. Even when formal rules and procedures apply, decision-making is greatly influenced by *informal norms*, such as consensus agreement (Mattila and Lane 2001, Heisenberg 2005), issue linkages (Dür and Mateo 2004, McKibben 2010), vote trading (Beyers 2005), vote selling (Golub 2012) or package deals. As Beyers and Trandal (2004:906) put it: "one should not attach too much explanatory power to formal rules". International negotiations as such have become more informal when it comes to the application of procedures and rules. Informal institutional rules in multilateral negotiations have become dominant (or are at least as important as formal rules) in explaining negotiation outcomes. The pre-agreement stage outside the formal decision-making scope is an informal norm that is facilitated by the increasing tendency towards informal cooperation prior to formal meetings (Tallberg 2008).

For example, in OSCE negotiations informal consultations and coordination in smaller groups often take place prior to formal negotiations involving all the members (Cameroon 2005:23). Such informal interaction in sub-groups has a certain advantage in terms of reaching preferred negotiation outcomes: informality often goes hand in hand with a lack of hierarchy that ensures general trust and rules out representation problems (Jönsson and Elgström 2006), thus providing information that reduces uncertainty about the expected behaviour of others (Hall and Taylor 1996:945). Within the EU framework, the number of scheduled meetings that are informal in nature has drastically increased, for instance informal Ministerial Councils, discussions "in the margins" of COREPER or Ministerial Councils, or adding AOB (any other business) agenda issues to Council meeting agendas. Lewis (2010:653) has calculated that the number of informal EU discussion formats has increased by 14.5 per cent per term over the past few years. The informal setting, for example informal "Gymnich" meetings (Dür *et al.* 2010c), provide the opportunity for a more open exchange of views to investigate the other parties' preferences, test their own positions and identify possible allies. Also, the media have no access to these discussions, thus ensuring more open exchange without fears that the positions expressed by the negotiators could be "checked" by their domestic constituencies. The effects of informal norms and rules are often explained using sociological constructivism theoretical tools (Lewis 2003, 2005). Yet, previous studies by Tallberg (2010b) and Niemann and Mak (2010) prove that institutions can also be approached from the rational choice perspective.

One common concept in institutionalist thinking is that "institutions affect outcomes" (Bjurulf and Elgström 2004). Institutions emerge as a result of actors' interaction in order to achieve commonly defined goals. There are three strands of logic for explaining what may lead to institutionalisation: functional logic, the logic of normative appropriateness and the logic of socialisation. According to functional logic, which this study also applies, creating institutions can help actors increase the efficiency of achieving their goals. The origin of institutions has been explained here by reference to "their capacity to help states overcome collective action dilemmas, related to high transaction costs and information asymmetries" (Tallberg 2010b:635).

The concept of institutional efficiency was initially discussed by North (1990:3), who argued that "institutions *are* the rules of the game"; since the institutions provide specific structures, the actors can take advantage of these institutional conditions in multilateral communication. According to North, the "major role of institutions in a society is to reduce uncertainty by establishing a stable structure to human interaction" (ibid.:6).

The logic of normative appropriateness focuses on norms and inconsistencies and views institutions as frameworks of norm-consistency guardians (Schimmelfennig, 2000, 2001, 2005). Finally, according to the logic of socialisation, actors are expected to reorient their attitudes and behaviours towards institutions' norms (Smith 2004:33, Lewis 2003, 2005) and be guided by shared ideas of what constitutes appropriate behaviour (March and Olsen 2009).

How stable are institutions? Once created, do they persist for ever? Actors may seek to change institutions over time; however, there may be reasons why actors decide to rely on existing ones. Smith (2004:30) explains that one of the prevailing strategic reasons is related to access to information, as "information problems prevent a direct calculation of ends and means when attempting institutional change". Therefore, actors may use existing institutions if the costs of membership are not too high. Indeed, this argument can be related to institutionalised coalitions in the Council. Despite claims by some scholars that the importance of persistent coalitions in EU decision-making has declined (Hosli 1996), member states evaluate the costs of such institutionalised cooperation as rather low compared to the benefits these institutions offer. To safeguard their political interests and to gain the bargaining advantage, member states are willing to cooperate with their "most natural peers" i.e.neighbours, provided there are pre-established institutional conditions that reduce the costs of such exchange.

2.2.1 On the notion of institutionalisation: shared goals, structures and interaction intensity

Based on the above discussion, how can we be sure that the institutional embeddedness of the cooperation is crucial in determining coalition members' bargaining power? What conditions does the cooperation framework have to fulfil in order to be considered as institutionalised?

In this study, institutionalisation is defined as the fulfilment of three conditions:

- shared goals,
- underlying structures and
- interaction intensity.

Shared goals: Numerous examples demonstrate common cooperation goals in the EU. The very idea of integration rests on the objectives of the internal market, environmental policy etc. Even projects extending to sub-groups of member states can follow common goals, such as enhanced cooperation in the field of the CFSP. This distinction between long-term and short-term goals is essential in distinguishing the patterns of coalitions. When aligning in *ad hoc* coalitions, member states share short-term goals to increase their voting power on a particular issue. By its very nature, the cooperation pattern does not provide for any defined agreement on the goals of cooperation.

Institutional coalitions demonstrate a much higher degree of formalisation in setting common objectives. For example, the long-term goals of the Benelux cooperation are defined in Article 41 of the Benelux Economic Union (BEU Treaty) (Rood 1997:14). The condition of defining common long-term goals becomes obvious at the level of political space (Veen 2011). Accordingly, on a broader socio-economic dimension the actors of an institutionalised coalition may exhibit more coherent positions. Goal-directed behaviour is a necessary precondition for bargaining success because it ensures that all sides "end up better off than they would otherwise be" (Milner 1992:468).

Institutions are established to solve general or specific problems. Consequently, the establishment of institutionalised coalitions follows functional logic: member states create coordination formats with particular structures and cooperation procedures in order to fulfill a concrete task, i.e. increase communication efficiency and generate a bargaining advantage through mutual exchange. Hence, the formation of institutionalised coalitions addresses shortcomings in the negotiation environment, namely uncertainty about others' positions, a shortage of expertise and/or power distribution imbalances.

Drawing upon its definition (see 2.1), coalition-building means that member states *coordinate* their behaviour in order to achieve goals they have agreed upon (Elgström *et al.* 2001:113). In a broader sense, coordination means an "act of working together" (Nedergaard 2008:3). In practical terms with regard to coordination on EU issues, this boils down to the interaction between the "individual departments, agencies, politicians, and officials, involved in a particular policy area or with respect to an activity or task" (Kassim 2001:7). For coordination to be effective, it has to ensure that goals, activities and interdependences are present (Nedergaard 2008:4); coordination that does not follow shared goals fails. Likewise, shortcomings in communication between the actors diminish coordination efficiency. Besides, effective coordination may counterbalance scarce resources because the mutual exchange is carried out rationally and in the most effective way. Thus, successful coordination depends on effective channels of communication, as well as on the skills and expertise of the actors. It is also indirectly correlated with the type of national EU policy coordination and its capacity to engage in intergovernmental cooperation. In the case of Council negotiations, coordination largely takes place amongst the public actors, i.e. government officials representing different policy sectors and levels of government.

Effective intergovernmental coordination may create common ground in regard to positions that is further "translated" into joint action. One of the practical ways for undertaking joint action is the presentation of a common statement or a common position paper in a Council meeting. Further, the institutionalised coalition may "nominate" a leader to voice the commonly agreed position on behalf of the group. "Outsiders", i.e. other member states, would perceive this message as the group's common position. One advantage that stems directly from such institutionalised cooperation is others' perception that the coalition is "speaking with one voice". This strategic power pooling grants bargaining leverage to the coalition members (Meunier 2000, Selck and Kuipers 2005, Smith 2006).

Underlying structures: Douglas North, who in 1993 won a Nobel Prize for his contribution to new institutionalism theory, pointed out that institution provides specific structures that may be strategically applied by actors in multilateral communication. According to the main concept on which new institutionalism is based, every institution can be characterised by an "institutional environment" consisting of particular structures, procedures, practices and paradigms. Approached from the new institutionalism perspective, institutionalised coalitions fulfil such conditions. They exhibit an underlying framework of (more or less formalised) interaction, are characterised by communication channels and follow established intra-group practices and procedures. Though pre-established, these practices can be characterised as informal cooperation networks as defined by Naurin and Lindahl (2007:4) and Börzel (2010:194) rather than as formalised intergovernmental structures. Coordination in informal networks is based on mutual resource dependencies and, as informal negotiation systems may share information, pooling resources, planning together and working in collaboration (Nan 2008:113). These networks can also be approached from a relational perspective, by focusing on the contacts, ties and connections of the individuals (Elgström and Jönsson 2004, Naurin and Lindahl 2007). From a geographical perspective, these institutional networks can stretch across borders and frame transgovernmental links. Accessibility is no longer contingent upon one's physical location (Elgström and Jönsson 2004), hence contacts with another country's officials can be just as natural and intensive as with domestic actors.

The application of institutionalism to coalition-building, as explained in previous sections, helps us to assess the effects of institutionalisation on bargaining power. Coalitions, approached as "institutions", are equipped with the structural tools needed for exchange. One of the important prerequisites in this regard is interaction routes. With regard to underlying communication networks, we can distinguish between two main interaction channels within institutionalised coalitions: the capital-to-capital route, i.e. between the officials who are in charge of the issue, and the coordination network comprising the member states' permanent representations in Brussels. The latter involves informal consultations involving the counsellors prior to working group meetings, contacts amongst the permanent representatives (COREPER ambassadors) or their supporting *Mertens* and *Antici* diplomats. Furthermore, institutionalised cooperation networks can act as "open systems" or "closed systems", depending on the tradition of the particular institutionalised framework or issues at hand. If an institutionalised coalition functions as an open system, it can invite additional member states to take part in the intra-coalition exchange.

Arregui and Thomson (2009:659) argue that networks give member states more bargaining power. As networks are limited to select participants, they create so-called "in-camera effects". Such an in-camera setting ensures a higher level of openness and insulation, i.e. "insiders" can speak more frankly about their positions and exchange other valuable information about "outsiders". Given that member states have incentives to disclose and misrepresent the information (Fearon 1995), the "veil of secrecy" in the in-camera setting may encourage officials to exchange information with a limited number of cooperation partners. Internalisation, thus, enhances both openness and diffuses reciprocity, and promotes the development of norm-guided rules. Schimmelfennig (2000:135) argues that norm-conforming behaviour may result in "habitualisation" if the structural conditions of the internalisation of norms remain stable. By habitualisation he means that on an individual level the persons and groups that regularly interact subsequently become habituated in reciprocal roles.

It should be noted that new institutionalism deals with norm-guided behaviour in the light of rational choice theory. Individuals do not adopt specific behaviour because it is perceived to be the "appropriate thing to do" but rather to avoid being punished by less advantageous deals in the future or simply because they do not see a better alternative.

Drawing upon the conditions of in-camera settings, we are equipped for explaining reciprocity phenomena amongst the coalition members. Internalisation provides a favourable environment for reciprocity. This is because actors reveal information while "expecting mutual responsiveness" from the others (Lewis 2010:652). It is acknowledged that institutionalisation enhances the conditions for diffuse reciprocity. As explained by Keohane (1982, quoted in Warntjen 2010:669), this type of reciprocity is particularly crucial in making concessions because it relies on the expectations of negotiation partners that "there will be a roughly equivalent action to one's […] sometime in the future". Despite short-term sacrifices, diffuse reciprocity allows more mutually beneficial cooperation deals within the context of institutionalised cooperation.

Interaction intensity: Finally, one of the key conditions for cooperation to be perceived as institutionalised is related to the degree of interaction intensity. In contrast to *ad hoc* coalitions, interaction within institutionalised coalitions is based on repeated and frequent interaction. There is a direct correlation that states that interaction intensity has an impact on institutional stability. This is because interaction intensity mirrors the frequency of the contacts and, hence, the degree of internalisation: the more frequent the interaction, the higher the stability of the institution (Barnett and Finnmore 1999). One could hypothesise that cooperation amongst those ministers who meet most frequently is more advanced compared to those Council configurations with a low meeting frequency. For example, we can expect contacts between the ministers of foreign affairs (who meet monthly) to be more institutionalised than those of the ministers of health and social affairs, who meet twice per presidency term.

Repeated interaction influences the efficiency of communication in two ways: by developing an "in-camera" setting and by affecting the "shadow of the future". Empirical studies demonstrate that when expectations regarding repeated interaction are high, the likelihood of cooperative moves is greater (Starkey *et al.* 1999). Cooperation theorists suggest that the institutional environment may contribute to extending the shadow of the future and thus enhance the cooperative behaviour of negotiation actors (Fearon 1998:270). It can be argued that in institutionalised cooperation, the "shadow of the future" is long enough to believe that concessions today will be "re-paid" in the future. This rational is also captured in the Prisoners' Dilemma, which draws on the classical cooperation model according to which the maximum gain for two parties can be reached by mutual cooperation. Nevertheless, this model has some limitations when applied to EU negotiation situations, partly because of the multilateral nature of the EU negotiation system compared to the bilateral model as presented in the Prisoner's Dilemma (Smith 2004), and also partly because of the multi-issue nature of negotiations (Odell 2010). However, the Prisoner's Dilemma model may be helpful in explaining that governments' behaviour emerges from the *expectations* of other actors' choices and the *willingness to interact* instead of explicit agreements (Axelrod 2000). This is an important precondition in coalition-building situations because decision-making takes place in the uncertainty about others' preferences and the actors have to rely on expectations and previous experiences about other member states' behaviour in negotiations.

2.2.2 Explaining the effects of institutionalisation: a theoretical framework

One can argue that coalitions, including institutionalised ones, are designed on the basis of power-seeking considerations. The idea that seeking power is a primary motivation behind coalition-building was acknowledged in early works on coalition-building theory (Riker 1962, in Selck 2006) and further elaborated by scholars dealing with EU policy (Winkler 1998, Meunier 2000, Reynaud *et al.* 2008).

Following power-seeking considerations, actors receive gains from coalition-building either by pooling votes or by strategic interaction that contributes to overcoming collective action dilemmas. According to voting power-pooling logic, by framing coalitions member states aim to achieve blocking minorities or winning majorities (Winkler 1998, Reynaud *et al.* 2008). This strategy is more common when decisions are taken under the QMV rule: by gathering enough votes to block a decision, member states can prevent an unwanted decision from being passed. Hence, "coalitions become necessary, almost inevitable" (Wallace 1990, quoted in Elgström *et al.* 2001). This trend has become even more evident since the adoption of the Lisbon Treaty, which provides that the share of legislative proposals adopted with QMV rule will considerably increase. While acknowledging the significance of the voting rule for strategies applied in coalition-building, one should also bear in mind that in practice, regardless of the formal voting rule, the consensus norm prevails in the Council (Lewis 2000, 2003, Heisenberg 2005). Because of this feature of Council work, some studies call it the "Consensual Council", emphasising the trend towards holding a formal vote only on salient issues (Høland and Hansen 2010). Golub (2012:151), for instance, provides evidence that "explicit voting takes place only about 20 per cent of the time".

Regardless of the voting rule, coalition-building behaviour is very frequent feature of day-to-day Council work. It is extremely rare for an individual country to openly demonstrate its dissent at the voting stage of the Council legislative process (Veen 2011:121). Voting against the majority carries a cost in terms of reputation, which is why member states strive to find allies to avoid reputation repercussions. Size is definitely a significant condition in explaining member states' decision to vote "no". Heisenberg (2005:74) has observed that large and populous states more often decide to vote against a proposal. Accordingly, following power considerations, smaller states strive to pool power by forming coalitions and thus to increase their bargaining power.

Voting power considerations, however, are not necessarily the only reasons behind coalition-building; coalitions are framed not only to attain specific voting thresholds, they are also based on affinities and ideas (Hayes-Renshaw and Wallace 1997:295). Indeed, member states can affect outcomes even when they are unable to block a decision, i.e. when the number of votes is insufficient to achieve the blocking minority thresholds. Low voting thresholds are in fact a feature of most territorially constituted institutional coalitions. Neither the Benelux nor the Nordic-Baltic coalition members can jointly reach thresholds to block a decision. This opens up the possibility of explanations of coalition-building that are based on considerations on how to affect the outcomes other than vote-pooling alone.

In the introduction of this chapter it was said that one of the most sustainable practices concerning cooperation with neighbours on EU policies are the prime ministers' breakfast meetings, which are held in Brussels before formal Council negotiations start. This is only one example of several ways in which neighbours cooperate. Other interaction networks range from consultations between the senior officials of different ministries, to exchange between experts who cooperate on specific issues. This section sheds light on the causal mechanisms by means of which the gains of this cooperation in terms of bargaining advantage can be explained. Based on the discussion of conditions for coalition formation, where we earlier distinguished between *ad hoc* and institutionalised coalitions, I will below elaborate a theoretical framework for explaining the effects of institutional coalitions.

It would, however, be inaccurate to claim that institutions are "wondrous" and that it is enough to institutionalise a given cooperation format in order to gain advantages in terms of the negotiation outcome. For instance, *ad hoc* coalitions that operate on a short-term basis and lack any structural and institutional environment can still be powerful power-pooling tools. Here we have to create a link to member states' policy preferences. This study has acknowledged the efficiency of interest-based coalitions formed among likeminded peers to aggregate voting power. Overall, such interest-based member state behaviour dominates the Council's day-to-day work. Member states' behaviour in the Council is predominantly guided by their policy preferences, which are transformed into negotiation positions around the negotiation table. This indicates that we have to take into account also another important background variable, namely member states' policy preferences. Institutionalisation is a necessary but not a sufficient determinant for coalitions to yield bargaining power for their members. In other words, if policy preferences (formulated by domestic constituencies of the individual member states) diverge, institutional embeddedness alone cannot ensure the effective output of cooperation. The role of preferences will be explained in more detail in 2.3. The causality mechanism below is constructed with respect to an advantageous option when the policy preferences of individual member states are close.

The theoretical model aims to answer the question "*Why* do neighbours cooperate?" The theory I advance here generates a hypothesis about the institutional embeddedness of cooperation amongst the members of coalition:

H1: The higher the degree to which a coalition is institutionalised, the greater potential it has for increasing its members' bargaining power.

In a nutshell, this hypothesis suggests that the institutional embeddedness of coalitions gives an additional advantage compared to sort-term *ad hoc* coalitions. To this end, this study develops a causality mechanism based on which institutionalised coalitions enhance bargaining power. The main argument here is that institutionalised coalitions give their members bargaining advantage by means of three mechanisms: (1) the *exchange of information*, which counterbalances the asymmetries in information distribution at pre-negotiation stages, (2) *expertise-pooling*, which allows member states to share resources and provide better argumentation for their proposals, and (3) strengthening the normative justifications that may lead to "*rhetorical action*" and normative entrapment of opponents.

Exchange of information: It is widely acknowledged that access to information and expertise provides a bargaining advantage. This study distinguishes between information and expertise as two separate concepts. Information is defined as an actor's knowledge about the strategic conditions of negotiations, for example preference information about other parties' interests, national resistance points, domestic constraints and actors' strategic moves during negotiations (Tallberg 2008:696–701, Bailer 2010:756). Besides this type of information, member states need to have information on content and decision-making goals, which they need to frame their own negotiation positions and develop negotiation strategies. Knowledge about the negotiation positions of others reduces uncertainty and improves the negotiation situation (Bailer 2003:7). Expertise (elaborated in the next section) is related more to a knowledge of the technical aspects, implementation consequences and an understanding of how the decision-making procedure works (Tallberg 2008:701).

The rational choice approach is based on the assumption that multidimensional decision-making entails an increase in the transaction costs (Moravcsik 1999:811, Zimmer *et al.* 2005: 407, Sharpf 2006:848). Ury and Fisher (1988:7) explain that, apart from typical transaction costs (in terms of time and energy devoted to negotiating), negotiation partners may experience asymmetries of power and information and dissatisfaction with negotiation results. Reducing one type of cost can increase another. Most scholars dealing with international organisations (IOs) acknowledge that actors may create and *use* institutions consciously in order to reduce transaction costs and, thus, to overcome uncertainty.

What kinds of uncertainties do member states face in EU negotiations? First, negotiations in the EU are multilateral, i.e. involve a large number of parties; the increasing number of participating actors raises transaction costs (Zartman and Berman 1982, Finke 2009, Odell 2010), leading some actors to be better informed than others. This creates asymmetries in information distribution. Access to information frames negotiation leverage (Dupont 1994, Shell 1999) because it gives an overview of the context in which the issue is discussed, what is at stake, and what the needs and preferences of other parties are. Parties that possess superior expertise and information are "better positioned to identify potential agreements and shape outcomes in their own favour" (Tallberg 2008:700). On the other hand, the scarcity of information hinders the efficiency of negotiations. Drawing on the study of EU treaty negotiations, Finke (2009:471) demonstrates that the effect of imperfect information has been evident in most IGC negotiations.

Second, according to rationalist explanations, actors may be unable to locate a mutually preferable negotiation settlement due to parties' incentives to hide or misrepresent information. Negotiators are often "dishonest about their true preferences" because then they can be easily "exploited" by others (Tallberg 2004:1001). The distribution of information itself can become a source of power (Bailer 2003, 2010) not only because of accessibility problems, but also due to the strategic dynamics that "result from the combination of asymmetric information and incentives to dissemble" (Fearon 1995:381). In the context of EU decision-making, member states can overestimate the success of their perceived strategies as a result of misjudging information provided by other member states. If their strategy is to achieve a favourable outcome by joining other member states' position (free rider tactics), they may rely on information about others' willingness to fight and they fail if the other party turns out to have misrepresented real intentions. This is one reason why member states continuously use "corridor exchange" to check if other allies are still of the same opinion (Meerts and Cede 2004:132, Delereux 2009:201). Drawing on rationalist explanations for war, Fearon (1995:397) notes that "to be genuinely informative about a state's actual willingness to fight, a signal must be costly in such a way that a state with lesser resolve or capability might not wish to send it". In other words, revealing or hiding information is a negotiation strategy. Delreux (2009) illustrates this in a study on environmental negotiations: Some member states succeed in keeping their fall-back positions secret, which generates an advantage because they can push decisions towards the lowest denominator even if they would have been able to accept stronger deals.

Accordingly, some actors have private information that is kept asymmetrically divided. Since negotiation parties have incentives to misrepresent information about their preferences (Risse and Kleine 2010:709), mutually beneficial agreements are difficult to achieve. Hiding information and member states' true valuations can be used as negotiation tactics. This creates uncertainty among other negotiation actors about the fall-back positions and the range of agreements that would be acceptable. In such situations actors may "use signals sent by others to estimate their resistance points" (Dür and Mateo 2004:5). In high-conflict situations, information about disclosed preferences becomes a strong asset. As Barnett and Finnmore (1999:710) point out, in regard to international organisations, "information is power"; withholding information gives the actor a better negotiating position.

One can further distinguish between public, private and secret information (Dupont 1994) according to the availability of information. Negotiations in the EU are highly secretive and only the final voting results are available for the public record (Hosli 1999). In the pre-negotiation phase, most information is either private (possessed by single member states) or restricted to groups of states. One can also observe information distribution asymmetries between member states and institutions, such as the Commission.

The link between information asymmetries and negotiation strategy is largely acknowledged. Odell (2010:621) claims that integrative bargaining tactics include communicating information more fully, including the "joint exploration for opportunities to create joint gains". However, this kind of cooperation is not altruistic and provides for compensation in terms of mutual gains. Drawing on negotiation theory, information exchange "expands the pie" (Dupont 1994). Another example of the link between information asymmetries and negotiation strategy is provided by Bailer (2010:750), who argues that, in information-rich environments where counterparts are well informed about each other's positions, it is much harder to "bluff" or to exaggerate constraints.

It is assumed that institutions and organisations are efficient solutions for solving problems of incomplete information (Barnett and Finnmore 1999:699). Institutions can act as "intervening variables" i.e. mediating between states' "pursuit of self-interest and political outcomes by changing the structure of constraints that states possess through their control over information" (ibid.).

Based on the aforementioned theoretical discussion, how can the variable of information asymmetries be linked to the causality of the explanatory framework adopted in this study? Institutionalised coalitions can facilitate information exchange and consequently provide additional bargaining power by means of two mechanisms: access to information and the processing of information. Access to information that would otherwise be restricted to individual actors is perceived by member states as a benefit (particularly while the costs of membership in the coalition are low). Member states cooperate within institutionalised coalitions because they provide access to information that counterbalances the asymmetries in information distribution at the pre-negotiation stage. The institutionalised set-up of cooperation enhances exchange because of the "similarity of actors" and their preferences (König and Bräuninger 1998:448), whereas access to information through well-established networks reduces their uncertainty about others' positions and helps to better frame their own positions. Institutions can provide actors with the additional resources for processing information, hence member states with scarce resources or little experience may have difficulties in consistently processing the flow of information. Mutual cooperation may be advantageous in helping them to sort and prioritise accessible information (Smith 2004:29).

Consequently, the exchange of information is directly correlated with the degree of institutionalisation. Interaction in smaller groups is based on strategic calculations of costs and benefits (Schimmelfennig 2005b:830). There is a clear correlation between the degree of internalisation and the effectiveness of information exchange. The ways in which the limited negotiation setting (in smaller groups) facilitates information exchange are discussed in 2.2.1. In short, the sub-group setting generates information benefits by enhancing distribution information asymmetries in favour of the insiders in a coalition (Delreux 2009:735). This is because the intra-coalition groups tend to develop internal cultures and views that do not necessarily match those outside the organisation whom it serves (Barnett and Finnmore 1999:723). For example, a study on EU coordination meetings in the UN demonstrates that countries that take part in information networking benefit from the exchange and openness of their partners. Networks of close allies that are open to sharing information "brings benefits for everyone involved by taking the level of information higher than any single member state can muster" (Degrand-Guillaud 2009:423). This example demonstrates that information exchange takes place more openly within less formal, in-camera settings.

The formation of institutionalised coalitions may have further consequences for overall decision-making in the EU. Cooperation networks may become quite independent, with a high level of mutual trust and conditions for diffuse reciprocity in exchanging sensitive knowledge. Such reasoning goes hand in hand with theoretical assumptions that an institution can become autonomous because of its control over information. Given the secretive nature of Council decision-making, internal trust among coalition parties may serve as a precondition for obtaining secret or restricted information (Bjurulf and Elgström 2004:254).

Expertise-pooling: In analysing power asymmetries, Habeeb (1988) noted that actors may compensate for the structural weaknesses that stem from size and scarce resources by using behavioural power in terms of mutual exchange and negotiation techniques, particularly in regard to specific issues, as EU legislation has become complex and technical in regard to content. Member states with richer economic and human resources have an advantage and better expertise in evaluating Commission proposals. In some policy fields, decision-making is characterised as "expertise-driven". This applies in particular to the regulatory decision-making mode (Hofmann 2009:484). Consequently, member states with richer resources not only gain a structural advantage, but also profit from the distribution of factual and technical information.

Tallberg (2008:700) distinguishes between two categories of expertise: content expertise and procedural expertise. Content expertise relates to technical knowledge of the issue, which is important in two ways: it allows member states to identify their preferences in a highly professional way and it allows them to evaluate the preferences of others. Procedural expertise helps the negotiators to be better equipped with an interpretation of different provisions that are defined in the treaties and that directly or indirectly affect the outcome. For instance, the Lisbon Treaty abolished the traditional comitology procedure, replacing it with two different articles in the TFEU, i.e. Art. 290 and Art. 291. These articles define how and under what conditions legislative power may be delegated to the Commission. As the Treaty itself does not explicitly define the possible consequences of the application of Art. 290 or Art. 291 in terms of legal basis, those negotiators who have expertise on these procedures are better positioned in Council negotiations. Furthermore, expert knowledge contributes directly to member states' issue-power because they can formulate more nuanced positions, apply credible argumentation and identify alternatives according to others' preferences.

Studies on small states suggest that the member states may counterbalance their structural disadvantages either by developing expertise on select prioritised issues (Panke 2010) or by exchanging and pooling expert knowledge with those member states with greater expert capacity on the given issue. In relation to the concept of professional knowledge in international relations, Haas (1992) introduced the term "epistemic communities" as networks of professionals who deal extensively with narrow issues and have consequently created well-established networks of competence (in Jönsson and Strömvik 2004, Beyers 2005).

As it is difficult to differentiate issue-knowledge from procedural knowledge, the two aspects are often linked. Jönsson and Strömvik (2004:54), for example, argue that EU networks rest on a combination of "know-how" and "know-who". It is not only important to have a good command of the technical details but also to know how to address concerns and positions. In other words, expert knowledge is an important determinant in contacts with supranational institutions, in particular with the Commission.

How can institutionalised cooperation contribute to a party's situation in negotiations and to what extent do institutional conditions matter? Countries that strategically involve "knowledge brokers" (Broman 2009:95) in framing their policy may share this knowledge rationally through interaction with other like-minded partners, yielding benefits in terms of increased bargaining power. Studying EU committees, Fouilleux *et al.* (2005) found that knowledge in terms of technical expertise may give member states an advantage due to exchange in networking at different decision-making levels. Furthermore, institutional theory acknowledges that institutional interaction may "transfer knowledge", in particular when approached from a micro-level. Individuals, through their interaction and knowledge transfer, may exert an influence on macro-level outcomes (Gehring and Oberthürn 2009:125).

Similarly, members of institutionalised coalitions may pool their knowledge on issue expertise and procedural proficiency because of the duration of the cooperation by establishing networks of the epistemic community level and through inter-ministerial contacts that link experts who are working on the same dossier. Nedergaard (2009:23) finds evidence of such well-developed expert networks among the Nordic countries in frames of cooperation within the strongly institutionalised framework of the Nordic Council of Ministers.

This study argues that the institutionalised set-up enhances expertise-pooling at different levels of Council decision making, in particular at the Council working group and COREPER levels, with rational choice institutionalism providing further explanations for this argument. Rational actors communicate through their networks in order to gain information and pool expertise; indeed, Elgström *et al.* (2001) have observed that knowledge is one of the most important determinants in choosing networking partners.

One can expect expertise-pooling to be enhanced through institutionalised cooperation. According to international organisation theories, professionalism serves as one of the preconditions for insulation (Barnett and Finnmore 1999:723), shapes the environment for normative orientation and creates communities of professional networks inside the organisation. Moravcsik (1997:534), on the other hand, refers to transnational communication and the dissemination of scientific information as a tool for cognitive ideological change.

Whilst information exchange is important throughout the negotiation process, expertise on the issue is particularly necessary at the initial phase of the decision-making process. When the draft legislative proposal is transferred from the Commission to the Council, i.e. to the member states, work on framing a national position starts in all EU capitals. Scholars dealing with negotiation theory acknowledge that expert knowledge is crucial during the framing phase of international negotiations (Shell 1999, Odell 2010) because experts have the capacity to evaluate and develop credible normative justifications for their positions (Risse 2000). From a rational choice perspective, arguing is the process of justifying one's positions and preferences (Risse and Kleine 2010:709). Expertise becomes an important determinant of a member state's bargaining power in Council negotiations because actors argue about *factual* claims (Warntjen 2010:674), whereas the institutional set-up allows the coalition to develop a mutual "goal-oriented and strategic interaction" (ibid.) in framing a better argument. Due to the frequency and duration of interaction, the preferences of member states within an institutionalised coalition are broadly known to all of its members, for instance Nordic neighbours are aware of Danish opt-outs in the field of migration policy, Swedish preferences in environmental policy, Finnish expert capacities in the field of forest preservation etc. Each of the members will have *expectations* about others' preferences, priorities and expert capacities. In long-standing relationships, actors reveal their positions more truthfully and explicitly, and may "justify their positions in order to increase the reputation and/or provide information relevant for future negotiations" (ibid.). Once the members of the coalition manage to present coherent (instead of constantly changing) justifications, this will give them an advantage *vis-à-vis* their opponents. Finally, as a group the actors cooperate in the environment of diffuse reciprocity, they may gain benefits from pooled expert capital and rely on exchange when it comes to factual and technical proficiency. Consequently, an institutionalised set-up enhances the conditions of exchange that equip the members of a coalition with better bargaining conditions.

Rhetorical action: The third mechanism by which the coalition members gain a bargaining advantage is related with the strength of the argument. Rhetorical action is a term that was proposed by Schimmelfennig (2001) and refers to the joint development of a set of claims and justifications of positions with the purpose of convincing an audience or depriving opponents of rhetorical materials (Schimmelfennig 2001, Morin and Gold 2010). This definition indicates two important conditions of rhetorical action: the presence of an audience and mechanisms for convincing opponents. The concept of rhetorical action in the tradition of rational choice accounts was originally applied by Schimmelfennig (2001) to illustrate normative arguments that have been used by member states in justifying their bargaining positions regarding the EU's enlargement to the East. As rational actors, member states are not interested in normative goals *per se*, they try to maximise their utility. They tend to conform to norms by following cost-benefit calculations in order to avoid punishment in terms of exclusion or reputation damages. Rational actors' motivation for entering negotiations is to achieve their preferences. The process of exchanging arguments is "mere window dressing"; what really counts is "persuad(ing) the public of the appropriateness of the bargaining position" (Grobe 2010:10) by making reference to a normative goal. One can assume that the general public are only partly informed and use cues in evaluating the actions of their governments. By using normative appeals, foreign governments may rhetorically address the public in other countries and rhetorically entrap their governments. It is acknowledged that the rhetorical action model only works when another party, i.e. an audience, is listening (Schimmelfennig 2001). An audience may, for example, be the "European public, who takes the role of an arbiter" (Grobe 2010:11). Risse and Kleine (2010:710) illustrate the effects of rhetorical action in the following way: "While instrumentally motivated speakers use arguments and justifications of their preferences, at least someone in the audience must listen and *adjust* her behaviour or rethink her understanding of self-interest accordingly so that strategic actors can advance their interests". That does not, however, mean that the actor deliberately changes preferences. By developing functional persuasion theory, Grobe (2010:12) explains argument-driven changes in the bargaining process from a rationalist perspective, proposing the concept of "functional persuasion". An important distinction to Checkel's model of persuasion is that functional persuasion occurs under conditions of uncertainty, i.e. when new causal knowledge becomes available. The persuader provides new causal knowledge as a justification of their position and may convince the persuadee of the validity of their claims. Grobe's model is helpful in explaining the mechanism of "convincing"; the persuadee simply "alters his initial beliefs *without* changing preferences" (ibid.).

It is worth mentioning that one additional condition has to be fulfilled in order to ensure rhetorical action, namely legitimacy. Legitimacy is an important prerequisite in the entrapment hypothesis. For a collective decision to be legitimate, it must provide for the opportunity to offer justifications that are consistent with the idea of a common good. An actor or state is regarded as legitimate if its behaviour corresponds with practices that are highly valued in the given environment (Schimmelfennig 2000:116). In this regard, the EU is considered to be one of the most "normatively structured systems" (Thomas 2009:344). Despite the diverging preferences of member states in this highly normative environment, decision-making is influenced by normative commitments that allow agreements to be reached even on mutually conflicting issues. Agreements are enhanced either by means of a reference to "meta-norms" concerning intrinsic values (e.g. the credibility of the EU as a global actor, human rights, support for democracy, high environmental standards, anti-discrimination etc.) or because of procedural standards, including informal practices such as consensus, reciprocity, confidentiality and exchange. According to the rhetorical action model, a single member state or a group of member states presents the justified position to the "audience" (the other actor/group of actors); "Once the audience is convinced by a particular position, the speaker opposing this position is literally left without a choice" (Grobe 2010:11) and outsiders have to accept their position because they cannot resist, unless they want to risk losing credibility.

If the government presenting convincing justifications for its positions uses rhetorical action strategically, this can provide a considerable bargaining advantage. A good argument here is not understood in light of the deliberative process that leads to preference shifts (as explained by sociological constructivism) (Risse 2000, Checkel 2002), but in rationalist accounts: approaching an argument as a means of leading to a "better understanding of the problem at hand" (Grobe 2010).

How can institutionalised coalitions enhance the mechanism of rhetorical action? In order to pool norm-consistent arguments, a "forum" is necessary (Thomas 2009). In other words, a single actor is less successful than a group where the physical environment of trust and norm-diffusion has a role to play (Manners 2002).

Morin and Gold (2010:567) argue that "participants must share a 'common lifeworld', i.e. a set of fundamental norms and system of beliefs against which they can weigh claims". This "common lifeworld" is framed through communicative action, a prerequisite of institutionalised coalitions. Due to the institutionalised embeddedness of coalitions, the parties develop mutual trust internally. Trust further creates incentives to be trustworthy and to engage in a process of argumentation. Thus, member states may use the institutional environment as an *intervening* mechanism in creating norm-based arguments. Members of an institutionalised coalition do not take norms and rules for granted, as their behaviour is "motivated by self-defined political preferences" and thus power-oriented (Schimmelfennig 2005:830). Provided that the members of an institutionalised coalition share converging preferences, they may jointly develop stronger normative justifications for their positions by acting as a group and thus rhetorically entrapping their opponents.

2.3 Brining preferences in

Asked about Nordic cooperation in the EU, the Finnish Foreign Minister Alexander Stubb said: "A Nordic bloc in the EU does not exist [...]. We exchange ideas and share information, but we do not necessarily always think the same way" (European Observer, 6 Dec. 2010). How does this statement relate to the argument put forward in this study, which has claimed the existence of a persistent territorially constituted coalition as a point of departure?

This section deals with preferences and explains how they relate to the causal mechanism presented in 2.2.2. The effects of institutionalised cooperation cannot be explained by ignoring preferences because preferences are a "fundamental raw material" when starting negotiations (Naurin 2008:20). Preferences reflect what individual actors want to achieve through negotiations (Thomson and Hosli 2006:6). If preferences change, outcome may change. Hence, preferences become additional variables that have to be taken into account. One of the main paradigms of rational choice institutionalism is that "political outcomes are the product of actor preferences and institutional arrangements" (Sullivan and Selck 2007:1153). Whilst institutions define structures, procedures and the rules of governance, preferences determine actors' ideal points regarding the outcomes.

Strictly speaking, preferences should tell us what the states want to get out of negotiations. In practice, however, it is not entirely unproblematic to establish this link. One of the reasons is the probability of so-called "hidden preferences". In his recent study, Thomson (2012:611) argues that "the distinction between actors' stated positions and hidden preferences is central". Nonetheless, it is not easy to identify preferences in practice. Both theoreticians and practitioners can experience some confusion in regard to terminology on the one hand and in regard to measuring preferences on the other. It may, therefore, be helpful to explain the meaning of concepts that are mentioned in relation to preferences and their representation in the negotiations.

In the literature we come across variety of terms, for example policy preferences, real preferences, hidden preferences, stated positions, negotiation positions etc. As regards terminology, this study draws on the classification by Thomson (2011), who offers two central concepts: policy preferences and policy positions ("positions"). Preferences and positions are conceptually distinct terms. Policy preferences are formulated by domestic constituencies and reflect "national economic and political attributes". By contrast, positions stem from policy preferences and are usually represented by negotiators at the outset of negotiations in the Council. By exposing their positions for other negotiation parties, the member states openly announce their underlying interests, i.e. they become "stated positions".

When judging positions (as direct reflections of underlying policy preferences), one needs to bear in mind that sometimes member states hide their real preferences for strategic reasons. It is said then that the positions are not "sincere" and it becomes almost impossible methodologically to identify the underlying policy preferences because the preferences do not correspond to the behaviour expressed by member states in negotiations. In general, however, member states do not have very many reasons to hide their preferences, and their positions mirror their underlying preferences. It is assumed that positions in negotiations reflect the economic interests of individual member states in the sector (Thomson 2012:611).

This approach is in line with the main theoretical assumptions of liberal international relations theory, which explains the positioning of governments in international negotiations. According to this theory, in negotiations states represent some "subset of domestic society; on the basis of whose interests state officials define state preferences and act purposely in world politics" (Moravcsik 1997:518). State preferences are first defined on the national level and then debated internationally to reach specific agreements. At the decision-making stage the preferences are transformed into negotiation positions. Governments, in fact, have little flexibility in making concessions beyond the lines of their national preferences, since they are not autonomous from domestic constituencies. As Moravcsik explains, these constituencies act as "principals"[6] and often represent national interest groups. However, the interests of domestic constituencies are not always coherent and "national interests [...] emerge through domestic political conflict as societal groups compete for political influence" (Moravcsik 1993:481). Thus, the position represented in negotiations is a compromise of national constituencies that is "recognised by governments". Thus, during negotiations governments act as agents representing their principals (interest groups) on the international

---

6   Principal-agent theory draws on rational choice reasoning and explains processes as interaction between two parties – "agent" and "principal". According to this model, the "agent" acts on the behalf of "principal". The theory is used to explain processes in political science and economics.

stage. Governments are constrained not only by the interests of their principals, but also by identities and the power of societal groups (Bailer 2005:5). The underlying motivation for following the agent's expectations is determined by the primary interest of governments "to maintain themselves in office" (Moravcsik 1993:483). Consequently, member states' preferences mainly reflect their economic interests. Governments often state their preferences publicly, for example on enlargement issues (Schneider 2011:11), which puts further constraints on their fulfilling their promises.

Accordingly, the EU policy adopted by member states is a "two level game", i.e. first governments formulate their positions that stem from the policy preferences and then they negotiate at the international level. When applying theoretical explanatory tools, one can identify the presence of Putnam's (1988) "two-level game model", which helps to explain the interrelation between the domestic and international domains.

Usually member states frame their positions at national level before the first meeting of the Council working group, with policy positions mirroring the general public's policy preferences, socio-economic development or, in other words, actors' political space (Veen 2011). On the international level the policy preferences are "translated" into negotiation positions on concrete issues. It should be noted that on the international level the member states may shift their negotiation positions according to external pressure from the EU institutions, other member states or by following their own strategic considerations. Position shifts are the prerequisites for reaching agreement, in particular when there is great heterogeneity of policy positions at the outset of negotiations. The final deal the parties reach in multilateral negotiations is achieved within the zone of agreement. The preferences of some negotiation actors may remain outside this zone, thus representing a distance between their ideal point of preferences and the real deal.

Figure 3: Zone of agreement

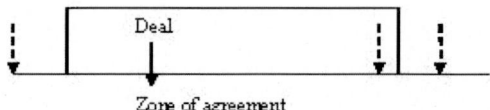

Source: after Odell 2000:26.

The discussion on reaching agreement outlines that "preferences are causally independent of the strategies of other actors" (Moravcsik 1993:519–520) and that the "configuration of independent state preferences determines state behaviour". In other words, negotiation actors not only "translate" their policy preferences into positions but also adjust their own positions to the positions of other member states in Council negotiations. This is the very rationale of the coordination process prior to formal negotiations that is the core argument of this study.

It is worth pointing out that the previous discussion reflects the *formation* of policy preferences, i.e. treats preferences as dependent variables. Though this knowledge is valuable and relevant for a general understanding of the background to coordination amongst the member states, it does not directly fit into the scope of this study. What is more important with respect to "bringing preferences in", is the extent to which member states' different preferences affect negotiations in the Council. As negotiations in the EU are by nature multilateral and thus characterised by a large number of actors with a broad range of preferences, it is crucial to know to what extent preference heterogeneity determines the member states' behaviour in framing coalitions. Thus, apart from approaching preferences as dependent variables, one should also examine their role as independent or intervening variables.

The second approach to dealing with preferences is to regard them as independent variables. Preferences can directly affect bargaining power when used strategically by negotiation parties in the international arena. For example, member states demonstrating high preference intensity and commitment to their preferences gain a bargaining advantage (Bailer 2005, Thomas 2009). Indeed, besides substance itself, preference intensity is regarded as the most important determinant in the analytical evaluation of the negotiation outcome. It is acknowledged that in case of high preference intensity and similar interests, it is easier to engage in joint activities. This has previously been observed in regional interest representation on environment issues (Tatham 2010).

In Council negotiations member states may opt for hard bargaining tactics particularly in the cases with high issue salience, thus shifting the negotiation outcome closer to their policy preferences. Dealing with the direct effects of preferences on bargaining power, Schelling (1960) hypothesises that heterogeneity of preferences can lead to a bargaining advantage. He labelled this phenomenon the "paradox of weakness" and explained it with the help of the pressure from domestic constituencies. When a government presents an extreme position in Council, it may get a response to its position, given the high domestic concerns. For instance, during the ratification of the Lisbon Treaty the Czech government became particularly powerful in giving its ratification agreement. According to Schelling's model, even a small state may become extremely influential when the effects of domestic constraints are revealed at the international negotiation table. Meanwhile, presenting extreme positions in the Council can be a risky tactic, since such "aggressive" member states may be simply ignored (Bailer 2005).

This study regards preferences as prerequisites of cooperation. In other words, policy preferences determine the choice of cooperation partners and the strategies they select in engaging in common action. After having identified their policy preferences and agreed domestically on the positions to be presented externally, governments approach peers and engage in consultations with them on different aspects of the dossier. One prevailing assumption is that selecting peers rests on the proximity of policy preferences (Saam and Sumpter 2009:359) or, as Naurin (2008:4) puts it, "preferences determine who is cooperating with whom". *Ad hoc* coalitions, by definition, rely on the convergence of preferences, i.e. member states select like-minded peers.

On the other hand, international negotiations are related to "learning process under uncertainty" (Moravcsik 1997:523), which means that before governments can form coalitions they have to acquaint themselves with the positions of other member states. This is partly realised in Council working groups, where the experts from member states report on their preferences in regard to the issue at hand and exchange views on possible agreement dimensions. In order to overcome problems related to asymmetrical information distribution in Council, the governments may also address those peers on the basis of geographical proximity that are "easy to contact". Saam and Sumpter (2009:360) explain this pattern of selecting peers in a study (2009:360). They explain the cooperation gains with the neighbouring states with the help of existing intensive transborder cooperation, for example the flow of services and goods. Intensive exchange may create international policy externalities, such as environmental threats and pollution, which are best combated by creating joint incentives for policy coordination.

When applied to explain the conditionality of institutionalised coalitions, policy preferences become a significant part of the argument. Where cooperation is more substantial, preferences serve as the conditions under which different institutional settings exert an influence on outcomes (König and Bräuninger 1998, Selck 2006). In other words, we need to be aware of the *correlation* effects between cooperation and the underlying preferences; if preferences diverge, no further interaction follows. To this end, this study applies preferences as *intervening variables*, i.e. it does not explain the direct effects of preferences on the bargaining outcome *per se* but approaches them as conditions under which institutional settings can exert an influence on outcomes (König and Bräuninger 1998). The effect of preferences on bargaining power is indirect, i.e. through the choice of cooperation partners. Hence, preferences determine how (and if) member states cooperate in power-pooling endeavours.

Since enlargement, the heterogeneity of policy preferences among the EU-27 has increased. This has contributed to the complexity of reaching a compromise on a proposal. Moreover, the outcome is determined not only by a single state's preferences and the government's capacity to pursue them, but it also puts constraints on finding the right strategy to pursue in Council negotiations. As Moravcsik (1997:523) has noted, governments must think about their positions "within a structure composed of the preferences of other states".

As intergovernmental bargaining is characterised by asymmetrical interdependence, it is assumed that negotiations will be more effective in environments where information is distributed widely. Actors need to cooperate to that end. Agreement to interact and cooperate is explained as a part of a strategic choice of rationally acting states. The question of "who cooperates with whom?" has continuously occupied scholars dealing with coalition theory. Interaction between governments can be conceptualised as a cooperative game of framing coalitions (Sam and Sumpter 2009:357). The logic behind selecting cooperation partners on preference proximity is very much power-based: rational actors aim to influence negotiation outcomes, therefore they select like-minded peers, i.e. member states with converging preferences, in order to aggregate voting power or to jointly shape future policies. A coalition framed by states that share preferences is perceived by outsiders as more credible, since it is less likely that "splitters" can fragment the group (Odell 2010:625). According to liberal intergovernmentalism, *agreement to cooperate* is an important part of the strategic reasoning of rational states. Hence, "collective outcomes are explained as the result of aggregated individual actors based on efficient pursuit of preferences" (Moravcsik and Schimmelfennig 2009:68).

Coming back to the statement by a Nordic minister ("A Nordic bloc in the EU does not exist"), it is worth taking a closer look at the statement using political science analytical tools. There is empirical evidence in the scholarly literature of a coalition among the Nordic states on EU policies. According to the study by Selck and Kuipers (2005:167), the Nordic countries not only share "hesitance" but also "joint success". The two scholars find empirical evidence for close proximity between the policy preferences of Denmark, Sweden and Finland that serves as a background for "jointly influencing EU policy-making". These statements form a puzzle that is worth looking at in more detail. The joint regional coalition is confirmed by the scholars and rejected by the politicians.

The solution to this puzzle is provided by a recent study by Veen (2011), who, instead of approaching policy preferences as a single concept, breaks them down into sub-levels. The main argument put forward by Veen is that the stability of coalitions differs across three levels: (1) political space level, (2) the policy domain level and (3) the issue level. It should be noted that this approach is best represented during the bargaining stage because here governments actively try to cooperate in order to gain more bargaining power. On the other hand during the voting stage the distinction between different analysis levels is less relevant because in open voting (which occurs quite rarely) governments mainly signal to their home constituencies.

Figure 4: Three-level cooperation

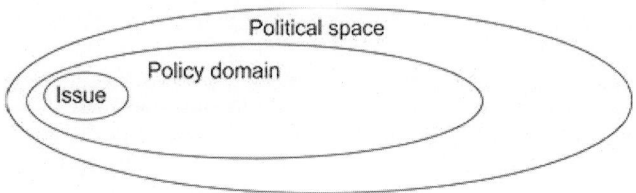

Source: after Veen (2011).

The most stable actor alignments at the bargaining phase are those on the political space level. Political space reveals underlying long-term interests, identity, language and broad socio-economic preferences within which the member states' alignments are quite distinct. Not surprisingly, we often find territorially constituted coalitions on the level of the political space. Accordingly, cooperation on the political space level may result in stable and well-established cooperation structures, for instance institutionalised coalitions. These cooperation forums differ significantly as regards the degree of institutionalisation, the coherency of member states' shared interests. One might expect that because of underlying long-term interests, neighbouring countries establish joint structures in order to enhance transborder exchange. In other words, on the political space level coalitions are more institutionalised. The frequency with which these exchange platforms across borders are used increases the bargaining leverage of institutionalised coalitions in EU negotiations (Panke 2010).

The policy domain level refers to particular policy areas, for example environmental, trade, budgetary issues etc. The stability of an alignment is here less distinct. Though there can be clear patterns in some particular domains, the empirical findings do not demonstrate consistent coalition patterns across domains (Zimmer *et al.* 2005 in Veen 2011:124).

Finally, on the issue level coalitions are both unstable and unpredictable. According to Veen's model, they do not form any persistent patterns across geographical dimensions. It is easy to agree with this statement, since preferences on narrow issues are not distributed according to territorial localisation.

By applying the three-level analytical approach the aforementioned puzzle resolves itself. The Nordic bloc does not exist when approached on the issue level; however, there is reason to believe that the territorially constituted coalition exists on the political space level. This distinction is important and helpful for explaining the empirical findings presented in the following sections of the book. Thus, this study hypothesises that:

H2: The higher the degree of homogeneity of policy preferences amongst the members of a coalition, the more likely it is that intergovernmental cooperation will produce a bargaining advantage.

For territorially constituted coalitions the homogeneity of policy preferences most likely occurs at the political space level.

The previous section explained the extent to which policy preferences affect the level of cooperation amongst member states in Council negotiations. It highlighted the role of policy preferences and defined them as conditions for cooperative behaviour of the member states when engaging in joint action. Though this study initially hypothesised that the institutional embeddedness explains the bargaining advantage of the member states in Council negotiations, we have now revealed the supplementary role of policy preferences. Is institutionalised embeddedness alone a sufficient condition for yielding bargaining power? Which combination of explanatory variables affects the dependent variable most significantly? Is it plausible to say that member states may have convergent preferences but refuse to engage in institutionalised cooperation?

This study assumes that instead of preferences themselves the *link* between preferences and the institutionalisation variable is of major significance. The author takes this into account when creating the research design for this study, which suggests that institutionalised embeddedness alone is not a sufficient determinant for explaining the effects on bargaining power. By adding the preference variable, the study hypothesises that bargaining power is dependent on the effects of institutionalised cooperation combined with preference convergence. Accordingly, three cases represent an explanatory relevance for this study:

1) high degree of institutionalisation + high convergence of preferences;
2) high degree of institutionalisation + low convergence of preferences;
3) low degree of institutionalisation + high convergence of preferences.

The fourth combination (low degree of institutionalisation + low convergence of preferences) is not valid, since no cooperation can be expected.

Table 3 outlines the research design for each set of independent variables. The study hypothesises that the highest bargaining advantage is gained where there is a high degree of institutionalisation and converging preferences. All other sets of independent variables, i.e. high institutionalisation with diverging preferences and low institutionalisation with converging preferences, are expected to yield low bargaining power.

One of the combinations in Table 3 offers quite an extraordinary arrangement, namely low degree of institutionalisation with a high convergence of policy preferences. This case deserves particular attention.

Negotiation situations are typically characterised by uncertainty about the outcomes. Each actor has to make a decision about whether or not to join a coalition. Joining a coalition may improve an actor's situation compared to unitary action and actors may even lower their demands away from their ideal point. Riker (1967) has labelled such tactical moves "quota shaving" (in Bottom et al. 2000:150). "Quota shaving" will occur when actors find themselves in a position of loss. Moreover, an actor's risk acceptance will increase if the threat of being outvoted or overruled increases (Dür and Mateo 2010b:681).

Table 3: Research design

Explanatory factors		Dependent variable
Institutionalisation	Preference convergence	Bargaining power
High	High	High
High	Low	Low
Low	High	Low
Low	Low	Not relevant

Source: Research design of the study.

Based on the aforementioned logic, member states may deliberately refuse to join a coalition if they realise that they would be worse off if they joined a coalition than if they did not. The reasoning behind such considerations can be explained by possible reputation costs (not being identified with unwanted perceptions, e.g. poor member states) or uncertainty about outcomes in general (whether the coalition will sustain or the allies "desert" them (Odell 2010:625)). Following such strategic considerations, governments can "calculate the value of an agreement [to cooperate] by comparing it to the gains from alternative solutions" (Moravcsik 1993:502). Most probable alternative solutions for a government refusing to join a coalition would be to "free-ride" on the policy outputs of like-minded member states (that belong to the coalition). By deliberately positioning themselves outside a coalition, the member state chooses a "solo position" (Bottom et al. 2000:154). Acting in a "solo position" brings with it the risks of being frozen out of a coalition and, accordingly, out of all interactions and information exchange that is part of the institutionalised cooperation. However, acting rationally, the member states evaluate the benefits of "not joining" as being larger than the benefits of institutionalised cooperation. This explains the paradox of the arrangement in which by having similar preferences a government still refuses to engage in institutionalised coalition. This case is less usual in practice, but a theoretically possible scenario. By drawing on the configuration of independent variables (a low degree of institutionalisation + high convergence of preferences), this study hypothesises that

H3: Preference convergence alone without institutionalised intergovernmental interaction cannot increase the bargaining power of a unitary actor.

This hypothesis will be tested in the empirical part of the book, in particular in the case of EU climate negotiations.

2.4 Rational choice institutionalism and alternative theoretical explanations

The main hypothesis (H1) draws on the assumptions of rational choice institutionalism that state that member states that engage in institutionalised interaction and frame durable coalitions act as "rational utility maximisers". The alternative hypothesis (AH) is grounded in the sociological constructivist approach that predicts that institutions shape the preferences of the actors. Both theoretical assumptions refer to the political behaviour of the negotiating actors and the outcomes. However, the logic of the mechanisms through which the behaviour is shaped differs across the two paradigms.

The section starts with explaining the theoretical paradigm of rational choice. Three essential elements characterise the rational choice approach: methodological individualism, goal-seeking utility-maximisation and acting under the constraints of external factors. The rational choice approach relies on the actions of individual actors and aims to explain collective behaviour as the "aggregation of individual choices" (Pollack 2006:4). Individual actors calculate the utility of their behaviour and act according to preferences that are assumed to be consistent or transitive (Warntjen 2010:667). One can expect rational actors to choose the action that maximises their utility. In this respect, the choice is perceived to follow the "logic of consequentialism" (March and Olsen 1998:949, Risse 2000:1). This logic (that is contrary to the "logic of appropriateness") suggests that action always includes an evaluation of the consequences of each step in the behaviour. Before undertaking an action, an actor weighs the benefits and costs of this action by evaluating each step: What are the alternatives, what are the values? What are the consequences of alternatives for the values? Accordingly, the actor chooses the action that has the best expected consequences (March and Olson, 2009:5).

This model can be straightforwardly applied to decision-making in the EU. Conceptualised as cost-benefit calculations when viewed against the backdrop of rational choice explanations, the behaviour of EU member states in the EU decision-making process can be seen as a utility-maximising behaviour. The rational choice approach is closely linked to liberal intergovernmentalism (Moravcsik 1991, 1993, 1997) and focuses on the role of preferences and interaction among the member states (rational actors) at international level. Liberal intergovernmentalism is a synthesis of theories of preference formation, bargaining and institutions and as such can be seen as an "application of rationalist institutionalism" (Moravcsik and Schimmelfennig 2009:67).

Rational choice institutionalism (RCI), as developed in the 1970s by political scientists in the United States to describe models of majority voting in the US Congress, has been widely applied to studies on EU decision-making, for example to explain EU politics, questions of Europeanisation, integration, public opinion, the principal-agent model of EU law implementation and the Council presidency (Hall and Taylor 1996, Pollack 2006, Tallberg 2004). RCI primarily focuses on the constraints of institutional factors (Tsebelis 1990), with the main paradigm here being to observe the kind of behaviour that the institutional constraints may cause.

According to RCI reasoning, the behaviour of political actors is shaped by the formal and informal rules and procedures within which they operate. Actors try to use institutions to their advantage in order to maximise their utility, calculate the best course of action and focus on the constraints that institutional structures impose on transforming their preferences. Actions are chosen not for themselves, but as means to a further end (Elster 1998:22). Thus, the outcomes are determined *not only* by the original preferences, but also by the institutional constraints on individual choices, where both formal and informal rules and procedures may constrain the choices of individual actors (Pollack 2006:5, Niemann and Mak 2010:727).

Four features distinguish the RCI approach from other theoretical strands:

(1) RCI employs a set of utility-driven actors' behavioural assumptions, i.e. actors behave "entirely instrumentally" so as to maximise achievement of their preferences;
(2) RCI approaches politics as "collective action dilemmas". Hall and Taylor (1996:945) explain it in the following way: "Collective action dilemmas can be defined as instances when individuals acting to maximise the attainment of own preferences are likely to produce an outcome that is collectively suboptimal". The presence of institutional arrangements may solve the problem of the collective action dilemma and encourages actors to take a collectively superior course of action (Tallberg 2010b:635).

(3) RCI emphasises the role of strategic interaction in determining outcomes. That means that the actors' behaviour is likely to be driven by strategic calculation and expectations of how others would act. Institutions *structure* the interactions of single actors. That is ensured by "providing information and enforcement mechanisms that reduce the uncertainty about the behaviour of others" (ibid.). It allows actors to expect gains from exchange in the form of a better outcome.

(4) Finally, RCI explains that the origins of the institutions are rooted in their efficiency preconditions. RCI assumes that actors create institutions to solve the joint problems of uncertainty during the negotiations. Institutions are created voluntarily because they provide more benefits in terms of gains from cooperation (Tallberg 2010, Hall and Taylor 1996).

To what extent are the RCI theoretical explanations applicable to coalition-building in the EU Council? Hall and Taylor (1996:944) attempted to apply RCI theoretical accounts to coalition-building in general. They argue that it is relevant in explaining both power-orientated and policy-based coalition-building mechanisms. In light of the power-seeking approach, coalition-building parties can be seen as "utility maximisers" who are motivated to oppose or block proposals. In light of policy-based explanations, actors' motivation in coalition-building can be explained by the parties' intention to influence policies that lie as close as possible to their own preferences (Elgström 2001:116).

This study applies RCI as a theoretical framework in explaining the origins and effects of institutionalised coalitions on bargaining power. According to RCI theoretical assumptions, the behaviour of actors in negotiations is shaped by rules and procedures within which they operate. This study draws on the rule-based model of institutions (Schimmelfennig 2005a) as a conceptual starting point. Member states voluntarily cooperate in informal networks of territorially constituted coalitions or like-minded groupings because they have realised that by doing so their goals can be achieved in the most effective way. Given that informal norms play an important role in EU negotiations, institutionalised coalitions provide an informal cooperation framework (networking, informal bilateral and multilateral consultations, exchange that constrains the behaviour of the member states and at the same time provides them with gains from cooperation (Aspinwall and Schneider 2000:11)).

Persistent coalitions are perceived as a strategic environment in which rational actors exchange information (Elgström *et al.* 2001:125), reduce their uncertainty about others' preferences (Bailer 2003, 2004), obtain more information about the views and expected behaviour of the EU institutions, and seek to attain increased bargaining power by aggregating their positions. Rational actors create institutions to address shortcomings and solve collective problems (Stacey and Rittberger 2003:864, Tallberg 2010b:635). It is widely acknowledged that member states negotiating in the context of Council decision-making face information asymmetries (both compared to other member states and EU institutions) and collective action dilemmas, related to high transaction costs and uncertainty about the "applicability" of their own negotiation positions. To this end, coalitions can help their members to reduce these uncertainties through exchange mechanisms and guarantee reliability, diffuse reciprocity and enhance cooperation efficiency that is aimed at increasing bargaining power. At the same time, engaging in institutionalised coordination leaves enough room for self-interest and strategic decisions.

As already indicated in the above, persistent coalitions can also be explained with the help of other theoretical approaches, for instance sociological institutionalism. In this study the latter is used as an alternative explanation framework.

The main difference between the RCI and sociological institutionalism (SI) is the way in which the two theoretical schools approach institutions. Whilst RCI defines institutions as the rules of the game, according to which rational actors adopt certain strategies in pursuit of their preferences, SI assumes that actors' behaviour is *shaped* by the norms and community, meaning that interaction at the systemic level changes states' identities and interests (Wendt 1994:384). According to the SI approach, actors do not necessarily adopt certain practices because they are the most effective, but because they represent collectively appropriate institutional models (Lewis 2003, 2005, Tallberg 2010b). In contrast to the RCI, actors and their interests are seen as the products of the social interaction, not as the aggregation of their individual interests and preferences. This is the main reason why SI rejects behaviour that is shaped egoistically. The central paradigm of SI deals with international actors committed in their decision-making to values and norms and who therefore choose behaviour that is "appropriate" (Hall and Taylor 1996:946, March and Olsen 1989:162). Rule-guided behaviour differs from strategic behaviour in the sense that actors are not striving to maximise or optimise their given preferences (Risse 2005).

In general, SI tends to define institutions in a broader sense than political scientists would otherwise do, i.e. including symbol systems, moral templates that "guide human action" and cultural explanations (Hall and Taylor 1996:947). Socialisation and repeated interaction are essential explanatory variables of SI. According to the socialisation hypothesis of SI, as a result of prolonged mutual exposure and interaction, individuals adopt "role conceptions" and develop as sense of "we-ness" (Beyers 2005:899). Following this logic, individuals who have been socialised in particular institutional roles internalise the norms associated with these roles and through these mechanisms institutions are perceived to shape their behaviour. According to SI, institutions are characterised by a high degree of durability; hence it is difficult to destroy such normative "investments" (Stacley and Rittberger 2003:866).

Applying SI logic to the study of coalition-building, it is no longer preferences or interest-based factors that motivate actors to build coalitions, but rather non-interest-based factors such as culture, language traditions and common historical legacies that engender the feeling of common identity that prevail. Mechanisms driving member states to build coalitions are the "duty to consult one's socially constructed fellows" (Naurin and Lindahl 2007:6). Moreover, institutions not only shape the behaviour of actors, they also change the preferences of actors towards the collectively preferred preferences. Thus, the preferences of actors appear to be socially constructed (Hall and Taylor 1996:949). Placing the emphasis on ideational, cultural and discursive origins of actors' policy preferences distinguishes SI from RCI accounts (Risse 2005). The actors' preferences may converge through persuasion. Checkel introduces a "thick" version of persuasion, which is a "process in which a communicator attempts to induce a change in the belief, attitude or behaviour of another actor" (2002:2). There are, however, institutional conditions that are necessary for persuasion to take place. These conditions are similar to the above-mentioned variables of the institutional groupings that may enhance "rhetorical action", i.e. an insulated, in-camera environment, repeated interaction and the un-hierarchal composition of community (Thomas 2009:352).

Research into EU decision-making has provided fertile ground for SI studies. This is because many institutions are involved in EU decision-making, these institutions are "externalised" from the domestic sphere and there are a great deal of informal rules that influence the decision-making mode and outcome. Nevertheless, findings regarding the impact of the institutional environment on the outcomes have not been homogenous: Lewis found support for SI explanations in empirical studies of COREPER and informal norms of Council decision-making (2003, 2005, 2010), whilst other studies on the Council working groups have not confirmed the hypothesis of supranational norm adoption by member states' officials (Beyers 2005).

This study applies SI as an alternative explanation of the effects of institutionalised cooperation of actors' bargaining power. Given the necessary institutional conditions, i.e. the high degree of institutionalisation and repeated interaction one might expect member states to shift their policy preferences after coordination within institutionalised groupings as a result of persuasion:

AH: The higher the degree of institutionalisation, the greater the increase in bargaining power through persuasion and convergence of preferences.

An alternative hypothesis suggests that the strength of institutionalised coalitions rests on common historical heritage and identity, which contribute to social interactions of member states' individuals and frame the social trust that results in the convergence of their preferences.

CHAPTER 3

3.1 Institutionalised coalitions in the EU

When describing coalition-building patterns in Council negotiations, the existing scholarship focuses on two main categories: interest-based coalitions (Hosli 1999, Mattila 2009) and culture- and identity-based coalitions (Faure 2002, Naurin and Lindahl 2008). Within these two categories this study has distinguished further sub-groups with four types of coalition-building patterns: interest-based, culture and identity-based, ideological affinity-based and territorially constituted. Regardless of the level of specification, two general strands of coalition-building in the Council deserve closer attention here, namely territorially constituted and interest-based coalitions. Since this book deals with those coalitions with a high level of institutionalisation (*ad hoc* coalitions are included in the analysis only for reasons of comparison), the focus on territorially constituted coalitions is understandable. Yet, how should interest-based coalitions be treated? To what extent can one include interest-based coalitions in the group of institutionalised coalitions?

The analysis set out in Chapter 2 pointed out that interest-based coalitions are formed when the actors identify close policy preferences. By their very nature issue-specific coalitions are unstable and therefore often characterised as *ad hoc* (Kaeding and Selck 2005). However, existing studies have overlooked an interest-based pattern of coalitions that share similar policy preferences and *are persistent* (in terms of interaction duration). Drawing on the model by Veen (2011), who proposes a three-level approach to analysing coalitions, i.e. the political space, policy domain and issue-level (see 2.3.), this study argues that interest-based coalitions can be persistent because of the degree of institutionalisation and as such improve their members' bargaining advantage. In other words, in this study I offer the same explanatory framework for territorially constituted and interest-based durable coalitions. Regardless of their proximity, both categories are treated with the help of rational choice explanations.

Table 4 illustrates the differences between territorially constituted and interest-based coalitions and outlines the concepts that are applied in this book.

Ad hoc coalitions are issue-based aggregations of member states that coordinate their action in order to achieve short-term goals. They are not fixed and their composition changes from issue to issue. When selecting peers for *ad hoc* coalitions, member states' behaviour is guided by preference-based reasoning, i.e. following an interest-based proxy. Cooperation between the states is not supported by any existing durable procedural or structural framework. With regard to the three-level approach, the *ad hoc* coalitions would best fit into an issue-level analysis (Veen 2011).

Table 4: Explaining the distinction between institutionalised coalitions

Coalitions		Stability and frequency of cooperation	Background conditions	Other coalition features
Ad hoc coalitions		Short-term Unstable Ad hoc	Like-mindedness on policy preferences regarding a particular issue	Issue-specific; Cease to exist after the the dossier is finalised
Institutionalised coalitions	Territorially constituted coalitions	Fixed Stable Regularly scheduled meetings; Formalised structures and procedures	Geographical, cultural affinity	Stretch across different issues; Stable in political space of cooperation (see 2.3)
	Task-specific coalitions	Fixed Stable during dossier; Less regular; 'when necessary' Less formal structures and procedures	Like-mindedness on policy preferences within the policy domain	Operate within a particular policy field amongst like-minded actors May become active when a particular issue comes up on agenda

Source: Literature review.

Institutionalised coalitions are defined as more stable (in terms of membership) and quite fixed alignments (in terms of durability) that consist of geographically proximal member states. Here policy preferences play an important background role.

The stability of a coalition is viewed as the degree of frequency and consistency of the cooperation. Most authors agree that alignments of decision-making actors are not fixed and that consistent patterns are rare (Tallberg 2008, Thomson 2009). Therefore, this study applies stability in relative terms. It is not expected that institutional coalitions will come together for each dossier at all stages of the decision-making; member states may calculate time-consuming costs or other practical costs and abstain from coordinating their positions. Furthermore, the decision to select peers depends on the salience of the issue and the distance between the preferences of the members of the institutionalised coalition. Stability is relative also with regard to composition of the coalition. It would be inaccurate to say that in institutionalised coalitions the same composition of actors meets every time. Coalitions are the tools of public diplomacy and operate as open systems, i.e. they may invite additional members to join the forum (Elgström and Jönsson 2004).

This study introduces a new concept, namely that of "task-specific" coalitions. The first part of the term characterises the significance of commonly agreed *long-term* goals. The second indicates that the coalition "specialises" in a particular policy domain. Thus, the task-specific coalition pattern can be best explained with the help of policy-domain (Veen 2011).

This study draws on the assumption that institutionalised coalitions in the EU operate in two modes: either on the basis of geographical proximity as *territorial coalitions*, for example the Benelux, Nordic, Nordic-Baltic, Visegrad partnerships, or as *task-specific coalitions* that are stable coalitions formed by member states that share similar policy preferences, for example the Aachen group, the Copenhagen group, the net contributors group etc. Examples of institutionalised coalitions according to the aforementioned classification will be illustrated in the following sections.

3.2 Territorially constituted coalitions

Territorially constituted coalitions are composed of the same members and are stable over time. The choice of coalition members here depends "not on what you want, but who you are" (Naurin 2008:2), with the choice of peers being very much guided by cultural affinity and common historical heritage: the factors that tend to produce in-group dynamics. Cooperation within a territorial coalition follows a certain logic: It is easier to contact the members of a socialised network of a territorial partnership than to seek contact with an unknown actor outside the regional cooperation framework. This section provides a closer insight into two territorial coalitions: the Nordic-Baltic and the Benelux cooperation and illustrates the conditions and historical background of the institutionalised nature of their in-group cooperation.

The enlargements in 1972, 1995 and in 2004 gave a boost to regionalisation in the EU (Antola 2009). The socio-economic conditions and challenges faced in different parts of the EU differ and this heterogeneity has contributed to the aggregation of policy preferences across the geographical axis. Numerous studies have acknowledged a distinct Nordic-South divide with relatively consistent and durable regional coalitions (Kaeding and Selck 2005, Thomson 2009, Veen 2011, Blavoukos and Pagoulatos 2011). Accordingly, one can roughly distinguish between four territorial coalitions[7] stretching from North to South: the region around the Baltic Sea (the Nordic-Baltic (NB6) partnership), the Visegrad group that emerged in 1991 comprising Poland, the Czech Republic, Hungary and Slovakia and gained impetus with enlargement in 2004 (Antola 2009), and the Benelux group comprising Belgium, the Netherlands and Luxemburg. Southern EU members: Greece, Spain and Portugal form a rather coherent Mediterranean bloc (Blavoukos and Pagoulatos 2011).

Figure 5: Institutionalised territorial coalitions in the EU: NB6, V4, Benelux and Mediterranean

Source: Author's illustration; Mediterranean group in the picture indicated with two circles.

All of these regional formations have common features: as relatively persistent coalitions, they operate within a regional framework of neighbouring countries (the Mediterranean bloc presents a slightly different pattern with alignment also stretching across socio-economic convergences, since Greece is not a neighbour of Spain or Portugal (Blavoukos and Pagoulatos 2011:572)). Apart from the similarities in the socio-economic policy space (Veen 2011), the activity of territorial coalitions largely stems from the pre-existing regional cooperation that rests on common regional identity bases, shared history, values and experiences before EU membership.

---

7   The author deliberately avoids including the German-French alliance in this section. Though often approached as a coalition of neighbouring countries, this coalition predominantly refers to structural power determinants.

3.2.1 The Benelux group

As founders of the European Community (EC) and resting on a highly formalised institutional framework, the Benelux countries (Belgium, Luxembourg and the Netherlands) constitute one of the most established geographical alliances in EU decision-making. Some scholars argue that this coalition recently "may have lost some of its significance" (Hosli 1996:259) after having acted as a bloc in the early decades of the Community's existence. The Benelux countries, however, continue to actively cooperate and have recently prolonged the cooperation agreement that entered into force in the 1950s. What allows this group to maintain its interaction activity? What are the institutional conditions and perceived gains of the collaboration, provided that the aggregated voting power of these three countries does not reach the threshold for blocking decisions by means of voting power-pooling? Currently the aggregated number of Benelux votes is 29 out of the 91 that would be necessary to block a decision (the Netherlands: 13; Belgium: 12; and Luxembourg: 4 votes).

Drawing on the Benelux example, this section examines the institutional framework of one of the most traditional and widely acknowledged territorial coalitions in the EU.[8] Despite some internal questioning of the value added of the Benelux cooperation (largely related to the general discussion prior to the expiry of the original Benelux Treaty on 31 October 2010), the Benelux coalition has a well-established reputation and is perceived by other sub-regional groups as a forerunner of the EU itself (Limonard and Piepenbrink-Lagerwaard 2010). An interview with a high-ranking official from the Baltic group supports this notion:

"Benelux is a much more established group than the others; it is a well-structured group. They all come with different opinions but they manage to discuss them internally and coordinate according to a pre-established mechanism. Consequently, they get further towards reaching agreement. Much attention is paid to reaching an in-group accord before any opinion is voiced externally" (interview no. 18, 19 February 2010, Riga).

There are at least two reasons why the Benelux group is perceived as a persistent geographical alliance: First, its institutional conditions are supported by a formal agreement (a trilateral treaty) and, second, its internal cooperation follows deep-rooted procedures that rest on well-established networking. In order to understand the possibilities offered by the institutional conditions of the Benelux coalition, the section starts with a review of its evolution and dynamics from a historical perspective.

---

8 This study does not include the empirical evaluation of the Benelux cooperation in regard to specific case studies. Here the example of the Benelux group contributes to a general understanding of institutionalised coalitions in the EU and it also serves for the generalisation purposes.

The Benelux cooperation is more than 60 years old and started with the establishment of a Customs Union by Benelux governments on 5 September 1944. The aim was to ensure more favourable conditions for the region by eliminating barriers to the free movement of persons, goods and services. In 1958 the Treaty on Customs Union was integrated into the broader scope of the Treaty establishing the Benelux Economic Union (BEU) that formed the basis for Benelux cooperation over the next 50 years. Benelux cooperation was initially aimed at strengthening economic cooperation and competitiveness *vis-à-vis* other countries. The original intention was to promote coordination and to pursue a joint policy in "economic relations with third countries" (Wouters and Vidal 2008:18). Apart from the formal treaty-based BEU cooperation framework, the Benelux cooperation encompasses a more informal scope of political cooperation (BPC) that is aimed at achieving coordinated positions in multilateral negotiations, such as in the UN, OSCE and G20. The exchange of views on EU policies is part of the informal agreement of the BPC. Its role has significantly increased since enlargement, as one interviewee confirms:

"In current EU decision-making member states almost never vote; there is a consensus culture. With 27 member states it is important to find strategic ways of exerting influence. Much is based on expertise and sharing ideas. The Benelux meetings before the EU Council negotiations have become a habit as they are an effective way of exerting influence" (phone-interview no. 26, 2 July 2010, The Hague).

The expiry of the BEU Treaty gave rise to lively debate amongst the Benelux governments on the value added of cooperation and its future forms given current global challenges and the decision-making framework of an enlarged EU. Three options opened up after the expiry of the BEU Treaty: (1) not signing the treaty, (2) extending it, or (3) drafting a new one. In order to select the most appropriate out of the above options, the Benelux governments launched several review initiatives, established advisory councils and nominated wise-men groups. The objective of these initiatives was to evaluate the benefits and challenges of Benelux cooperation and submit future recommendations. Based on the reports and political evaluation, the decision was made to extend the Benelux Treaty in a revised form. In June 2008 the governments of Belgium, Luxembourg and the Netherlands signed a new Treaty of Benelux Union (BU)[9] that replaced the BEU. The changed name indicates the substantial adjustments to the goals of the "new BU", which in its new shape focuses more on transborder cooperation across a range of policy fields. The revised treaty deals with three pillars: 1) the internal market, 2) sustainable development and 3) justice and home affairs. Contrary to the previous treaty (BEU), it is less reminiscent of an economic partnership.

---

9   The full name of the treaty – 'Treaty Revising the Treaty Establishing the Benelux Economic Union signed on 3 February 1958.'

Partly this can be explained by the fact that the EU has taken over the tasks that were originally defined in the BEU Treaty. Accordingly, the new Treaty of BU explicitly refers to cooperation within the EU framework in order to enhance the influence of the Benelux members on EU decision-making after enlargement. As defined by Art. 2 of the Treaty of BU, "The purpose of the Benelux Union is to deepen and expand the cooperation between the High Contracting Parties so that it can continue its role as a precursor within the European Union and strengthen and improve cross-border cooperation at every level". Thus, the Benelux cooperation, in the context of cooperation within EU policies, is a continuation and extension of pre-existing bodies that were instituted by subsequent agreements and treaties since the 1950s.

Though the Benelux Union is not considered to be an organisation (Wouters and Vidal 2008), the Treaty provides for the structural and procedural elements that demonstrate a high degree of institutionalisation. According to the Treaty of BU (Art. 24–33), the cooperation framework is supported by five internal "decision-making bodies", namely the Benelux Council of Ministers, the Committee of Ministers, the Consultative Benelux Parliament, the Benelux Court of Justice and the Benelux General Secretariat that contributes on a daily basis to the "realisation of common interest […] and offers valuable intellectual, administrative and logistic service on the basis of a neutral position towards the standpoints of the partners" (Wouters and Vidal 2008:9). The institutional conditions are further supported by the fact that the BU has its own budget for fulfilling operational objectives. The annual budget of the Benelux Union is estimated to be €7–8 million (Limonard and Piepenbrink-Lagerwaard 2010). Furthermore, the goals of the institutionalised cooperation are jointly defined by framing a work programme. The current programme sets out the tasks of cross-border cooperation for the period 2009–2012 and can be seen as a transition from the old to the new treaty.

Apart from internally well-defined goals and procedures, Benelux cooperation has established a legal link between the trilateral treaty between the Benelux countries and EU law. The so-called "enabling clause" grants the Benelux cooperation a particular position such that Art. 233 of the 1958 Treaty of Rome enabled integration between the Benelux countries without qualifying it as discrimination *vis-à-vis* other member states. Benelux states have further negotiated including this reference in the Lisbon Treaty (Art. 350 of the TFEU),[10] retaining the enabling clause for Benelux cooperation in the future. Interestingly, Art. 350 of the TFEU is *not* extended to include other territorial coalitions in the EU, such as the Visegrad, Nordic or Baltic partnerships.

---

10 "The provisions of the Treaties shall not preclude the existence or completion of *regional Unions* between Belgium and Luxembourg, or between Belgium, Luxembourg and the Netherlands, to the extent that the objectives of these regional Unions are not attained by application of the Treaties" (author's empahsis).

The formal institutionalised agreement provides the relevant background for cooperation in the EU policy context because it creates a permanent consultation structure and defines the channels of cooperation. Meanwhile, one has to acknowledge that the Benelux cooperation has "outlived" the original objectives of the Benelux Economic Union and that the current cooperation channels are much more informal and flexible (Wouters and Vidal 2008). When consulting on the positions for EU decision-making, inter-state coordination does not engage the Secretariat-General. The permanent Secretariat can, however, support the activities of broader information and expertise exchange. According to the interview with a Dutch official:

"The Benelux Secretariat organises the meetings for EU officials on a regular basis. They are not working with EU issues primarily, but they invite us to discuss issues and to exchange views" (phone-interview no. 25, 2 July 2010, The Hague).

Cooperation on EU issues is adjusted to suit the actors of EU decision-making, i.e. political leadership, EU coordination offices, COREPER ambassadors, staff of the permanent representation to the EU and line ministries in charge of specific dossiers. According to the testimonies of respondents:

"Relations between the three capitals are very intensive. The ministers and the EU directors know each other very well. You need to have good contacts both in the capitals and among the Permanent Representatives in Brussels. These are two parts of the same streamline. We meet more often within the COREPER and exchange views on our positions" (phone-interview no. 25, 2 July 2010, The Hague).

In the EU context, the Benelux group operates in its informal cooperation scope, i.e. the Benelux Political Cooperation (BPC), *outside* the formal treaty framework. However, one could claim that the formal agreement has an impact on the intensity of interaction. While maintaining the freedom of action in selecting cooperation peers, the treaty favours the notion "to consult each other" or even "give priority to consulting Benelux first" on the topics that are on the EU agenda (Altes *et al.* 2007:23). The most common consultation framework (as in other territorially constituted coalitions) is the "breakfast meeting" format for prime ministers, the ministers of foreign affairs and other ministers of different Council configurations. These meetings are held prior to Council meetings in Brussels. The "Benelux breakfast" that was started in the 1970s possibly inspired other institutionalised territorial coalitions across the EU to establish their cooperation mode.

"The Benelux Breakfast is a traditional format of cooperation but it is more like a "tip of an iceberg". The exchange has already taken place at the lower level amongst the experts, capitals and diplomatic missions. We exchange information all the way to the Council meeting. [...] Ministers and prime ministers rather discuss the agenda of the coming Council meeting and, if possible, decide who will speak on behalf of the group" (phone-interview no. 26, 2 July 2010, The Hague).

The tradition of cooperating has spill-over effects to other interaction levels and covers a broader range of policy fields. Comprised of small member states (with the possible exception of the Netherlands), the Benelux group has expressed concerns about the marginalisation of their influence in EU decision-making.

One of the corner-stones of the Benelux cooperation: the spirit of forerunners[11] and the "laboratory for initiatives" (Wouters and Vidal 2008) has been threatened by two tendencies in the EU: increasing intergovernmentalism in EU bargaining and the shifting of decision-making channels to more informal formats of interaction. In this regard, the Benelux governments have adjusted their traditional cooperation to new decision-making challenges and have applied their institutionalised cooperation as an instrument in "joining the forces of Benelux countries to exert more influence than by acting in isolation" (in Limonard and Piepenbrink-Lagerwaard 2010). Contrary to the assumption that Benelux cooperation is a "fossil from the 1940s" (in Jobse 2010:8), the interviewees argued that exchange between the capitals in the Benelux framework has recently increased. Interaction with other Benelux colleagues helps to overcome information distribution asymmetries, which has become a common problem of small countries, particularly since enlargement.

"Responding to the situation that more and more information is exchanged beyond formal EU decision-making structures, we have recently introduced new routines. European correspondents of the Benelux countries now have weekly exchanges either on the phone or by video conference. They share information that has been acquired through individual channels. Without information, you are unprepared for meetings. This applies in particular to the small sates" (phone-interview no. 24, 28 August 2010, Luxembourg).

The Benelux cooperation has a distinctive role within EU decision-making due to its jointly issued political statements, the so-called "Benelux memoranda" (Lehtonen 2009:68). Most notably on institutional issues, the three countries present themselves as a coalition with a common view that is often articulated by one country on behalf of the country grouping. It should be noted that in the field of institutional issues the three Benelux countries are "supporters of the Community", i.e. they all support strong supranational institutions, which they consider as the "friends of small states". This view may possibly have its origins in history, since the Benelux countries, as the founders of European integration, were comparatively small compared to the influence of Germany, France or Italy. The first Benelux memorandum was issued in 1955, ending the stalemate of negotiations during the Messina meet-

---

11 According to the Preamble of the Treaty of the BEU "...basing themselves on their cooperation, they have been able to successfully implement initiatives *which had a favourable impact on international developments*, particularly within the European Union." http://www.benelux.int/pdf/pdf_en/act/20080617_nieuwVerdrag_en.pdf (author's empahsis).

ing. Driven by common concerns about the influence of small countries in the EU, the Benelux group initialised an extended format of the "Benelux breakfast" with the aim of creating a united "front" amongst the heads of state of 18 small states on the eve of the European Council in Athens (EU-Observer, 16 Apr. 2003). Furthermore, the Benelux group was active in producing joint memoranda during the IGC negotiations on the Amsterdam and Nice Treaties (Wouters and Vidal 2008, Lehtonen 2009). The best examples of the Benelux countries' power-pooling can be found on institutional issues and in the fields of justice and home affairs and crisis management. The Benelux group is seen by the rest of Europe as a forerunner in the field of food security and has actively engaged in removing obstacles to the internal market. A concrete example of Benelux cooperation is the pooling of resources and sharing the navy headquarters by Belgium and the Netherlands within the joint battle group initiative. Issuing common statements is the strength of institutionalised coalitions in two senses: The joint memoranda are acts of successful internal coordination (thus being the means of mitigating the internal disparities of the policy preferences) and as intentional strategic negotiation instruments, where the joint statements help to pool power through legitimate arguments that other member states find difficult to resist. According to the interview testimonies, preference proximity is one of the most significant conditions for undertaking joint action:

"In order to influence the decision, we prepare common papers, but not on every dossier. In recent years we came up with joint memoranda mostly on institutional issues. Our argument has to be strong and convincing; not to lose the credibility of the group; if we internally find a common goal (sometimes not by choosing the same way), we may convince the others to join our ideas" (phone-interview no. 26, 2 July 2010, The Hague).

The institutionalised provisions, even the most formalised ones, cannot yield bargaining power for its members if the governments do not share similar policy preferences. For example, negotiations on the Lisbon Treaty demonstrated a clear division between the positions of Belgium and Luxembourg vs. the Netherlands on institutional issues. The unity of the group was further challenged by the negative result of the referendum in the Netherlands on the Treaty establishing a Constitution for Europe in 2005 (Wouters and Vidal 2008). Nevertheless, on 7 October 2009, the Benelux group issued a memorandum that included proposals on the role of the European Council and the positions of the High Representative and the President of the European Council (interview no. 25, 2 July 2010, The Hague). To further demonstrate Benelux unity, the heads of the Benelux governments travelled to the EU Lisbon Summit on the same plane (EUObserver, 22 Nov. 2007). Nevertheless, the Benelux members are cautious about making joint statements and do it rather rarely, paying much attention to convincing arguments that, in case of failure, would harm the credibility of the group.

Preferences (unless converging) are, accordingly, the main limiting factor of the regional Benelux cooperation. It is said that cleavages in the group have existed since the very start of the cooperation. Interviewees acknowledged that there is, in fact, not always common ground in all policy domains. In policy fields such as budgetary issues, agriculture, tax law and economic orientation the countries tend to represent different positions. For example, they do not share common standpoints on issues in the multiannual financial framework, as the Netherlands is a part of the net contributors group (phone-interview no. 26, 2 July 2010, The Hague). The Benelux countries' views also differ on enlargement (EU-27 Watch, July 2010).

Nevertheless, the political recommendation for the revised Benelux Union that was issued by the authors of the evaluation report points out that "Benelux cooperation (even if currently rather loose) has the potential of influencing EU decision-making by acting jointly" (Altes *et al.* 2007:23). That means that there is distinct internal *political support* for institutionalised cooperation, in spite of the heterogeneity of preferences in several issues. The conferences on the future of the Benelux cooperation pointed out that "despite its occasional diverging opinions [...] the Benelux remains the most stable sub-group of the Union" (Conference on the future of the Benelux cooperation, 2007)[12].

Analysts consider that Benelux could serve as "a laboratory and mediator of dissent between other countries" (ibid.). Interviewees acknowledged that institutionalised cooperation within the territorial coalition helps the countries with different views to explain their arguments and to gain acceptance for their positions (interview no. 26, 2 July 2010, The Hague).

One of the instruments that is increasingly being used by the Benelux group is the so-called "Benelux-plus cooperation" (Benelux+). Acting as an open system, the Benelux coalition cooperates with other regional formats, for instance the Visegrad group, the Baltic group, France and Germany, and the Nordic group. In the Benelux+ strategy, the Benelux group opens up to the exchange of information with other territorial coalitions across the EU. Originally, following strategic considerations, cooperation was extended to larger neighbouring countries, i.e. France and Germany. After enlargement, Benelux has expressed an interest in engaging in partnerships with the Baltic and Visegrad groups, by arranging consultations prior to Council meetings (interview no. 26, 2 July 2010, The Hague). Despite the differences in their own positions the Benelux group, together with the Visegrad group, has called for solidarity with poor member states on budgetary issues (EU-Observer, 15 Dec. 2005). This confirms that the strength of the Benelux

---

12 The conference on "The future of the Benelux cooperation in a changing Europe" was held in Luxembourg in 2007 with an aim of defining the future shape of Benelux cooperation before drafting the new legal framework for cooperation. Ideas were exchanged among the governments and the think-tanks of three countries.

group partly lies in the strategic and purposeful use of the institutionalised cooperation structure in favour of its members. Using the reputation advantage, the individual members of the group can further complement Benelux cooperation by establishing bilateral channels of communication with partners outside the alliance. As one of the interviewees put it:

"It is useful to have an institutionalised setting. We have the structure for internal cooperation but it does not help much if we do not complement it with ad hoc contacts in the margins" (phone-interview no. 25, 2 July 2010, The Hague).

Benelux is perceived by other member states as a well-structured and established coalition. Enlargement and developments in the EU have created further opportunities for the Benelux countries to present itself as influential actors. The external visibility of Benelux actors could also be traced through the personal leadership of nationals representing the Benelux group in high-level positions, for example Herman van Rompuy, the President of the European Council, and Jean-Claude Junker, the Euro Group President.

3.2.2 Nordic-Baltic cooperation: evaluating the regional potential

As in the case of the Benelux group, the present cooperation in the EU context among the Nordic-Baltic states has its origins in 'traditional' regional cooperation. This section introduces the structures and objectives of the territorially constituted coalition, providing a systematic overview of cooperation from a historical perspective. Based on the line of argument put forward in this study, the institutionalisation embeddedness of coalitions stems from pre-existing transborder cooperation with neighbouring countries, which consequently fosters the formation of institutional structures, procedures and practices to make the cooperation more effective. In the case of the Nordic-Baltic cooperation such structural adjustments have undergone periods of boom and decline and current cooperation in the EU context should be evaluated in the light of this historical development.

Serious systematic efforts to build up a cooperation network of Nordic countries took place after World War II with the formation of different temporary groups to solve issues of common interest. This cooperation framework was a kind of reflection of the 19th century "Scandinavianism" that some authors have characterised as an early sign of "Nordic nationalism" (Andrén 1984:252). Focusing on representing national preferences, the early foundations of institutionalised Nordic cooperation attempted to assert common interests when preferences converged rather than to create a single, homogeneous identity. Applying Veen's three-level analytical approach (2011), at the outset of the Nordic cooperation joint action was based on common interests on the level of the political space (for details on the three-level approach see 2.3.). Common underlying interests foster the formation of the so-called "Nordic model" in promoting democratic traditions, progressiveness and the compromise model in labour markets. Internationally, the Nordic model advocated equality and solidarity with developing countries and the promotion of stringent environmental standards (Moritzen 1995, Bergman 2006, Musial 2009). These common interests provided a solid basis for establishing even stronger cooperation that some scholars describe as a "Nordic bastion". The tradition of cooperation was transferred from the regional level to multilateral diplomacy, where the Nordic countries presented themselves a group. This spirit of cooperation further corroborated the group's institutional consolidation. Consequently, the Nordic Council was created in 1952, the first real attempt to institutionalise regional cooperation (Musial 2009:295). Since then, the Nordic Council has served as a major forum for parliamentary cooperation amongst the national parliaments of Sweden, Denmark, Finland, Norway, Iceland, the Faroe Islands and Aland by means of a large number of committees and working groups that focus on inter-state cooperation in different policy areas. After the establishment of a common framework for political (parliamentarian) cooperation, the attempt to institutionalise economic cooperation followed in the 1970s with the creation of NORDEK: a common Nordic economic market. Nevertheless, efforts to create a comprehensive Nordic community by means of economic cooperation failed when Finland decided to opt out (Andrén 1984:252). Partly due to long-range disagreements on the institutions' aims, partly due to the different underlying interests of the individual actors, NORDEK could not justify the functional efficiency of the institution and did not satisfy its members' expectations.

The cooperation within NORDEK failed because the interests were too different (interview no.2, 22 January 2010, Stockholm).

Some scholars claim that the NORDEK framework could have served as an "instrument for improving the negotiating strength of the Nordic countries" in relation to the Common Market, which was due to emerge in Western Europe (Andrén 1984:254). Indeed, drawing on the well-established political cooperation framework within the Nordic Council, it would have merely been the logical next step of joint action on the international level. Yet, this did not happen. There are several explanations for this failure: The first relates to the diverging interests of individual Nordic states in framing their domestic policies. The second refers to the differences in international perspectives that governments envisaged for their countries. Possibly at this stage NORDEK failed because Denmark joined the EEC, only one of the Nordic countries. Thus, the fact that the Nordic community had to choose between satisfying domestic interests on the one hand and fulfilling international commitments on the other hand led to the turning point in the Nordic cooperation model.

After some unsuccessful efforts to create a consolidated Nordic community on the regional level during the 1970s, the Nordic countries instead created an active cooperation and consultation process within the framework of the UN. According to Laatikainen's study (2003), the Nordic countries established a strong coalition within the bloc system of politics in the UN. Relying on the common values of a democratic tradition, i.e. pluralism, solidarity with vulnerable states and environmentalism (Bergman 2006), they developed a strong "Nordic voice" in terms of voting cohesion. Laatikainen (2003:429) identifies that within the UN framework, the Nordic countries were voting the same way in 85 per cent of all votes. This voting coherence was ensured with the help of internal coordination and a large number of joint statements. The coordination practice of the Nordic group in the UN was further formalised by the Nordic Treaty of Cooperation (also known as the 1962 Helsinki Treaty). The aim of further institutionalising the cooperation framework was to enhance cooperation across several policy domains. First, it aimed at strengthening intra-regional political cooperation; second, it envisaged the establishment of a passport-free zone; finally, its objective was to enhance the Nordic labour market. Article 30 of the Treaty of Cooperation defined that the "countries *should consult* one another" regarding questions of mutual interest that are dealt with by international organisations. Seen from the perspective of institutionalism, the formalisation of the cooperation framework was just another complementary provision in the mechanism of intergovernmental consultations. The study of cooperation patterns amongst Nordic delegates in the UN demonstrates that officials never articulated a position in UN meetings that was not coordinated with other Nordic states prior to the meetings (Laatikainen 2003). Thus, a distinctive Nordic profile in UN negotiations created a reputation and an external heritage of a "Nordic bloc"; individual Nordic states were seen primarily as part of the *Nordics* before being viewed as independent countries (ibid.). Provided that the perception of power is an important bargaining advantage for territorially constituted coalitions (Klemenčič 2011:10), the question arises of whether the *Nordics* have also transferred this consultation practice to other frameworks of international cooperation, for instance to the EU.

With its distinct Nordic voice in the UN, further strengthening of the regional Nordic cooperation took place in 1971 with the establishment of the Nordic Council of Ministers. Apart from the objective of further strengthening and formalising the regional cooperation, the rationale was also to keep up the regional framework in case individual states chose the European future perspective (as was the case with Denmark and Norway,[13] who held referenda on EU membership in 1972).

---

13 Norway twice held a referendum on EU membership, the first in 1972 and the second in 1994. Both failed http://www.eu-norway.org/eu/.

The objectives of the Nordic Council of Ministers have subsequently deepened and broadened. Being highly institutionalised, with headquarters in Copenhagen, the Nordic Council of Ministers is currently responsible for joint policy planning, the coordination of activities and implementation of projects in different policy areas. This institutionalised cooperation has undoubtedly played an important role in strengthening Nordic cooperation and representing the "Nordic brand" outside the region (Browning 2007). Implementation of numerous projects has reinforced the "Nordic model" in the fields of social policy, environmental policy and development policy. The "Nordics" have been presented as progressive and "different from the rest of Europe" (Musial 2009:288). Policy consolidation, institutionalisation and the continuity of interaction have served as an advantage for strengthening the Nordic voice. The question is whether and how the regional cooperation network and structures have been applied to exerting joint influence in the EU. A debate in the Nordic and Baltic capitals was sparked by the Swedish columnist Gunner Wetterberg, who proposed the formation of the "United Nordic Federation" (Wetterberg 2010), meaning that a revitalised Nordic "bloc" would help the region to compete with larger EU member states, including intergovernmental bargaining in the EU.

The integration of the individual Nordic countries into the EU has created a new situation for Nordic regional cooperation, with Denmark becoming an EU member in 1972, followed by Sweden and Finland in 1995. It is argued that membership of the three Nordic countries in the EU shifted their identity away from the "Nordic bastion" (Musial 2009). There are at least two explanations for this shift: First, after the accession of the Nordic states to the EU, the geopolitical position of the Nordic countries has shifted from being placed in the core between the Eastern and Western blocs (Browning 2007:33) to the periphery of the EU. In 1995 Sweden found itself at the external border of the EU. The second change relates to the political and economic interests of the individual Nordic states, which suddenly became mutually contested as they realised that each of the countries had become part of the intergovernmental decision-making mechanism with voting powers being rationally allocated according to their population size. In other words, under the EU institutional framework the former partners became rivals by individually pushing for more influence in EU decision-making. While in the early 1970s Denmark had taken on the role of "bridge-builder" between the Nordic community and the EU, with the accession of Sweden and Finland in 1995 "the Nordic label was replaced with the EU identity" (ibid.:43). Sweden, which had initially acted as a forerunner and a leader of the Nordic model, announced shortly before acceding to the EU that "the time for the Nordic model has passed" (Mourizen 1995:14) and that "[Sweden's] policy will be one with a clear European identity" (in Musial 2009:295).

Yet, after being hit by a deep economic crisis in the early 1990s and with a non-socialist government winning elections in 1991 (for the first time in 35 years), Sweden turned its face more towards the EU. Sweden began focusing on EU policies and realised the potential for influencing decisions that EU membership offered. In the first years of its membership, Sweden selected hard bargaining tactics in EU negotiations, thus trying to exert an influence by acting alone. According to Mattila's study (2001), Sweden demonstrated one of the highest records of "no" votes when the Council took a decision by unanimity. In comparison, Finland has been characterised as a "good pupil", with a strong tendency to respect the rules and willing to promote common aims while supporting strong institutions (Lehtonen 2009:73). One of the Finnish interviewees supports this notion:

"Finland is a consensus-based country. We have always acted as a "nice guy", this is how Finland functions" (interview no. 13, 12 January 2010, Helsinki).

Despite quickly adhering to the rules of intergovernmental bargaining in EU decision-making, the Nordic countries soon realised that their individual bargaining tactics were insufficient, particularly when decisions were made by QMV (Elgström *et al.* 2001). The attempt to reconstruct the Nordic bloc and strengthen its common voice as a useful instrument and a tool *vis-à-vis* non-Nordic partners was reassumed during preparations for the Swedish (2001), Danish (2002) and Finnish (2006) Council Presidencies.

Several years after the Nordic countries acceded to the EU, the cooperation pattern also changed to a more cooperative mode in the field of EU decision-making. One study on cooperation patterns among the Nordic EU members indicates that after their accession to the EU, clear cooperation patterns appeared between Sweden, Denmark and Finland (Naurin 2007). By pinpointing the United Kingdom and the Netherlands as the most frequent cooperation partners for the Nordic countries, these findings confirm that some more permanent cooperation patterns exist within the Northern part of the EU and that the dividing line is along the North-South axis (Zimmer *et al.* 2005, Kaeding and Selck 2005).

EU enlargement in 2004 brought further changes in regard to regional cooperation. The Baltic States' accession to the EU was a clear political priority of the Nordic countries. They have undoubtedly been the keenest supporters of the "big bang" enlargement scenario, when all three Baltic States become members of the EU on 1 May 2004 (together with eight other new member states). The motivation behind this support for enlargement partly relates to the normative explanations of enlargement (Schimmelfennig 2001) and partly to Nordic self-interest in terms of economic and financial expansion in the region (in Bergman 2006:84).

With the accession of the Baltic States to the EU, the "reference" to the regional identity space changed. The former post-communist countries were now part of the EU, shifting the external border of the EU further to the East. Consequently, it was more natural to refer to the Baltic Sea region, i.e. countries around the Baltic Sea, instead of remaining fixed in the Nordic cooperation space. This was the reason for shifting the regional core from the distinct Nordic group to the Nordic-Baltic geopolitical space that, since enlargement, comprises a new European macro-region. The newly emerged spatial reference after enlargement was labelled "NB6". What does this acronym indicate?

Since the origins of Nordic cooperation and throughout the evolution of the regional cooperation framework, an "organisational jungle" has emerged in terms of different institutional formations that were established by, in essence, the same participants. The list of institutionalised regional structures and constellations contained six different acronyms.[14] Apart from the well-known acronym for Nordic-Baltic cooperation (NB8, also known as 5+3)[15] comprising Sweden, Denmark, Finland, Norway, Iceland, Estonia, Latvia and Lithuania, the review also identified 3+3 (NB6), which refers only to EU members in the region. In 2009 the Finnish Ministry of Foreign Affairs launched an initiative to review the regional cooperation framework in line with the regional and global economic and political challenges. The proposal was to create a new acronym (B8) with a spatial reference to the Baltic Sea (interview no. 16, 12 January 2010, Helsinki). Apart from the Finnish initiative to systematise the acronyms of regional cooperation, the Nordic Council of Ministers also took the initiative in 2010 and gave the "wise men group" a mandate to analyse the efficiency of the existing institutionalised regional structures. The final report of the "wise men group" suggested keeping the NB8 acronym for regional countries (EU members and beyond). They also recommended strengthening coordination on EU policies within the framework of the NB6 (Birkavs and Gade 2010:12).

This study focuses on the NB6 in particular because two countries in the NB8 framework (Norway and Iceland) are not members of the EU. NB6 is a relatively new formation. It was established in 2004 on Sweden's initiative with the goal of integrating the Baltic States into EU decision-making routines:

---

14 The most frequently used institutionalised cooperation formats in the Baltic Sea region: 3+3, 3+5, NB8, NB6, NB6+2, B8.
15 The 5+3 framework comprises two former institutionalised networks in the Nordic and the Baltic countries, i.e. the Baltic Council (regional governmental cooperation format involving the three Baltic countries) and the Nordic Council of Ministers. In the EU policy framework, this format is limited to 3+3, excluding Norway and Iceland, although these countries are often invited as observers, in particular after Iceland applied for EU membership.

"The NB6 breakfast was an initiative started by Anna Lindh.[16] Initially it was more likely an attempt to introduce the rules of EU procedures to the newcomers from the Baltic States than to agree on common positions" (interview no. 13, 12 January 2010, Helsinki).

Starting in the first year of Baltic EU membership, regional cooperation included interaction among the Nordic and the Baltic ministers and prime ministers. The interview data emphasise the informal nature of the NB6 cooperation:

"NB6 format is well-established but at the same time very informal. Usually it is held as a minister's or prime minister's breakfast in the morning before the meetings in Brussels. Most highly established NB6 consultations take place before the Foreign Affairs Council. Ministers meet monthly and these consultations have become a tradition" (interview no. 2, 25 January 2010, Copenhagen).

Apart from institutionalised cooperation in the run-up to Council meetings, there is a broad range of meeting formats in the capitals and in Brussels. In contrast to the highly institutionalised Benelux cooperation, the NB6 does not follow any formal guidelines on how to proceed with the institutionalised coordination of EU policy. Hence, the intensity of cooperation and organisational patterns vary across different policy fields. One example of NB6 interaction on the senior official's level is cooperation amongst the EU directors, who convene for consultations twice a year before the start of each presidency term. This interaction facilitates exchange between the EU coordination headquarters during the intervals between consultations. One of the meeting participants puts it in the following way:

"We attach a lot of weight to the EU directors' meetings that take place once during the term. These consultations are particularly important because of the exchange of information on the priorities of each country and the stakes they attribute to different issues. Initially, these regular consultations started among the Nordic and Baltic countries. Once we also decided to invite Germany and Poland, which belong to the Baltic Sea region anyway. Besides, both are large countries. By inviting Germany or Poland to the NB6 political directors' meetings, we see a mutual advantage. They are important players and it is a good opportunity for them to meet six countries together. Everybody wants to come to Berlin or Warsaw to exchange views" (interview no. 28, 22 January 2010, Stockholm).

EU directors' meetings have borrowed some organisational principles from the organisational structures of the regional institutions, such as the Nordic Council of Ministers or the Baltic Council. It is general practice to share the administrative burden and to rotate the chair. Like these regional institutions, the members of the NB6 "rotate" responsibility for hosting meetings in their capitals, including agenda setting and selecting participants.

Apart from the EU directors' network, another high-level cooperation network comprises the advisors to the prime ministers of the Nordic and the Baltic countries. Having direct access to the political leadership, these net-

---

16   Former Minister of Foreign Affairs of the Kingdom of Sweden.

works serve as effective and operational coordination mechanisms of a highly informal nature. As the political advisors to the prime ministers accompany them to the NB6 coordination meetings in Brussels, they have created their own operational network that continuously operates via e-mail or telephone communication channels. An interview respondent confirms that:

"It is always good to have the feeling that we can ask for support in critical situations. In such cases, the NB6 solidarity brings us closer. If we use the informal channels through the prime ministers, they are soon "multiplied", as each of them has their own contacts and political networks" (interview no. 18, 19 February 2010, Riga).

In some cases, the NB6 network has been extended to include external actors, for example the United Kingdom, the Netherlands and Germany:

"Once during each presidency term Denmark participates in the meeting of the so-called Northern Light group. This group comprises the advisors to the prime ministers of the Nordic EU members, the Netherlands, the UK and Germany" (interview no. 2, 25 January 2010, Copenhagen).

The interview data show that the institutionalised NB6 cooperation framework functions as an "open system". According to institutional theory, institutionalised cooperation networks can operate either as "open systems" or "closed systems" (Elgström and Jönsson 2004). The flexibility of the cooperation format is indirectly linked to the institutional set-up and the degree of formalisation. This "openness" is perceived by members as a positive component, though the participants are hesitant to further formalise the structure of the NB6 framework (interview no. 13, 12 January 2010, Helsinki).

Several interviewees indicated that governments try to coordinate their positions at the outset of decision-making, i.e. NB6 consultations on the Commission proposal take place before the first discussions in the working group in Brussels. This is because the bulk of the technical details of the dossiers are negotiated at the working group level. Interaction frequency amongst the experts is the highest. Usually, the same officials are engaged in the negotiation of one dossier throughout the entire legislative process. With an average meeting frequency of one to two times a week and a negotiation length on one dossier of between 20 to 80 weeks, the Council working group level constitutes the most solid institutional environment in terms of inter-personal network.

The working group level in Council is particularly significant in terms of coalition-building. According to the rules of procedure, the member states present their preferences in one of the first working group meetings. Then discussions on reaching agreement start. On the inter-personal level the frequency of meetings provides the opportunity for mutual exchange. First, delegates identify the colleagues who are in charge of the issue in other member states; second, they may informally exchange views on technical details with these focal points about the issue and exchange information about their preferences. Along with work on the legislative proposal, the member states select their most preferred cooperation partners and frame coalitions. In most cases, a coalition has a "lead country" that takes the initiative for organising an intra-coalition meeting. Usually, this "lead country" has a particular stake in the dossier or is interested in coordinating the partners for other reasons, for instance in the context of an upcoming Council Presidency. Once the coalitions are framed at the Council working group level, their participants continue to cooperate on the subsequent decision-making levels, i.e. COREPER and minister level.

The EU decision-making procedure provides that 70 to 80 per cent of all issues are settled before they reach the Council of Ministers (Beyers 2005:904). Indeed, the role of the COREPER as a diplomatic forum for reaching agreement on political as well as technical disputes has increased in recent years (Bostok, 2002). Some interviewees point out that the COREPER format is the most important for inter-state cooperation in the search for allies:

"If we speak about coalition-building, then their formation is most visible on the CORE-PER level. The positions "crystallise" and like-minded groups are exposed. Permanent representatives meet regularly and have created a good discussion atmosphere" (interview no. 19, 18 February 2010, Riga).

With respect to considerations explained in the previous section, it is natural that the NB6 takes the opportunity to network in Brussels and cooperate on the COREPER ambassador's level. Whilst the ministers mainly address politically sensitive questions, the COREPER discussions are often narrowed down to particular issues and concrete wording in the documents. The intensity of interaction between the permanent representatives is much higher than among ministers, namely several times per week. COREPER is embedded within extensive and highly informal networking, including corridor talks before meetings (Meerts and Cede 2004), informal lunches and telephone communication. The COREPER ambassadors are also supported by their counsellors, i.e. the Mertens and Antici group. Cooperation amongst the permanent representatives of the Nordic and the Baltic countries follow a pattern that has been labelled by scholars as "thick trust" (Lewis 2003:106).

"We used to have COREPER lunches. The institutionalisation of the NB6 format at the COREPER level is rather vague. If we share common interests or realise a problem, we discuss it over lunch – it is more like the exchange of views and sharing background on our positions. For COREPER II it is easier to get an understanding from others on their positions, but in the case of COREPER I geographical proximity does not mean that we can agree on common positions over lunch. Permanent representatives have good personal relations; it is just a useful format of exchange" (interview no. 20, 19 November 2009, Riga).

This interview confirms that policy preferences are important background variables. The homogeneity of preferences varies according to different policy domains and across different issues. According to the interview testimonies, the NB6 Ministers of Foreign Affairs continue to convene in Brussels because they can touch base with each other.

"Actors in each policy field create the cooperation constellations that they consider purposeful. We have fruitful discussions in the NB6 institutionalised framework in those issues where we identify common interests, e.g. neighbourhood policy, the Baltic Sea Strategy, Eastern partnership etc." (interview no. 28, 22 January 2010, Stockholm).

Prior to their accession to the EU, the Nordic states' institutionalised cooperation framework focused on areas of shared interests among the Nordic countries, particularly on environmental policy, welfare policy and development policy, *bypassing* issues where preferences diverged, for instance some Nordic states' neutrality policy. Enlargement has further increased the heterogeneity of policy preferences amongst the members of the NB6 by bringing in new member states with less prosperous economies and less advanced social welfare systems. This further translates into different policy preferences on the issue level.

When explaining regional cooperation on EU policies, it is helpful to approach coalitions by using the three-level analysis approach as suggested by Veen (2011) (for more details see 2.3.). Policy preferences may conflict when approached on the issue level, whilst, when viewed from a socio-economic perspective, the preferred negotiation outcomes may be similar. For instance, all member states express concerns about global climate change and agree that action should be taken. Nevertheless, their views on how to share the burden of financing climate policies differ once discussed on the issue level. An interview with a Nordic senior official supports this distinction of three-level cooperation:

"In the Nordic-Baltic area we share a common view. Some countries have undergone a difficult process, but we all have a common footing for internal exchange, which enhances the flow of information across the region. However, looking one level lower – at the level of concrete negotiations – one can immediately observe that each country has its own interests and it is no longer obvious that Sweden, Latvia and Finland can support each other. When evaluating details, different issues emerge to which the member states attach different attention and importance. [...] and it is normal because each country is bound by its political system and preferences" (interview no. 48, 3 June 2010, Stockholm).

The previous section illustrated that the members of the NB6 do not share similar preferences on all issues. What, then, binds the NB6 together? Geographical location is most likely only one of the underlying conditions. Though some authors emphasise the territorial aspect of cooperation proximity (Panke 2010), geography is possibly an overarching concept for some broader explanations of what keeps the regional partners cooperating. Asked what keeps the territorial coalition together, one interviewee said:

"Geography is not enough to build a coalition. It may be a common history, similar natural resources, similar GDP level or similar structure of legislation. (interview no. 13, 12 January 2010, Helsinki)"

Given the limited amount of knowledge about the underlying proximity conditions of territorial coalitions in general, in the first round of interviews in the Nordic and the Baltic countries interviewees gave their opinion about the institutional conditions of the territorial coalition. It is usually pointed out that identity is a unifying factor for cooperation (Lewis 2003, Naurin 2008). Identity often means different things to different people (Browning 2007:30), as it can be explained by a common language (Elgström *et al.* 2001), shared historical experience (Andrén 1984) or cultural affinity (Elgström *et al.* 2001, Naurin 2008). There are different scholarly views on the role of language in identity formation. Linguistic affinity is considered a strong determinant of identity in sociological constructivism thinking. "Language fellowship" can certainly be applied to the Nordic region (Sundelius 1977:73). "Scandinavian" is basically understood by the Nordic members (provided that Finnish representatives take advantage of using Swedish as one of the official languages in Finland). The Nordic countries' membership of the EU has affected the use of language internally in the region. Interestingly, English has replaced Scandinavian, becoming a common language of Nordic civil servants dealing with the EU (interview no. 29, 22 January 2010, Stockholm). Interviewees in the Baltic States also denied that language was the unifying condition for regional cooperation.

Apart from language, identity can be explained by culture, i.e. the beliefs, values and norms that a social group shares. From the sociological perspective, culture is interpreted more in ethnic or ideational terms. This study interprets culture in terms of societal and behavioural factors. In the negotiation context, culture can be related to occupation, education and regional substructures (Dür and Mateo 2010b:689). Culture may be seen as the "way of doing things" or the "way of approaching things" in terms of norm-conforming behaviour. The professional culture and the way of doing things is pointed out by interviewees from the Nordic states as an underlying value for cooperation networks (interview no. 3, 25 January 2010, Copenhagen), with neighbours being perceived as the "most natural partners" (interview no. 2, 25 January 2010, Copenhagen).

When norms become stable, interaction reaches a degree of "habitualisation" and helps actors to behave in conformity with shared values (Schimmelfennig 2001). The institutionalised cooperation in the Nordic and Nordic-Baltic region is largely shaped by such habitualisation within the common cultural *milieu*. Actors create some kind of a "corporate culture" that is attributed to the cooperation framework. The perception of the "in-group" community encourages more exchange between officials within the regional coalition than with outsiders. Identity thus creates the conditions that determine the *choice* of cooperation partners. Consulting partners of the territorial group are characterised as being as "natural as breathing" (Laatikainen 2003:416). Interviewees identified that, in the process of selecting cooperation peers, they chose the peers following the logic of "neighbours first":

"My natural reaction is first to contact Estonians and ask what they think about the proposal (interview no. 18, 19 February 2010, Riga)."

This section described the evolution of regional cooperation in the Baltic Sea region by highlighting significant turning points in the framing of the NB6, the current cooperation format in EU context. Particular attention was attached to the development of regional institutions and structures, which according to the argument of this book ensure the institutional embeddedness of the regional coalition. The conditions under which the coalition operates, i.e. common historical heritage, identity, culture and language, were also briefly touched upon.

This study hypothesises that the degree of institutionalisation (supported by converging preferences) matters for bargaining power in Council negotiations. The theoretical framework has explained the notion of institutionalisation by highlighting the conditions under which institutions affect outcomes. Empirical research provides interesting data in this regard. Asked about the NB6 meeting format, interviewees emphasised that meetings are highly informal and restricted only to members of the group without the presence of a large number of civil servants. When held on the prime minister level, the NB6 breakfast meetings include the prime ministers and possibly one senior civil servant per country:

"The NB6 breakfast is limited only to the Prime Ministers, possibly 1+1. Actually, we [in the capital] know that the meeting is taking place but few of us have the insights of the proceedings there. From our ministry we do not send any speaking notes; it is highly informal" (interview no. 36, 15 January 15, Stockholm).

The advantage of limiting the number of participants is that the in-camera setting encourages governments to exchange information, thus promoting the spirit of diffuse reciprocity. In the complex system of Council negotiations with a large number of actors, the uncertainty about possible negotiation outcomes is high and depends on the asymmetries of information distribution and asymmetries in resources to acquire enough technical and procedural knowledge about the proposal. It is likely that the ministers who discuss issues in a friendly, informal atmosphere shortly before the Council meeting will gain more common ground than if they discuss issues in the large EU-27 group. Thus, the members of institutionalised coalitions recognise two groups of actors: the insiders, i.e. members of the sub-group, and outsiders. Insiders can speak about the positions of the outsiders more openly. They acquire knowledge about the emergence of other alliances and learn about the intentions of the institutions. The insulation and the group-spirit create a feeling of "us" and "them". Consequently, those taking part in the meeting become more cooperative in exchanging the information they have accessed through their individual channels. Diffuse reciprocity encourages mutual deals and concessions between insiders; however, these remain within the margins of their policy preferences. Indeed, interaction within the NB6 demonstrates a high degree of norm-confirming behaviour. Interviewees acknowledged that the in-camera setting allows them to discuss highly sensitive information:

"Sometimes we give and take information about those who are not present. Perhaps one of the colleagues has recently been in Poland, or another country: what can we expect from the Poles?" (interview no. 2, 25 January, 2010, Copenhagen).

During the mutual exchange in in-group constellations the member states may find acceptance of their positions or "test" their own positions. This reasoning is supported by several interviewees across the NB6:

"The NB6 is a framework for exchanging information. First we identify how the other members of the group position themselves. If the positions are similar, we may think about building a coalition" (interview no. 20, 19 November 2009, Riga).

"We exchange information on how one expects the others to position themselves, what their red lines on certain issue are. We exchange our analysis of the dossiers" (interview no. 2, 25 January 2010, Copenhagen).

"We use the institutionalised format to acquire information about their positions. Sometimes it is not about coordinating how to present a common view; rather it is about explaining what we think. I would call it a format of sharing and exchange" (interview no. 7, 21 January 2010, Tallinn).

As the decisions in the Council are mostly adopted by consensus even when QMV is applied (Heisenberg 2005), the member states try to explain their positions, including the domestic political and economic constraints, in order to gain the acceptance and understanding of other EU members prior to the meetings. This may help them to get support from those who do not have particular stakes in the issue:

"Often it is enough if we get an understanding for our position. We explain our situation and our arguments. Even if they do not join us, it is important that our partners gain an insight into our concerns" (interview no. 20, 19 November 2009, Riga).

In some cases, the governments formulate initial positions that are too extreme (possibly under pressure from their domestic constituencies). On the one hand, the member state presenting an extreme position may draw the negotiation outcome towards its own position (Bailer 2003), whilst, on the other hand there is the risk of reputation costs if the extreme position is not supported by others. When QMV is applied, the reluctant member state can be simply ignored. Therefore, countries use the territorial partnership as a pre-negotiation forum to test the viability of their positions:

"My impression is that the important advantage of the territorial cooperation framework is that we can check our own positions. If I can get support for my positions on the level of my most natural partners, it would be feasible to proceed with such a position in the Council negotiations" (interview no 2, 25 January 2010, Copenhagen).

Most of the EU states that participate in institutionalised cooperation are small- or medium-sized countries. When the issues are highly specific or technical, they may lack the resources to identify all the possible implications of the proposal. For instance, in some foreign policy issues, they may simply not have a presence in the region, which limits their expertise and output capacity. By sharing resources and expertise, institutionalised coalitions solve such distributional problems. My interviewees mentioned the advantage of expertise-sharing and of supporting each other in situations of resource scarcity:

"The NB6 network supplements the capacity and resources of the Baltic countries in regard to the EU's policy towards Africa. Sweden has a large presence in the region; we can share expertise and support our Baltic neighbours" (interview no. 28, 22 January 2010, Stockholm).

Another example of pooling expertise relates to technical knowledge. Some countries develop more advanced knowledge on particular issues that is important on the national level either for economic reasons or due to political priorities in regard to domestic policies. Pooling expert capacities is one of the main principles of regional cooperation in the Nordic Council of Ministers' cooperation framework, as numerous projects deal with transferring expert knowledge across the region. The rationale behind these initiatives is to efficiently use regional resources by sharing capacities and thus increase regional competitiveness internationally *vis-à-vis* other regions. In EU cooperation, member states act rationally and focus on their national policy preferences. Still, regional solidarity in pooling expertise is mentioned by several respondents, with the countries relying on the expertise of more competent partners of the group becoming "free riders" of their technical competence (interview no. 19, 18 February 2010, Riga).

By including interview data, this section explained the causality through which institutionalised territorially constituted coalitions enhance the bargaining power of their members in the Council. Apart from realised power, the existence of territorial institutionalised coalitions (or the perception by others that regions act together as blocs) *per se* is an advantage. In 2011 the British Prime Minister, David Cameron, took the initiative of hosting a summit for the NB6 in London (The Economist, 20 Jan. 2011). The follow-up meeting was held in Stockholm in 2012, which the media named the "Northern Future Forum" (Dagens Nyheter, 9 Feb. 2012). This example illustrates the fact that the Nordic-Baltic partnership is perceived by external players as a group.

3.3 Task-specific coalitions: beyond the territorial framework

Degree of institutionalisation is an important explanatory variable of bargaining power. The more institutionalised a coalition is, the more bargaining advantage its members have. This correlation is particularly powerful in cases when the underlying interests of coalition parties are close. In territorially constituted coalitions that is not always the case. Is it possible to pinpoint any interest-based coalitions in Council decision-making that are more permanent in terms of stability and do not follow the *ad hoc* logic? An answer to this question will be provided in the following section by looking at a distinct type of coalition that is interest-based and persistent. Contrary to the conventional view, which approaches interest-based coalitions as short-term member state aggregations, this study explains their stability by means of institutional conditions.

Table 4 shows that institutionalised, persistent coalitions can be formed by drawing either on geographical proximity or on preference proximity. In other words, by applying the explanatory variable of the degree of institutionalisation, this study goes beyond the territorial framework. In order to avoid any confusion in terminology, the study at hand labels persistent, interest-based coalitions as "task-specific coalitions". Inspired by the concept of "task-specific institutions" (Bellamy and Palumbo 2010), the term "task-specific coalitions" clearly points to common long-term goals and makes reference to a specific scope of issues or policy domain within which these goals have to be achieved by like-minded governments.

Scholarly knowledge of persistent, interest-based coalitions is limited. Theoretically, scholars dealing with interest-based coalitions usually describe them as issue-specific and short-term aggregations. On the policy domain level, the coalitions tend to demonstrate patterns that are more persistent than at the issue level. The coalitions are not resolved but, instead, continue to exist in "latent mode". The principles of legislative work in the EU mean that proposals within a particular policy domain return to the Council once the Commission or the Council presidency proposes the dossier through their agenda-setting powers. This study argues that task-specific coalitions "follow a dossier" and thus take up their activity again as soon as the issue is put on the EU decision-making agenda. Empirically, there are broadly acknowledged difficulties in capturing the on-going processes in Council negotiations, particularly if the coalitions are not exposed in final voting results. Task-specific coalitions are difficult to study because their existence is limited to informal contacts amongst the sub-groups of a small number of member states. Size is more manageable and provides the good institutional conditions of an in-camera setting for the effective exchange of information.

The most prominent examples of task-specific coalitions are the Salzburg group, the Aachen group, the net contributors group, the Quadro group etc. Task-specific coalitions are often named after the place of their first meeting. Often, however, they are not given any name at all and are highly informal. Provided that task-specific coalitions are established on a preference proximity basis, the main objective of these durable coalitions is to exchange information and pool bargaining power in order to achieve jointly defined goals. Paradoxically, though they are preference proximity-based, these groups may experience internal disparities and fail to agree on a common position in Council negotiations.

This section describes the composition, institutional conditions and functional specifics of task-specific coalitions in decision-making in the Council. To start with, task-specific coalitions are probably the least institutionalised formations in terms of their structure and composition. They comprise an indistinct number of member states that have similar policy preferences on a particular policy domain or issue. So far, the definition of task-specific coalitions has, to the same extent, also been applied to *ad hoc* coalitions. Task-specific coalitions may interact repeatedly and durably whenever the issue in their policy scope comes up for discussion. For example, the net contributors' group takes up its work as soon as budgetary issues are discussed (or scheduled for discussion). This was confirmed by one of the interviewees:

"In the field of budgetary issues there is a clear example of a like-minded group. The countries that are net contributors meet from time to time to exchange their positions both in the capitals and in Brussels. This group is restricted to the net contributors and becomes active when budgetary issues are discussed" (interview no. 44, 7 June 2010, Stockholm).

The degree of institutionalisation in task-specific coalitions is lower than in territorially constituted coalitions. There is certainly no formal intra-coalition agreement (as in the case of the Benelux group). Using the terminology applied by Emmanouilidis (2007:3), one could say that task-specific coalitions are "loose coalitions", i.e. they are established to fulfil a single task without defining the means. Though loose, the institutional conditions of task-specific coalitions provide at least some internal operational procedures. A coalition emerges when member states with similar preferences "realise the need" for more intensive information exchange with like-minded peers. As is the case with all interest-based coalitions, a like-minded group may initially be chaired by a lead country that is randomly selected from amongst its members. As the group continues to meet and coordinate positions and activities, its members may agree on the chair rotating between its members. This principle is most clearly illustrated in the Salzburg group: The participating countries hold six-month presidencies beyond the formal decision-making structures and procedures of the EU. Other groups, for example the Aachen group or Copenhagen group, are much more informal and select their lead countries on an *ad hoc* basis. Thus, the degree of institutionalisation and specific operational procedures vary from group to group.

It can be said that task-specific coalitions are less fixed in terms of their members. Their membership may be extended if additional states identify policy preferences close to those shared by the like-minded group. On the other hand, a member state may leave the like-minded group if its policy preferences change. The latter may happen in the event of a preference shift, for instance following elections. Thus, based on the previous classification (see 3.1.), task-specific coalitions can be characterised as open systems.

The logic behind cooperation within task-specific coalitions is to maximise utility in terms of creating an advantage for coalition members compared to "solo" action. In some cases, when the size of a coalition in terms of aggregated votes is sufficient to achieve the threshold of a blocking minority, the task-specific coalition may be used as a voting power-pooling instrument. Otherwise, the group's main rationale rests in framing justifications for common arguments by coordinating positions internally and by targeting external actors through joint activities, such as common statements or position papers.

Task-specific coalitions are difficult to study. As Council negotiations are generally restricted to the insight from outside, these formations of like-minded governments are particularly difficult objects for research because of their highly informal nature. Given the scarcity of knowledge on this type of coalition, some examples of task-specific coalitions will be provided in the following. The evidence was largely gained through in-depth interviews with government officials.

The Salzburg group, also called the Salzburg Forum, comprises seven EU member states: Austria, Hungary, the Czech Republic, Poland, Slovakia, Slovenia, Romania and Bulgaria. Croatia holds observer status in the group. The group was established in 2000 on Austria's initiative. The main objective for creating the group was to support the efforts of countries from the macro-region to join the EU. More specifically, the focus was on internal security with the scope of the Justice and Home Affairs (JHA) Council.[17] The structure and operational procedures of the Salzburg group are much more institutionalised than in other task-specific coalitions, with the high degree of operational continuity being ensured by the rotating presidencies. Each country holds the in-group presidency for six months. The current sequence of presidencies in the Salzburg group is as follows: Czech Republic (1st half of 2012), Bulgaria (2nd half of 2011), Austria (1st half of 2011), Slovenia (2nd half of 2010), Slovakia (1st half of 2010) etc. It should be noted that the rota-

---

17 Source: http://www.salzburgforum.org

tion sequence in the Salzburg group does not correlate[18] with the Council Presidency. Thus, one could agree with Emmanouilidis (2007:2), who said that task-specific coalitions serve as examples of "intergovernmental cooperation outside the EU framework". There are, however, several procedures that are "borrowed" from EU decision-making. The presidency of the Salzburg group presents the work programme that is implemented for an 18-month period. The group's presidency acts in the capacity of agenda-setter and schedules meetings within its term. The presidency also defines the Salzburg group's priorities in political cooperation, strategic cooperation and operational cooperation.

The interaction framework within the Salzburg group is more strictly defined than in other task-specific coalitions. Member states interact on the ministerial level, civil servants' level and expert level. Taking the Slovenia presidency in 2010 as an example, the Salzburg group held a ministerial conference in Austria, a minister-level meeting on the margins of the JHA Council in Brussels, a civil servants' meeting on the margins of the Council working groups on JHA issues (CATS, SCIFA, COSI) in Brussels and several expert meetings in Ljubljana to prepare a joint draft document to be adopted by the ministers of the Salzburg group. In terms of strategic cooperation, the Slovenian presidency focused on the adoption of the joint internal strategy – the Salzburg Forum Vision 2020.

Since the establishment of the Salzburg group in 2000, its objectives have changed and have been adjusted to meet the current challenges of EU decision-making. As defined on the group's website (a sign of institutionalisation *per se*), "The political dialogue between the Ministers of the Salzburg Forum helps to define common positions within the European Union and enables the members of the forum to actively participate in EU decision-making". Based on the theoretical framework of this study, the Salzburg group is a perfect example of institutionalised coalition, since it satisfies the conditions for institutional embeddedness, for instance structure, frequency of interaction and commonly defined goals. As regards frequency of interaction, for example, during the Slovenian presidency member states in the group met weekly to monthly. Since the Salzburg group does not have a permanent secretariat, the group must have well-advanced coordination routines to ensure smooth operations.

Finally, similar to territorially constituted coalitions, task-specific coalitions are open systems *vis-à-vis* external actors. The inclusion of an additional member with observer status illustrates the knowledge transmission and information exchange with actors outside of its core. Croatia was invited to the high-level meetings within the framework of "Friends of the Salzburg

---

18   CATS – the Co-ordinating Committee on the area of Police and Judicial Cooperation in Criminal Matters, SCIFA – the Strategic Committee on Immigration Frontiers and Asylum, COSI – the Standing Committee on Internal Security.

Forum". It should be noted that the choice of external participants in "Salzburg plus" followed preference proximity considerations.

Since 2000, the Salzburg group has acted jointly in response to several EU initiatives, such as supporting Bulgaria and Romania in joining the Schengen Area (Ministry of Administration and Interior of Romania, press release, 15 May 2008), presenting a joint statement on the working group and COREPER level on the asylum package (interview no. 50, 20 August 2010, Riga) and coordinating the seven members' position both in Brussels and in the capital of the Council Presidency prior to the adoption of the Stockholm Programme (interview no. 29, 22 January 2010, Stockholm). Furthermore, during the adoption of the M.A.D.R.I.D. report[19] on the working group level held in Brussels in May 2010, the Salzburg group submitted a joint paper on the procedure for initiating joint measures, which was followed by another joint initiative, the Sarajevo Declaration, on intercultural dialogue and internal security (Council Doc. 9224/10 JAI 375) as a follow-up to the "Salzburg plus" cooperation. The Salzburg group supports the argument that a high degree of institutionalisation enhances group members' means of exerting an influence on decision-making mechanisms in Council negotiations.

The Aachen group is less institutionalised and less "visible" in EU decision-making than the Salzburg group. It nevertheless has a distinct role in negotiations on health and social policy. The Aachen group was established in 2006 and has features of a task-specific coalition in terms of structure and objectives. Though it started as an *ad hoc* coalition of like-minded states during negotiations on the Service Directive[20], it was framed following the divide of member states governments according to left-right ideologies. It got its name from the place where the first internal discussions were held. At the initial stage of operation, Germany acted as lead country. As European Social Policy (2006) reported, "The health ministers, mainly Social Democrats, are now forming a group around Ulla Schmidt, the German Federal Minister of Health and Social Security. Sharing concerns over the issue, they hold regular meetings in Aachen, where Minister Schmidt is based. Thus their group has come to be known by the name Aachen group."

The Aachen group's original members were Germany, Spain, Belgium, Luxembourg, Portugal, Sweden, Italy and the UK. Its initial objective was to exchange information and background knowledge in order to frame a common line of argument in the Council. According to a study by Baeten (2007), the objectives of the eight like-minded countries were to "safeguard the common values and principles and to argue for a legal framework that pro-

---

19 M.A.D.R.I.D report is the EU's internal strategy on the threats and challenges to internal security adopted under Spanish, Belgian and Hungarian presidencies.
20 Directive 2006/123/EC of the European Parliament and the Council on services in the internal market.

vides a basis to justify the use of management tools to steer the health systems and guarantee their quality and accessibility". One interviewee, a representative from a member state that was initially a part of the group said:

> "The Aachen group came together for the first time in Aachen to discuss the Service Directive and to discuss the issue of the mobility of healthcare services. Later, this group continued to coordinate positions until the Service Directive was adopted. As an established structure, the group later gathered again when the Directive on patient movement came up" (interview no. 47, 16 June 2010, Stockholm).

After the internal exchange and coordination of their positions, the Aachen group issued a joint non-paper that was presented at the Informal Council meeting on Employment, Social and Health Ministers in Helsinki (6–8 July 2006). The non-paper proposed clearer rules governing the reimbursement of care provided in another country and further definitions of patient rights and safety. In line with social democratic ideology, the Aachen group managed to keep the legal framework that provides a basis for the mobility of patients separate from the scope of the Service Directive. Consequently, patient mobility was a subject of a separate legislative project that followed after the Service Directive.

Having established its institutional framework, the Aachen group continued to exist independently of the Service Directive dossier. The institutionalised coalition resumed its activity as soon as an issue of relevance to its scope was put on the EU decision-making agenda. For example, it gathered informally on the margins of several EPSCO[21] meetings in 2007 to discuss the free mobility of patients, with participating member states of the Aachen group meeting mainly in Brussels on the fringes of scheduled ministerial meetings, COREPER or working groups. As an open system, the task-specific coalition can either be extended to include additional members or reduced in the event of an ideological shift in one of the capitals, as was confirmed by one of the interviewees: Sweden was the member of the Aachen group only during the previous [Social Democrat] government (interview no. 47, 16 June 2010, Stockholm).

The **Copenhagen group** is another example of a task-specific institutionalised coalition. It operates in the field of competition policy and financial policy and comprises Sweden, Finland, Denmark, the Netherlands, the United Kingdom and Ireland. The members of the Copenhagen group share similar preferences on market liberalisation. The rationale behind this task-specific coalition relates to the broader debate on market liberalisation vs. regulation. Since the completion of the single market, the policy preferences of the member states have been divided in two major blocs: those supporting more regulation in the internal market and those advocating market liberalisa-

---

21 Council for Employment, Social Policy, Health and Consumer affairs.

tion. Basically, the preferences have been distributed along the North-South divide, with the Nordic countries, the Netherlands, the United Kingdom and Ireland supporting "market-making", principle-based and competition-friendly ideas, and the Mediterranean countries, France and Belgium advocate a more "market-shaping", rule-based and investor protection approach. Germany shifts between these two positions, stands between these two coalitions, depending on domestic debates.

It is interesting that the name of the Copenhagen group is known only by insiders and was mentioned to the author by one of the interviewees. It cannot be found on the internet or by studying the rules of procedure of the Council. Some studies call this coalition simply the "Northern coalition" (Quaglia 2008). As regards stability, this task-specific coalition is very stable and has existed since the adoption of the Single European Act in the 1980s. From the coalition theory point of view, the Copenhagen group demonstrates a classical preference distribution, namely two distinct interest blocs. First a common position is agreed internally within the coalition and then negotiated (as if it were a bilateral negotiation situation) with the other coalition representing an opposite view (Elgström *et al.* 2001). Because of its stable composition and similarity of policy preferences, the Copenhagen group meets from time to time in order to update information. Accordingly, the parties of the coalition are well-informed about the preferences of the group and can base their strategic moves in negotiations on expectations in regard to others' behaviour. According to an interview with a government official representing the group, meetings are held two to three times per year on the senior civil servant level in the capitals and additionally on the margins of formal EU meetings in Brussels (interview no. 45, 10 June 2010, Stockholm).

The Quadro group comprises four member states (hence the name) from the EU's southern part, which is particularly affected by the influx of third-country migrants to the Mediterranean region. The members of the Quadro group (Malta, Cyprus, Greece and Italy) initiated a common action in 2008 aimed at attracting the EU's attention to finding EU-wide solutions to the influx of migrants. Since then, the group has been internally coordinating positions on the technical and political level. The main political objective of the Quadro group is to call for member states' solidarity in sharing the burden of immigration and asylum. Part of the group's concerns are addressed to other member states nevertheless, a great deal of the measures have to be dealt with by the Commission, for example the reconsideration of current regulation (Dublin II system), the strengthening of the Frontex boarder agency and the establishment of the asylum support office. During the 2009 Czech Presidency, the Quadro group delivered a joint statement on the effective implementation of readmission agreements. The group's activity was expected to increase in relation to the Stockholm Programme dossier that was scheduled on the basis of the Swedish Presidency and aimed to set the political goals for the EU's action in the JHA area for the next five years. As the interviewee of the Presidency said:

"The Quadro group is a typical and visible group in the field of immigration and asylum policies. We expected them to increase their voice during the negotiations under the Swedish Presidency" (interview no. 29, 22 January 2010, Stockholm).

The group was established on Malta's initiative (Times of Malta, 13 Jan. 2009); yet, current operational activity relies on shared leadership, i.e. meetings are held in the capitals of the members on the rotation principles. A lot of work is done on the technical level; experts prepare proposals that are discussed internally amongst the group's politicians. The consistency of the group, however, experienced some major problems during negotiations on the Stockholm Programme (see 4.3.). This once again supports the argument that institutionalised arrangements alone cannot provide a bargaining advantage if the preferences of the group members differ.

The net contributors' group is one of the widely acknowledged coalitions that "pops up" when the EU Financial Framework is discussed, as well as in relation to issues concerning the EU budget, such as the reform of the Common Agricultural Policy (CAP). Since budget debates often focus on the question of how much each country pays and how much it gets back, the common desire of the net contributors' group is to keep overall expenditure below 1 per cent of GDP. Governments' preferences are mainly due to the domestic situation, since the budget debates are relevant to their electorates (Schneider 2011:9). The net contributors' group comprises six countries (Germany, Sweden, the Netherlands, Luxembourg, Austria and the United Kingdom). Belgium and France are considered minor net contributors (EurActiv, 29 Jan. 2010). The group is perceived as a strong and visible actor in Council negotiations, outlining the distinct cleavages between the net contributors and net recipients in terms of their policy positions (Thompson 2009:756). Some studies have observed that the net contributors' group pursues a joint negotiation strategy, opting for hard bargaining in order to increase bargaining power when negotiating the financial perspective (Dür and Mateo 2010a:565). As pointed out by interviewees, the net contributors' group uses interaction channels both between the capitals and the permanent representations, and in terms of its institutionalised structure is a well-established group (interview no. 44, 7 June 2010, Stockholm)

The like-minded group on trade is a highly informal group with a loose structure. This task-specific coalition does not have a specific name and the group is framed according to preferences in regard to support for free trade policy, confirming the general trend of preference division along the North-South axis. The like-minded group on trade comprises Sweden, Denmark,

Finland, the United Kingdom, the Netherlands, Germany, the Czech Republic and Estonia. Its composition demonstrates a mixture of small and large, old and new member states that distinctly illustrates its emphasis on preferences as a main prerequisite of cooperation. Given its structure, the like-minded group on trade operates as an open system and sometimes operates beyond the core countries, extending invitations to Austria and Ireland (interview no. 46, 16 June 2010, Stockholm). The group meets both by consulting in Brussels on the margins of the decision-making bodies as well as in the capitals on the initiative of one of its members.

The like-minded group on agricultural issues demonstrates a similar trend for preferences being divided across the North-South divide. The task-specific coalition on agricultural issues comprises Sweden, Denmark, the Netherlands, Germany and Estonia. Like the task-specific coalition on trade, it demonstrates a low degree of institutionalisation and meets once every four months. The meetings on the level of senior civil servants take place in one of the members' capitals (interview no. 38, 1 July 2010, Stockholm).

The G5 is a "different case". The G5 includes Germany, France, the United Kingdom, Spain and Italy and follows a different logic of formation. The G5 can be partially considered as fulfilling a specific task, as it focuses specifically on the issues of internal policy and security and therefore deals with cooperation in the field of JHA; on the other hand, the group exclusively comprises large member states. Therefore, the G5 is often called the "big EU 5", indicating the size of the members rather than the perceived policy goals. The initial objective of the G5 was to combat terrorism and reduce crime. This can be partially seen as the big EU member states' response to the terrorist acts of 9/11, as it defined terrorism as the "biggest threat to all European nations" (EurActiv, 26 Oct. 2006). After enlargement, the group was upgraded to G6 by including Poland; the extended structure is not, however, fixed. Even after enlargement, following the invitation of the Council Presidency chaired by Nicolas Sarkozy, the ministers of the interior of the G5 gathered in Evian for an informal meeting to discuss the "threat from immigration" in the previous "setting" without inviting Poland (EurActiv, 5 July 2005). In contrast to other task-specific coalitions, the G5/G6 serves as a political leadership instrument that deals with operational tasks on the EU decision-making agenda. Meetings are mainly held on the political (ministerial or prime ministerial) level and attract media attention, thus also serving as reputation aggregators for the domestic and external image of the G5 members. That is particularly true given that immigration issues are high on the participating countries'[22] domestic agenda.

This section introduced some task-specific coalitions that represent institutionalised cooperation forms beyond the territorial framework. On average, a task-specific group comprises four to eight members, a number that is "easier to handle" (interview no. 28, 22 January 2010, Stockholm). Table 5 presents an overview of the task-specific coalitions discussed in this study.

Task-specific coalitions are difficult to trace and to study because they operate in a "grey area" of decision-making, i.e. beyond formal negotiation structures. No media records are available on the activities of these inter-state cooperation formats and exchange is restricted to members, with their operation often being limited to internal interaction without issuing a joint statement to the Council. Nevertheless, the role of task-specific coalitions has increased since enlargement and will possibly further increase under the decision-making provisions of the Lisbon Treaty. As one of the high-level officials interviewed put it:

"I would say that the inter-state collaboration in Council negotiations is an increasing tendency and covers more and more policy areas. One can observe this pattern especially in preparation for European Council meetings. Sometimes cooperation takes place in the capitals, sometimes we meet bilaterally and consult with one of the members of the group more specifically" (interview no. 45, 10 June 2010, Stockholm).

The overview of task-specific coalitions in Council negotiations demonstrates two distinct tendencies: First, the groups of member states are stepping up cooperation outside formal decision-making formats across almost every Council configuration; second, in spite of the different degrees of institutionalisation, these coalitions create a kind of "in-camera island" that exchanges information and formulates strategies for dealing with distributional asymmetries on a continuous basis. These coalitions are restricted to a limited number of like-minded partners that frame the "insiders club" and are difficult to access externally. The above list of task-specific coalitions is perhaps not exhaustive, and it is possible that more overarching results could be obtained by interviewing representatives of the southern regions of the EU. Yet, the data available so far confirm the hypothesis that cooperation within an institutionalised setting is strategically applied by member states in order to gain a bargaining advantage in Council negotiations.

---

22   AT – Austria, HU – Hungary, CZ – Czech Republic, PL – Poland, SK – Slovakia, SI – Slovenia, RO – Romania, BU – Bulgaria, DE – Germany, ES – Spain, BE – Belgium, LU – Luxembourg, PT – Portugal, IT – Italy, UK – the United Kingdom, SE – Sweden, FI – Finland, DK – Denmark, NL – the Netherlands, IRL – Ireland, CY – Cyprus, MT – Malta, EL – Greece, EE – Estonia.

Table 5: A list of some task-specific coalitions in Council decision-making

Name of the task-specific coalition	Members	Task-specific scope
Salzburg group	AT, HU, CZ, PL, SK, SI, RO, BU	Justice and Home Affairs
Aachen group	DE, ES, BE, LU, PT, IT, UK, (SE)	Employment, Social Policy and Heath Affairs
Copenhagen group	SE, FI, DK, NL, UK, IRL	Single market
Quadro group	CY, MT, EL, IT	Immigration and Asylum
Net contributors	DE, SE, NL, AT, UK, LU	Budgetary issues
Like-minded group on agriculture	SE, DK, NL, DE, EE	Agriculture
Like-minded group on trade	SE, DK, FI, UK, NL, DE, CZ, EE	Trade
G5/G6	DE, FR, UK, ES, IT/ PL	Internal security

Source: interview data.

3.4 Do neighbours cooperate? Evidence from EU negotiations cases

The theoretical framework for explaining the effects of institutionalised coalitions on bargaining power was introduced and examples of institutionalised coalitions in the EU presented in previous chapters. The study at hand has argued that institutionalised coalitions give their members bargaining power that can be explained by means of the institutional conditions. The institutional embeddedness of cooperation enhances three processes that help the member states to overcome information asymmetries and deal with transaction costs because: (1) institutional coalitions enhance information exchange, (2) the internalisation of the expert networks promotes the pooling of expertise, and (3) they increase the strength to normatively justify the coalition's positions through rhetorical action.

In this chapter methodological concerns will be outlined in brief and then three cases studies introduced. In order to test the hypotheses, the study applies the qualitative methodological approach. As Council negotiations in general and coalition formation in particular are highly restricted domains, semi-structured elite interviews combined with process tracing seemed to be most appropriate methods for supplying reliable data. Empirically, the study draws on 51 interviews conducted in Sweden, Denmark, Finland, Latvia, Estonia, the Netherlands and Luxembourg between November 2009 and July 2010. Anonymity was granted to all interviewees, which explains the limited information provided in the Annex on interview background. The list of interviews in the Annex indicates interview number, date and place. Eighty-five per cent of all interviews were carried out in face-to-face mode and lasted for an average of 45 minutes.

The research design draws on small-n design. It offers three case studies selected with regard to variation of the independent variable using John Mill's method of difference. The research design treats degree of institutionalisation as an independent variable. As explained in 2.3., the impact of preference convergence also has to be tested, thus the degree to which the policy preferences of coalition members converge is also taken into account as a background variable. Possible sets of variables and the expected outcomes are presented in Table 3 (see 2.3.). In sum, the cases that are interesting in regard to an empirical evaluation are the following combinations of independent variables:

1) High institutionalisation + high preference convergence;
2) High institutionalisation + low preference convergence;
3) Low institutionalisation + high preference convergence.

The study focuses on three negotiation dossiers: the Baltic Sea Strategy, the Stockholm Programme and EU negotiations on climate change. All three dossiers have high political salience for the member states and for the EU in general. As Bailer (2005:13) noted, a legislative proposal needs to raise at least some kind of controversy in order to be considered. The selected dossiers cover highly sensitive policy fields (migration, environmental issues, burden-sharing and cohesion policy) and have a high coalition-building potential. One might expect to encounter North-South cleavages (e.g. the Baltic Sea Strategy) that demonstrate the consolidation of coalitions along geographical proximity lines. The dossiers also represent policy domains in which there are likely to be task-specific coalitions.

The dependent variable in the study is bargaining power. Chapter 1 was devoted to the discussion of the power determinants in the Council and their measurement, focusing in with on the effects of coalition-building. The hypotheses were developed deductively (see 2.2.2.), with their origin in the theoretical underpinnings of rational choice institutionalism and the contribution of previous studies (Schimmelfennig 2000, 2001, 2005, Tallberg 2008, 2010b, Bailer 2003, 2004, 2010, Odell 2000, 2010, Naurin and Wallace 2008, Dür and Mateo 2004, 2008, 2010a,b). Figure 6 summarises the argument and outlines the causality mechanism that leads to the variation of the dependent variable.

Figure 6: Causality mechanism through which the degree of institutionalisation causes the variation in bargaining power

Independent variables	Causality chain	Dependent variable
Institutionalisation	Information-exchange	Bargaining power
+	Expertise-pooling	
Preferences	Rhetorical action	

Source: Research design.

Empirical findings obtained from three negotiation dossiers in the Council (the Baltic Sea Strategy, the Stockholm Programme and climate change negotiations) will be presented in the following.

CHAPTER 4

4.1 The Baltic Sea Strategy

The Baltic Sea Strategy, one of the priorities of the Swedish Council Presidency, was adopted in December 2009 as a new model for cooperation on a macro-regional level. The commissioner for EU Regional Policy, Paweł Samecki, called it a "new animal" in the EU (EurActiv, 21 Sept. 2009) because of its innovative and experimental governance mode (Schymik and Krumrey 2009). The strategy, which focuses on coordinating policies in the region, was apparently largely supported by the member states of the Nordic-Baltic region, which predictably had converging preferences in regard to Council negotiations on the dossier.

Figure 7: The Baltic Sea region: NB6+2

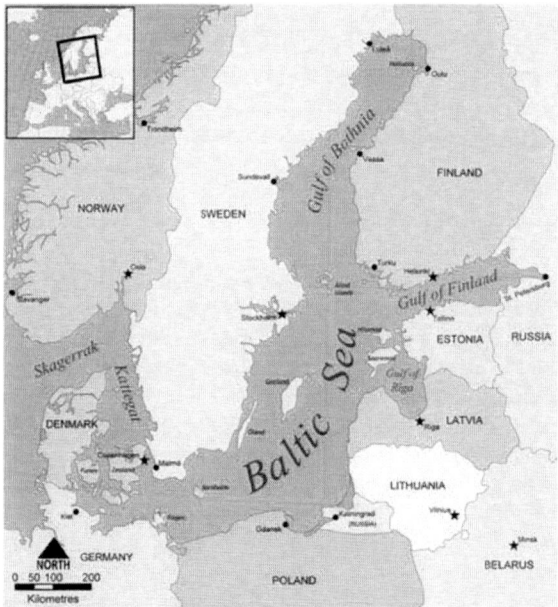

Source: http://en.wikipedia.org/wiki/Baltic_region.

The Baltic Sea region, as defined by the strategy, comprises eight EU member states: Sweden, Denmark, Finland, Estonia, Latvia, Lithuania, Poland and Germany, with an additional external link to regional partners outside the EU, i.e. Russia, Norway and Iceland (EurActiv, 4 Nov. 2008). Six of the countries engaged in the macro-region comprise the core of the NB6 (see 3.2.2.). Poland and northern Germany border on the Baltic Sea, but in terms of historical and cultural proximity they are placed outside the Nordic-Baltic region. Based on these considerations, the study at hand labels the coalition that was formed during negotiations on the Baltic Sea Strategy the "NB6+2".

This territorially constituted coalition includes old and new EU member states. With reference to socio-economic differences and regional challenges in terms of environmental problems and infrastructure disparities across the region, the Baltic Sea Strategy was called a "test case for macro-regional cooperation" (Bengtsson 2009:1). Indeed, representing 23 per cent of the total EU population, the region's aggregated GDP amounts to 16 per cent of the EU's total GDP (speech by Danuta Hübner, then European Commissioner for Regional Policy, 30 Sept. 2008). The economic crisis of 2008/2009 severely affected economic growth in the Baltic States (EurActiv, 5 Oct. 2009). The strategy aimed to improve the region's economic and social disparities and to increase its competitiveness.

The Baltic Sea Strategy was meant to be a pilot project in regard to developing macro-regional strategies in the EU, and it therefore created great uncertainty among the member states. There have been some previous attempts to focus on the Northern region. In 2005 the EU launched the Northern Dimension, aiming to focus on the external aspects of Baltic Sea regional cooperation, in particular cooperation with Russia. However, internally the macro-region around the Baltic Sea did not have any existing policy instruments for increasing competitiveness and for consolidating the partners.

The initiative started in 2005 with a proposal from an informal group of the European Parliament (Europe Baltic Intergroup) to launch a comprehensive approach to the Baltic Sea region within the EU. The European Parliament resolution on this issue was adopted in November 2006, inviting the Commission to draft a proposal for the macro-regional strategy and aiming to "create a brand for the region as one of the most attractive and competitive areas in the world" (European Parliament resolution on the Baltic Sea Region Strategy for the Northern Dimension 2006/2171(INI)). It encouraged the EU to deal with regional challenges by means of joint action by eight Baltic littoral states in order to strengthen the region in terms of sustainable economic growth, environmental standards and infrastructure (*Regeringskansliets-faktapromemoria* (Swedish position), 2008/09: FPM151). In other words, the European Parliament endorsed a strategy for reinforcing the "*internal pillar* of the Northern Dimension". The resolution proposed a considerably wider scope for the new strategy.

The objectives of the strategy were particularly significant for the Swedish government, and from the outset Sweden took on the role of lead country after Finland in 2006 and Germany in 2007 had expressed little enthusiasm in including the dossier in the Programme of their Council Presidencies

(Schymik and Krumrey 2009:5). In December 2007 the European Council invited "the Commission to present an EU strategy for the Baltic Sea region at the latest by June 2009. This strategy should *inter alia* help to address the urgent environment challenges related to the Baltic Sea" (Council Conclusions, 13 Dec. 2007).

Having launched the public consultations in November 2008 (EurActiv, 4 Nov. 2008), the Directorate-General for Regional Policy (DG REGIO) took responsibility for drafting the proposal, which was supported by the Directorate-General of Environment (DG ENV), the Directorate-General of External Relations (DG RELEX), and the Directorate-General of Maritime Affairs (DG MARE) (Joenniemi 2009). The proposal covered a broad range of policies, involving a total of 19 Directorates (Schymik and Krumrey 2009). Public consultations were supplemented by stakeholder conferences in Stockholm (30 Sept. 2009), in Rostock (6 Feb. 2009) and the round tables in Kaunas, Gdansk, Copenhagen and Helsinki. The Commission published its proposal on 10 June 2009, shortly before the start of the Swedish Council Presidency. Sweden, as leader in preparing the Baltic Sea Strategy, positively evaluated the fact that the text was "close to the vision that the Swedish government had put into the proposal" (Cecilia Malmström, Swedish Minister of EU Affairs, press release, 10 June 2009). This statement indicates that many proactive and coordinated efforts were already put by the lead country before the strategy was formally published by the Commission.

In its Communication the Commission pointed out that the macro-regional strategy was the EU blueprint in terms of the governance model and the horizontal approach of the policy solutions is similar for regions in the EU, for example the Danube, Alpine macro-regional strategy.

The main objective of the strategy was to bring the Baltic Sea region closer to the EU by improving economic and social integration, developing the infrastructure and jointly facing environmental challenges. By offering an innovative strategy, the Commission proposed a new governance model that involved flagship projects that were coordinated by individual member states around the region. The Commission maintained its responsibility for monitoring, reporting on and facilitating implementation (Bengtsson 2009:5). In the early stages of the proposal, environment policy was the first and "most obvious field" for involvement of the regional approach (speech by Cecilia Malmström, Swedish Minister of EU Affairs, 12 Dec. 2007). In regard to environmental policy, the new member states still had to catch up and therefore were granted several transitional periods until 2015 (Juknys *et al.* 2005), and were primarily concerned with their economic growth records.

The Baltic Sea Strategy rests on the existence of common regional institutions and policy instruments (the Nordic Council, the Council of Baltic Sea States, the Northern Dimension) and favourable conditions regarding regional identity that enhances cross-border cooperation and coordination of the actions (speech by Danuta Hübner, then European Commissioner for Regional Policy, 5 Feb. 2009).

Furthermore, it was claimed that the Baltic Sea Strategy should not call for additional funding from the EU structural funds, but should instead make use of existing funding resources by better coordinating policy priorities. Member states of the Baltic Sea Strategy are encouraged to use €55 billion of EU cohesion policy funding that is available for the period 2007 to 2013. According to the Commission, €27 billion will be allocated for making the region attractive and accessible place, €10 billion to the sustainable environment, €6.7 billion to competitiveness and €697 million to security and cross-border crime prevention (EurActiv, 11 June 2009). The EU institutions had different views on the financial issue. The European Parliament, for instance, called for an "own budget line" for the Baltic Sea Strategy that would apply at least during the initial phase of implementation (speech by Diana Wallis, Stockholm conference, 18 Sept. 2009). This was later rejected by the Commission, claiming that the involved member states should apply for funding from the development banks (Helsingin Sanomat, 17 Sept 2009).

Formally, the Council began negotiations on the Baltic Sea Strategy after publication of the Commission Communication with the annexed action plan on 10 June 2009. In practice, however, informal consultations among the member states of the macro-region had begun long before that. Table 6 illustrates the ways the NB6+2 were already channelling their preferences to the European Commission from 2008. Each country submitted proposals to the Commission according to their policy preferences.

Table 6: A list of government input during the drafting of the Baltic Sea strategy by the Commission

National government	Submitted document	Date
Denmark	Danish thoughts on the EU strategy for the Baltic Sea Region	24 Sept. 2008
Sweden	A Healthy and Prosperous Baltic Sea Region – A Swedish contribution to the preparation of an EU Strategy for the Baltic Sea Region	14 May 2008
Finland	Preparation of the EU's Baltic Sea strategy: Finland's objectives for the priorities of the Strategy	25 Feb. 2008
Latvia	The EU Strategy for the Baltic Sea Region – A Latvian Version	14 July 2008
Estonia	Ideas for the Baltic Sea Strategy	July 2008
Lithuania	Lithuanian proposals for the EU Baltic Sea Strategy	30 May 2008
Germany	Preparing an EU Strategy for the Baltic Sea Region – A Contribution from Germany	25 Sept. 2008
Poland	Cohesion and competitiveness of the Baltic Sea region – contribution from the Government of Poland	1 June 2008

Source: Schymik and Krumrey 2009:18.

The Baltic Sea Strategy was one of the "fast-track" issues in EU decision-making. The Council negotiation agenda outlined short and effective negotiations on the dossier from July to October, 2009. The strategy was supposed to be adopted in the European Council meeting in October, 2009. Given its horizontal nature, the proposal had to pass through two GAERC[23] meetings in July and October 2009. The presidency also planned discussions at the Environmental Council. The main Council body for negotiations was the *ad hoc* working group Friends of Presidency group (FoP) comprising representatives from the 27 member states' capitals at the senior civil servant level. The Presidency had scheduled only six meetings for the FoP group before the COREPER and the Council meeting. Furthermore, the Presidency planned to hold a minister level conference in Stockholm on 18 September 2009. The aim of the conference was to discuss the general concept of macro-regional strategies and the objectives of the Baltic Sea Strategy (Baltic Review, 25 Sept. 2009).

The negotiations on the Baltic Sea Strategy demonstrated a strong territorial coalition with a high degree of institutionalisation and a high convergence of preferences. This case illustrates two important aspects of EU decision-making that were effectively applied by the NB6+2 coalition:

(1) *informal preparatory work* prior to formal negotiations in the EU Council of Ministers, and
(2) *internal coordination* within the smaller group of actors thus enhancing their bargaining advantage *vis-à-vis* other negotiation actors.

The informal preparatory work on the Baltic Sea Strategy was launched on the initiative of the Baltic Parliamentarian Intergroup. The intergroup collaboration within the European Parliament was soon overtaken by intergovernmental cooperation among the Nordic-Baltic countries. By identifying the Baltic Sea Strategy as one of the core priorities for the forthcoming 2009 Council Presidency, the Swedish government became one of the strongest advocates of the initiative and from 2007 it acted as the coalition's lead country on this dossier. This commitment was clearly expressed by the Swedish Minister for EU Affairs, Cecilia Malmström, in her speech to the European Parliament as early as 12 December 2007: "We need to build support for the strategy in the region. We have come a long way already and we are pleased with the warm welcome by which these ideas have been received so far. *My government will now continue an open and even closer cooperation with our partners.*[24] I am planning a meeting in Stockholm with all Baltic ministers in charge of European affairs next spring". Accordingly, the coordinated action of the NB6+2 started about one and a half years before the publication of the

---

25 The dossier was negotiated before the adoption of the Lisbon Treaty, hence the acronym GAERC (General Affairs and External Relations Council).
24 Author's emphasis.

Commission proposal on the strategy. In its capacity as lead country, Sweden realised coordination activities along two "tracks": contacts with the member states in the region and contacts with EU institutions, in particular the Commission, which was invited by the Council in 2007 to draft the proposal. The coordination work included lobby activities not only through political and governmental actors, but also those of stakeholders and academia. Since the aim was that the macro-regional strategy was to become a pilot project for subsequent EU strategies of this kind, the involvement of stakeholders was essential.

Table 7: Discussion agenda on the Baltic Sea strategy in the Council

July	August	September	October
FoP group meeting	-	FoP group meetings Informal Ministerial conference in Stockholm, 18 Sept. 2009	FoP group meeting COREPER II meeting GAERC, 26 Oct. 2009 European Council, 29 Oct 2009 Implementation aspects: Environmental Council, 22 Dec. 2009 EPSCO 1 Dec. 2009 Economic and Financial Committee

Source: Council Presidency agenda

A year before the publication of the Commission proposal, the governments of the coalition nominated their "contact points", i.e. civil servants of ministries with responsibility for the dossier. Most often the "contact points" were the ministries of foreign affairs, with the exception of the office of the Swedish Prime Minister, for example. Acting as focal points for their respective governments, these civil servants were assigned the role of internal coordinators at the national level among the involved line ministries and other stakeholders (interview no. 22, 11 Dec. 2009, Riga). Neither the Commission Communication nor the action plan indicates the nomination of the national contact points. This network was established on the basis of intra-coalition agreement and was part of the informal networking procedures at the working level during the pre-negotiation stage. Table 8 outlines the informal pre-negotiation work that, in the case of the Baltic Sea Strategy, took place in advance of the start of formal negotiations.

Apart from the broad involvement of stakeholders, the NB6+2 governments exchanged views and ensured mutual support for positions that were represented externally by organising bilateral consultations and including the issue in regular meetings at the political and diplomatic level. According to one interviewee:

"We successfully coordinated the Baltic Sea Strategy within the NB6 format that is built on the principles of regional identity. EU directors from the Nordic and Baltic countries meet twice a year and officials from the EU coordination units usually take part" (interview no. 49, 17 June 2009, Stockholm).

Table 8: Informal consultation work on the Baltic Sea Strategy

Activity	Time	Actors/Framework
Conference of the Baltic Sea States Subregional Cooperation (BSSSC)	Kaunas 18 Sept. 2008	*Working level* Governments BSSSC framework
Round table on environmental issues	13 Nov. 2008 Gdansk	*Working level* Governments, experts, stakeholders, European Commission
The Baltic Sea Programme Conference	26 Nov. 2008 Tallinn	*Working level* Experts, governmental actors Nordic Council of Ministers
Stakeholders Conference	30 Sept. 2008 Stockholm	*High political level* EU institutions, governments, non-governmental actors
Round-table on safety and security issues	9 Dec. 2008 Helsinki	*Working level* Governmental actors
Baltic Development Forum Summit	1 Dec. 2008 Copenhagen	*Political level* Governmental actors, Stakeholders
Stakeholders Conference	5 Feb. 2009 Rostock	*Working level* Governments, business partners, experts, academia, European Commission
Conference on financial instruments	11 June 2009 Visby	*Working level* European Commission governments, managing authorities
START OF DECISION-MAKING IN THE COUNCIL		

Source: website of the EU Strategy for the Baltic Sea Region, interviews.

This informal preparatory work was followed by intra-coalition exchange and coordination once the formal negotiations had started. Despite general support from the EU-27 on the Commission proposal, four issues caused controversy among the EU-27: (1) the idea of macro-regional strategies, (2) the definition of macro-regional strategies, (3) the governance model, and (4) priorities and implementation.

The "macro-regional strategy" initiated a debate on the idea of macro-regions in the EU in general. Firstly, there was, in 2009, no one standard definition of macro-region. The definition had to be developed along with preparations for the EU Strategy for the Baltic Sea region and would consequently be applied to subsequent macro-regional strategies in the EU. To this end, the conceptualisation of cross-border cooperation was of great importance both for the coalition and "outsiders". The emergence of new macro-regions raised two concerns among the negotiation actors in the Council.

Firstly, the Commission, supported by some member states, for instance Belgium and Portugal, wanted to ensure that there would be no fragmentation of EU cooperation. Such fragmentation could arise from the emergence of smaller groups of states aggregating their particular interests beyond the overall EU cooperation framework. Most of the criticism came from those countries that could not identify themselves as a part of any future macro-region. These countries, for example Slovenia, Italy and Greece questioned the value added of new regional instruments, which in the worst case could duplicate existing structures and take away resources from other initiatives managed by the Commission. They also wondered what was the "critical mass" in terms of number of countries after which such a regional instrument should be initiated. In the context of the Baltic Sea Strategy, the macro-regions are defined as an "area comprising territory from a number of different countries or regions associated with one or more common features or challenges" (Interact-EU 2009). Accordingly, the scope of the macro-region applies to cooperation within the EU, based on EU funding and the *acquis communautaire* (speech by Diana Wallis, MEP, 18 Sept. 2009). This means that EU macro-regions do not automatically include third countries. For some member states, for example Austria and Hungary, which saw the opportunity presented by upcoming macro-regional strategies, this clarification was of significant importance, since the possible Danube region strategy would most likely stretch to the Balkan countries (EUObserver, 13 Apr. 2010). Accordingly, those countries that faced the prospect of being affected by future EU macro-regional strategies had specific policy preferences.

The second concern that was expressed by member states outside of the macro-region related to use of the term "macro-regional strategy" in the Council Conclusions. The lack of a clear definition created uncertainty regarding how to relate the strategy instrument to cohesion policy and to the next multiannual Financial Framework of 2014–2020. The new macro-regional strategy was without doubt linked to the debates on the cohesion policy, though indirectly. The strategy proposal was launched in 2009 when the discussions for the forthcoming Financial Framework (2014–2020) were due to start (interview no. 22, 11 Dec. 2009, Riga). Some member states, for example Portugal and France, proposed replacing the term "macro-regional strategy" with "territorial strategy" considering it to be a more appropriate wording in terms of the cohesion policy instruments. Countries expressed concerns about the "pot of money: if the macro-regional strategies would become a tool of taking money" (interview no. 6, 26 January 2010, Copenhagen). Discussions on the use of "macro-regional" or "territorial" continued until the late stage of negotiations.

The third concern related to the new governance model, as the strategy was the first of its kind. The new governance model implied stronger regional interaction amongst the member states, each of which was assigned responsibility as lead country for particular policy actions. The action plan was kept "open", meaning that each of the regional partners could add a new project in the course of action (Terk 2010). The Commission's intention was that the action plan should be updated on a regular basis (Schymik and Krumrey 2009). Discussions involved the issue of nomination of the "high level group" that was to include the Commission and the EU-27 representatives (interview no. 22, 11 Dec. 2009, Riga). The fact that the Baltic Sea Strategy covers 78 different actions to be monitored by the Commission caused eyebrows to be raised among member states outside the macro-region. The hesitant countries were concerned about the capacities and resources that would be taken away from other initiatives and projects, provided the Baltic Sea strategy was claimed to make use of the existing resources without adding in human or financial capacities (interview no. 6, 26 January 2010, Copenhagen). Another criticism of on the governance issue concerned the unclear mandate of the high level group. Neither the Commission Communication nor the annexed action plan outlined the mandate and the composition of the high level group. It was also unclear to which Council configuration the macro-regional participants should account during implementation of the actions. One option could have been to report annually to the General Affairs Council. Once adopted, the Baltic Sea Strategy needed a continuous procedural framework, for instance a review during the upcoming Council Presidencies. The fact that Poland was scheduled to have its Council Presidency in the second half of 2011 with two other presidencies representing the Baltic Sea region (the Danish Presidency in 2012 and the Lithuanian Presidency in 2013) ensured the coherency of the planned action (Schymik and Krumrey 2009). In general, however, the "outsiders" were positive about the new governance aspects of the macro-regional strategy, mainly due to the potential benefits of extending this model to other regions in the EU.

Finally, the member states' preferences differed in regard to the policies and priorities that the Baltic Sea Strategy aimed to tackle. This discussion mainly consolidated the "insiders" of the strategy since they were directly affected by implementation of the actions. Poland, for instance, placed more emphasis on economic measures and instruments that were intended to enhance economic growth. The Baltic States were particularly concerned about energy supply because of their dependence on Russia's energy resources, as well as about their isolation from the EU energy networks. Nordic countries, for example Denmark and Sweden, called for stricter environmental standards to preserve the vulnerable Baltic Sea environment. Finland offered to coordinate activities on maritime safety and sustainable agriculture, fisheries and forestry.

Having demonstrated the coherence between member states' preferences and actions, the dossier provides an adequate basis for an analysis of the effects of both independent variables: degree of institutionalisation and convergence of preferences. The dossier represents a case where both factors demonstrate a high degree, i.e. *high degree of institutionalisation + high convergence of preferences.*

How do member states take advantage of their institutionalised cooperation? The negotiations on the Baltic Sea Strategy demonstrate the effects of cooperation, namely the informal exchange of information and expertise, as well as rhetorical action. Internal consultations and coordination started well in advance of the formal negotiations in the Council, thus members of the territorial coalition were in a privileged position compared to member states outside the region:

> "The national "contact points" meetings preceded the negotiations in the Council. The concept of macro-regional strategies was new. The implications of using a term like "territorial strategy" or "macro-regional" first had to be understood within the group" (interview no. 11, 21 January 2010, Tallinn).

Member states outside the region experienced considerable information distribution asymmetries at the first working group meeting. Insiders were better informed about the political priorities of the proposal (since it was largely drafted based on *their input* to the Commission). They were also better equipped with regard to procedural tools, having held internal meetings beyond the formal negotiation framework. Finally, the Council Presidency acted on behalf of the member states in the region.

Understandably, this situation gave rise to dissatisfaction among the outsiders. There were "critical voices on the fact that the already agreed-upon paper was on the table" (interview no. 35, 11 June 2010, Stockholm). By the time discussions were held in the FoP group, there were almost no remaining internal disparities within the regional alliance. It was able to operate as an institutionalised coalition *vis-à-vis* other negotiation actors. In working group negotiations the regional participants often acted as a coalition by supporting each other's interventions. Opposition from member states outside the coalition was directed at three main issues: the use of the concept of "macro-regional strategy", the nomination of the high-level group and the value-adding benefit of such a strategy.

In general, the Ministerial Conference on the Baltic Sea Strategy was a tactical element in the negotiation process, since on the political level member states rarely express their objections with the same intensity as at the working level. Indeed, most of the participants expressed general support for the initiative. The success of the NB6+2 was further established by issuing a joint declaration that was drafted internally by the members of the group prior to the conference (Joint Declaration on the implementation of the EU Strategy for the Baltic Sea Region, 18 Sept. 2009). The declaration contained the main elements of the macro-regional approach, the governance structure, finances, the external dimension and implementation. In its conclusion, the joint declaration called for the development of "this Strategy in ways that allow it to serve as an example and inspiration for all EU Member States as to how challenges and opportunities of a macro-region, may be addressed by an EU-internal integrated multi-sector strategy" (ibid.).

Preparations for the ministerial conference on 18 September 2009 in the member states' capitals practically overlapped with preparations for the GAERC on 14 September 2009, which, according to the Council Rules of Procedure, had to adopt the agenda for the European Council of 29/30 October 2009. Discussions on the agenda of upcoming European Council meetings usually provide the opportunity for member states' governments to voice their concerns on specific dossiers. Accordingly, the ministerial meeting in Stockholm was a milestone for further negotiations in the Council. It was also expected that the countries outside the Baltic Sea region would contrast insiders' views about the value added of the strategy with the definition of the macro-region concept. The outsiders would therefore possibly use the opportunity to raise these concerns during the conference. The Ministerial Conference in Stockholm confirmed the bargaining success of the NB6+2. The Baltic Sea Strategy was supported by all delegations. The Hungarian Minister of Foreign Affairs pointed out that up to the Baltic Sea Strategy "no appropriate decision-making, covering areas smaller than the entire EU" was available. He also promised to include the issue of the Danube Strategy in the agenda of the upcoming Hungarian Presidency in 2011 and to organise a "Danube Summit" in Budapest (speech by the Hungarian Foreign Minister Péter Balázs in Stockholm, 18 Sept. 2009).

Despite the informal character of the ministerial meeting in Stockholm and the participation of delegates beyond the Council structure (speakers were invited from the European Parliament, the Commission and the European Investment Bank), the conference identified general support for the initiative and paved the way for its smooth adoption in the Council. Discussions at the two remaining meetings of the FoP groups following the ministerial conference in Stockholm did not address any controversial issues and only engaged in some fine-tuning on implementation and monitoring. The member states that identified the future benefits of the adoption of such a pilot project in the text of the Council Conclusions invited the Commission to draft future macro-regional strategies.

The dossier was passed through the COREPER meeting and the GAERC without any major discussions. In order to secure the financial aspects of the strategy, on the initiative of the Swedish Presidency, the strategy was discussed within the Economic and Financial Committee, which invited the European Investment Bank to further support the Baltic Sea Strategy (*Regeringens skrivelse*: Memorandum by the Swedish government 2009/10:159). The Council Conclusions on the Baltic Sea Strategy were unanimously adopted by the ministers of foreign affairs during the GAERC meeting on 27 October 2009. The Council recognised the potential of macro-regional strategies in the context of the territorial cohesion. Further, meeting the interests of the outsiders, the Council outlined "the Danube region as the next macro regional strategy [...] and possible future macro regional strategies" (press release, General Affairs Council, 26 Oct. 2009) Figure 8 illustrates the distribution of the policy positions of the negotiation parties. As the Baltic Sea Strategy is a conceptually new model of macro-regional cooperation, the SQ is situated closer to the endpoint 0. The Commission proposal offers a new concept of macro-regional strategies; however, this proposal has to be 'defended' by the like-minded territorial coalition (Sweden, Denmark, Finland, Latvia, Lithuania, Estonia, German, Poland). The position of Belgium, Slovenia, Italy and Greece on the axis demonstrates their hesitance in regard to the new macro-regional concept. The coalition NB+2 got support from the countries that may in future profit from the next macro-regional strategies, for example Austria and Hungary. It should be pointed out that the intensity of preferences[25] plays a significant role here. The NB+2 represent converging and intensive preferences on the issue.

Figure 8: Effects of NB6+2 coordination on the bargaining outcome of the overall deal on the Baltic Sea Strategy

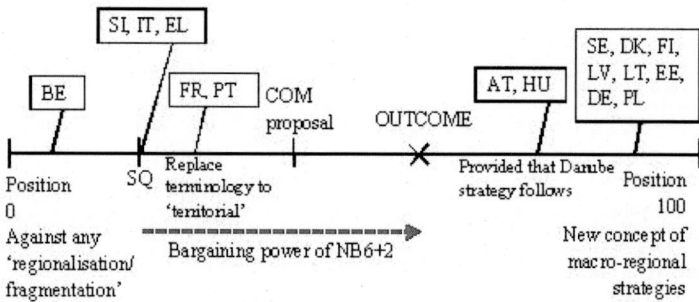

Source: Interviews, media reports, Council Conclusions – doc. 13744/09.

Figure 8 illustrates that the territorial coalition NB6+2 managed to shift the outcome towards the preferences of its members. Taking advantage of the existing regional framework and, in addition, supporting it with a newly established network of contact points, the coalition framed a pre-agreement that granted its members considerable advantage before the issue was discussed by the EU-27. Accordingly, the coalition managed to shift the outcome away from *status quo* (SQ) with "strong wording" on the objectives and references to "macro-regions" without any changes to "territorial re-

---

25 The author acknowledges the significance of the preference intensity variable; however, in this study it does not serve as an explanatory variable and is, thus, kept constant.

gions".[26] The NB6+2 could 'improve' the overall attitude of the member states towards the macro-regional strategies in future, as compared to the Commission's proposal. By ensuring the adoption of the first pilot project of this kind, the regional coalition demonstrated the value-added of regional approach.

The findings support the argument on rhetorical action. Though the preferences of the NB6+2 members were similar on the "political-space" level (see Veen 2011), i.e. with a common objective of increasing the competitiveness of the region and jointly mitigating environmental damage to the Baltic Sea, priorities on particular actions and visions regarding implementation of the strategy differed. Estonia focused mainly on the "old bottlenecks" in terms of market hindrances, energy interconnection problems and the transportation network (Estonian non-paper, January 2009). Lithuania and Poland prioritised internal market mechanisms, i.e. business networks, innovation and R&D, whilst Latvia called for a Baltic energy interconnection plan (interview no. 22, 11 Dec. 2009, Riga). The Nordic countries' proposals to the Commission contained an incentive to make use of the existing institutional frameworks such as the Helsinki Commission (HELCOM), the Nordic Council of Ministers and big commitments regarding environmental standards and regional competitiveness (Norden, News and Events, 10 June 2009).

Compared to the Baltic States, the Nordic view on environmental policy and sustainability was much more ambitious. Nevertheless, these disparities were overcome by framing common long-term visions for the macro-region (interview no. 35, 11 June 2010, Stockholm). The big normative commitments in terms of increasing environmental and safety standards were able to "reduce extremalities" in the new member states' positions by counteracting narrow national economic interests. This consequently increased the credibility of the strategy as a whole (and definitely the credibility of the coalition), since the highly ambitious objectives of the strategy fostered normative aspects of the adopted actions. The arguments of the insiders rhetorically constrained the attitude of the outsiders.

"We stressed the macro regional value of the strategy, for example in the environmental policy. It was significant for everybody. All member states were able to identify with these objectives" (interview no. 11, 21 January 2010, Tallinn).

---

26 On 29/30 October the European Council adopted the Baltic Sea Strategy without further discussions on the content of paragraph (4) of the overall text of the European Council Conclusions. The wording was as follows: "The Council adopts the EU Strategy for the Baltic Sea Region and endorses the Council conclusions on the subject (doc. 13744/09). This Strategy constitutes an integrated framework to address common challenges, i.a. the urgent environmental challenges related to the Baltic Sea, and to contribute to the economic success of the region and to its social and territorial cohesion, as well as to the competitiveness of the EU. [...] The European Council calls upon all relevant actors to act speedily and ensure full implementation of the Strategy, which could constitute an example of a *macro regional strategy*." (Council conclusions, 30 October 2009; author's emphasis).

The empirical evidence gathered through the elite interviews supports the hypothesis that institutionalised cooperation within institutionalised territorial coalitions gives its members bargaining power. One overall conclusion that can be drawn from the Baltic Sea Strategy dossier is that institutionalised coalitions maximise their bargaining advantage most effectively when policy preferences converge across the coalition members. Actors' preferences converged not only on the political space level but largely also on the majority of issues. Consequently, the cooperation involved all elements of the causality chain: the selection of peers on the basis of geographical proximity, the exchange of information and pooling of expertise, justification for the positions and, finally, engaging in joint action (e.g. joint declaration at the ministerial conference). Proactive information exchange was facilitated by establishing a specific "institution", a network of national contact points. At the bargaining stage the exchange on the political level took place between EU directors before the Swedish Presidency and between the ministers of foreign affairs and prime ministers when the dossier was part of the informal "breakfast meeting" agenda.

The theoretical section of this study proposed that coalition members gain a bargaining advantage through the mechanism of rhetorical action. This requires additional explanation in relation to the Baltic Sea Strategy. Environment policy was one of the key areas of the strategy. Given the strong normative content, the Nordic countries, in particular Sweden, actively endorsed high standards in regard to sustainable environment in the proposal. According to the interviews, the framing of common objectives in the environmental actions encouraged the new member states of the NB6+2 to aim for more ambitious environmental standards (interview no. 35, 11 June 2010, Stockholm). This joint regional commitment, together with a vision of strengthened internal market mechanisms and cross-border security, served as a normative pull for their rhetorical action *vis-à-vis* outsiders. The countries that were initially critical of the emergence of new macro-regions made concessions because of the presence of a clearly normative commitment. Consequently, the institutionalised territorial coalition was able to reach a more credible deal in line with its preferred negotiation outcome.

4.2 EU negotiations on climate change

"Often it is enough if we get understanding for our position from our neighbours. We explain our situation and our arguments. Even if they do not join us, it is important that our partners gain an insight into our concerns" (interview no. 20, 19 November 2009, Riga).

This interview quoted above summarises the complexity of the dossier on climate change negotiations and the context in which the territorial partners operated. Due to its "in-built" controversy, climate change represented a field of high variation across the member states' preferences. The climate issue can be seen as highly controversial for EU member states, since it has the potential to impose significant costs on their economies and thus to jeopardise competitiveness *vis-à-vis* internal and external actors. In particular, this affects those countries with heavy industry sectors, which are highly dependent on energy use, or countries still using coal. In other words, climate negotiations can be characterised as hard interest-based bargains (Vogler 2009). As such they also carry great potential for coalition-building, since the negotiation parties have high reputation awareness because of the normative character of the climate change issue. It would be most unlikely that a single member state would veto agreement for an EU-internal deal on climate policy. Before focusing on the coalition patterns in climate negotiations, the background to the dossier will first be presented.

In the autumn of 2009 the Swedish Council Presidency had the ambitious task of taking the EU to the COP15 conference in Copenhagen in December of that year. It should be noted that the EU aimed to demonstrate its aspirations as a global leader in regard to climate change policy. The objective of COP15 was to agree on the creation of a unified global regime during the post-Kyoto phase on the combating of climate change (Haug and Berkhout 2010). International agreement following the Kyoto phase was to lead to a "comprehensive, ambitious, fair, science-based and legally binding treaty from January 2013" (Council Conclusions, 30 Oct. 2009). The internal EU negotiations in preparation for the EU's mandate for COP15 were based on two general negotiation documents:

(1) Communication from the Commission to the Council, the European Parliament, the Economic and Social Committee and the Committee of the Regions – Towards a Comprehensive Climate Change Agreement in Copenhagen, COM (2009)39, 28.01.2009 ("Commission Communication of 28 Jan. 2009"), and
(2) Communication from the Commission to the European Parliament, the Council, the European Economic and Social Committee and the Committee of the Regions. Stepping up International Climate Finance: A European Blueprint for the Copenhagen Deal, 10.09.2009 ("Commission Communication of 10 Sept. 2009").

The **Commission communication of 28 Jan. 2009** defined the political objectives and the necessary action (by the EU and international community) that should be agreed at COP15 in Copenhagen. The agreement in Copenhagen was to serve as the basis for further international action after the Kyoto Protocol's first commitment period ended in 2012. Drawing on the political decision of the European Council in June 2008, the Communication called for the following action:

- Developed countries should reduce their emissions in order to collectively deliver 30 per sent emission reduction in 2020 compared to 1990;
- Emissions from aviation and shipping (that were not covered by the Kyoto Protocol) should be included;
- Among the market instruments the Communication mentions the carbon market, the Clean Development Mechanism and Emission Trading System (Commission, press release, 28 Jan. 2009).

The **Commission communication of 10 Sept 2009** set out a concrete proposal for scaling up finance to help developing countries combat climate change. According to the Commission's calculations, the developing countries would need €100 billion by 2020. This figure was spelled out for the first time by the Commission and was subject to lengthy discussions in the Council. The international carbon market could cover around 40 per cent but about 20 to 40 per cent would be needed from public and private finance in developing countries (i.e. €22–50 billion a year). The methodology offered by the Commission on how much each country should pay was based on GDP and responsibility for emissions. Accordingly, the Commission communication proposed the following financing commitment:

- The total EU contribution: €2–15 billion a year by 2020 (i.e. 10 to 30 per cent of global contribution).
- Breaking down the total EU contribution of €900 million by periods, the EU would contribute €2.1 billion a year (2010–2012) – (also called "Fast-start" funding), €3.9 billion (2013) and €2–15 billion a year (2014–2020).

Taking up the Presidency from the Czech Republic in the second part of 2009, Sweden faced the demanding task of consolidating the member states around a strong mandate that would maintain the EU's "standard-bearer reputation" (Parker and Karlsson 2010:924) and by its example encourage the international community to agree on an ambitious commitment for the post-Kyoto phase. Each individual member state entered the internal EU negotiations uncertain about the international players' level of ambition and with worries about how to fulfil the goals and commitments defended by the EU. There was enough reason for the Presidency to be "afraid of the new conflict between the old and new member states" (Aftonposten, 27 Oct. 2009). Another factor that threatened successful EU-internal preparations for the climate negotiations prior to the Copenhagen Conference was a delay in appointing a new Commission (Financial Times, 20 July 2009).

Climate policy is a particularly complex dossier because it is negotiated not only amongst the 27 EU member states but also simultaneously at the UN level within the G8, G20 etc. Because of the global nature of this issue, its "architecture" stretches across several international formats. From the negotiation theory perspective, negotiations on climate change are "plurilateral", i.e. seeking a compromise between several multilateral institutions. Accordingly, the EU's internal negotiations were part of global agreement, where the EU-27 agreed on a common position (a mandate for the Presidency) to be presented at COP15.

The main global framework for climate change policy is defined in the United Nations Framework Convention on Climate Change (UNFCCC). Its long-term objective, as formulated in Art. 2, is the "stabilization of greenhouse gas concentrations in the atmosphere at a level that would prevent dangerous anthropogenic interference with the climate system. Such a level should be achieved within a time-frame sufficient to allow ecosystems to adapt naturally to climate change, to ensure that food production is not threatened and to enable economic development to proceed in a sustainable manner" (UNFCCC, Art.2). International agreements on the UNFCCC are reached at the annual Conferences of Parties (COPs). The key legal instrument is the Kyoto Protocol, which was agreed during COP3 in 1997, but because of the delay in ratification could not enter into force before 2005.[27] The Kyoto Protocol stipulates that the signatories of the Kyoto Protocol must reduce their emissions by (at least) 5 per cent below 1990 levels by 2012 (accordingly, the climate change ambitions *after 2012* had to be defined). As from the late 1990s, the EU demonstrated "directional leadership" in regard to international climate policy, i.e. leading by good example (Kilian and Elgström 2010:265). Since the early 2000s, the EU has adopted a number of binding measures in order to demonstrate its global leadership role in climate policy, for example the EU emission trading scheme in 2005, the so-called "20-20-20 plan"[28] in 2007 and the EU energy and climate package in 2008.

In general, negotiations on climate change in the EU demonstrate a division between the "forerunners" and "hesitant" countries. More specifically, several like-minded groups of member states can be identified. The first group comprises "advanced green" states (the Nordic countries, Germany, Austria and the Netherlands). The second group includes rich countries with

---

27 Protocol requires its ratification by 55 per cent of signatories, including the parties listed in Annex I of the Protocol (industrialised developed countries), which are responsible for 55 per cent of emissions. The reticence of Japan, Canada, Russia and the United States to ratify the Kyoto Protocol put severe constraints on the credibility of international determination to take concrete and effective measures in combating climate change. In 2001 the United States, under the incoming Bush Administration , refused to sign the Kyoto Protocol. Following increased scepticism from Australia, the Kyoto Protocol experienced a major setback. From seemingly effective multilateralism from the initial negotiations, the ratification process was faced with parties' domestic policy preferences and resulted in the international climate regime crisis (Costa 2008:537). To some extent this served as a driving condition for the emergence of the EU's leadership role in further climate change negotiations.
28 The commitment covered three activities: (1) reducing emissions by at least 20 per cent by 2020, (2) increasing renewable energy by 20 per cent by 2020, and (3) improving energy efficiency by 20 per cent by 2020.

historically high stocks of emissions (France, the United Kingdom, Italy, Belgium, and Luxembourg). The third group comprises "cohesion countries" that are eligible for financial assistance and low emissions per capita (Spain, Greece and Ireland). Finally, since enlargement in 2004 a new group of countries has emerged comprising transitional economies still lagging behind the group of prosperous EU member states. Energy production in several of the new member states is largely based on coal (Vogler 2009).

Thus, negotiations on the mandate for COP15 provided evidence for a distinct task-specific coalition that was framed between like-minded member states during the EU energy and climate package in 2008, and took up its work during internal EU negotiations in 2009. Most prominently, it was demonstrated with the emergence of the coalition of new member states, which coordinated joint action. One interviewee explains the emergence of the new coalition of member states in the following way:

"The coalition emerged in 2008. At that time two countries (Poland and Slovakia) took the leadership of the internal coordination of the member states' positions. In the 2009 climate negotiations the core of the group was the same. Some countries joined, others left. For example, Estonia was not a part of this new group. But generally speaking members shared similar negotiation outcomes" (interview no. 21, 11 December 2009, Riga).

Applying the theoretical framework of this research project, the coalition of nine new member states[29] may be considered a task-specific coalition that begins its operational activity as soon as the dossier that is relevant to its specific policy scope is put on the decision-making agenda. During internal EU negotiations before COP15, the task-specific negotiation demonstrated resistance to its forerunners' ambitions and favoured careful climate policy commitments. The reason behind the cleavages was a different view of the future of the Kyoto framework and particular aspects of the climate deal. Firstly, the "hesitant group" shared the same view of the future of the Kyoto framework. The issue was essential both legal and political, and there was a link between the EU's internal concerns and the preferences of the international community. The main objective of the Copenhagen Conference was to agree on the establishment of a comprehensive, ambitious and legally binding global treaty (Haug and Berkhout 2010). The issue that was of a legal nature to the climate policy instrument was still open for discussion. There were two options: continuing the Kyoto Protocol or creating a new overarching legal instrument. The latter could also have been constructed as a "two-track approach" by creating a special legally binding instrument separate from the Kyoto Protocol for the US and sceptical major developing countries (Spencer et al. 2010). In this context, the new member states favoured the continuation of the Kyoto Protocol framework. Their position was grounded in the fact

---

29   Poland, Hungary, Slovakia, the Czech Republic, Slovenia, Lithuania, Latvia, Bulgaria and Romania.

that those member states that had joined the EU after the signing of the Kyoto Protocol (1997) were not included in list of the signatories of the Annex II of the Protocol and were treated as transition economies (Vogler 2009:482). Therefore, they were entitled to voluntary commitments without binding themselves to numerical financial targets (The Economist, 15 Oct. 2009).

With reference to the research design of the study, the Council negotiations before COP15 revealed variation across the independent variables, i.e. degree of institutionalisation and preference convergence, and provide rich data for empirical analysis. Accordingly, three cases can be observed within the climate dossier:

- High degree of institutionalisation + high preference convergence;
- High degree of institutionalisation + low preference convergence;
- Low degree of institutionalisation + high preference convergence.

The negotiation structure will be outlined in the following and empirical evidence offered in accordance with the aforementioned combinations of independent variables.

Under the Swedish Presidency, work on the dossier was carried out by three main actors: The Council Working Group on International Environmental Issues (WPIEI/CC), the Council Secretariat and the Commission. The European Parliament was not included in its legislative capacity, though continuous exchange on the climate negotiation process was taking place through Presidency channels (Swedish Presidency website).[30]

The negotiations on the internal EU mandate on climate change were largely intergovernmental, with the Council playing a major role in decision-making. The dossier was passed through three Council formations (Environmental Council, ECOFIN[31], GAERC[32]) and then adopted by the European Council by unanimous vote. The Commission played a role in drafting the proposal and outlining the basic elements of the EU's commitment that were further integrated by the Council Secretariat into the main negotiation document, i.e. the Council Conclusions.

The WPIEI/CC served as a key decision-making body on the expert level of the climate negotiations. Taking into account different aspects of climate policy, the WPIEI/CC was further split into 10 subordinate working groups. The subordinate expert groups dealt with specific and often highly technical aspects of the climate issue. According to the data of the Swedish Presidency Secretariat, the work of the WPIEI/CC expert group included subgroups on

---

30 After the European Council on 29/30 October, the Swedish Prime Minister, Fredrik Reinfeldt, reported to the European Parliament on the results of the Council negotiations.
31 Economic and Financial Affairs Council.
32 Climate change negotiations were carried out under the provisions of the Treaty of Lisbon before splitting GAERC (General Affairs and External Relations Council) into GAC (General Affairs Council) and FAC (Foreign Affairs Council).

budget, legal issues, science aspects, aviation and maritime effects, reporting, LULUCF (land-use, land-use change and forestry), technology, technical and economic analysis, and further action. Since climate policy stretches across several policy fields, the dossier was discussed in several Council configurations. The complexity of the task was further increased by "switching" the dossier from the COREPER I to the COREPER II, each of the bodies comprising different staff members of the permanent representation in Brussels[33] and the national instructions being prepared by the member states' Ministry of Environment and the Ministry of Finance, respectively. Furthermore, the differences in voting procedure across different negotiation levels enhanced the process of coalition-building at the level of the Environment Council. In spite of the QMV rule applied in the Environmental Council, the possible "threat of a veto" in the European Council determined "the rules of the game" in Council negotiations from the start. Moreover, internal cleavages during the adoption of the EU energy and climate package in 2008, with several countries threatening to veto the final agreement, encouraged a similar negotiation atmosphere in 2009. In other words, the highly complex formal setting, decision-making procedures and pressure of time led to the emergence of smaller groups beyond the EU-27 framework that exchange information and positions prior to formal meetings.

Table 9 shows that the climate negotiations were simultaneously held within several Council formations and shifted from one Council configuration to another at short intervals (sometimes only one day) between the discussions within different Council configurations. This leads to two observations that are important in regard to the argument put forward in this study: (1) the member states coordinate their positions prior to the peak of negotiation activity in the Council (as the agenda above shows, three Council of Ministers meetings and the European Council negotiated on the climate dossier within the space of one week), and (2) since the climate issue covers topics that stretch across different policy fields, the possible member states' coalitions for enhancing bargaining power have to operate across several Council configurations. In other words, the coalition "follows" the dossier. This, in turn, increases the number of actors with different professional profiles and calls for good internal coordination (nationally and intergovernmentally among the coalition members). Consequently, coalition-building, coordination of positions and the exchange of information on the technical aspects of the climate negotiations followed several paths: (1) exchange on the expert level among the ministries of environment and ministries of finance, (2) exchange among the EU coordination units of the member states either at the prime ministers' office, or within the ministries of

---

33 COREPER I, supported by *Mertens*, discusses issues channelled to the Environment Council; COREPER II, supported by *Antici*, discusses issues channelled further to ECOFIN and the GAERC.

foreign affairs, (3) cooperation on the political level, i.e. ministers and prime ministers.

Table 9: Agenda of the climate negotiations

	July	August	September	October	November	December
EU meetings	Informal Environvironment Council 24 July 2009		Informal European Council 17 Sept. 2009	ECOFIN, 20 Oct. 2009 Environment Council, 21 Oct. 2009 GAERC, 26 Oct. 2009 European Council, 29 Oct. 2009	ECOFIN 10 Nov. 2009 GAERC 16 Nov. 2009 Extra. Env. Council 23 Nov. 2009	European Council 10 Dec. 2009
UN Meetings		Informal climate meeting in Bonn	International Climate meeting in Bangkok		Informal Climate meeting in Barcelona	COP 15 in Copenhagen
Political meetings	G8		UN General Assembly meeting G20	Major Economies Forum	G20 EU-US and EU-Russia summits	

Source: Council Presidency agenda.

Three main issues shaped the debates among the "forerunners" and the "hesitant" countries prior to the October Environment Council and the ECOFIN meeting in 2009: commitment to moving from a 20 to 30 per cent emission target, assigned amount units (AAUs) and climate financing (the scale of the public funds); agreement on when funding should start; and the method for calculating burden-sharing.

The policy preferences of the member states on the 30 per cent target demonstrated extensive disparities in the Council. The "environmental willingness" demonstrated variation across the North-South and the West-East divide. The new member states' policy preferences on the 30 per cent target could be explained by two domestic conditions: they saw the far-reaching measures to reduce emissions as a threat to their economies (Parker and

Karlsson 2010:934) and expressed concerns about their competitiveness *vis-à-vis* third states.

Member states on the external border of the EU believed that the unitary EU commitments on emission targets would jeopardise their competitiveness chances compared to countries outside the EU that were not bound by the climate change commitments. Accordingly, their energy dependency on Russia might increase (interview no. 21, 11 December 2009, Riga). The coal-dependent member states were reticent to accept the 30 per cent target for different reasons: their widely available energy sources were responsible for high levels of emissions. For example, Poland's economy is 90 per cent dependent on coal (Parker and Karlsson 2010:935), whereas Estonia mostly produces electricity from locally extracted oil shale (interview no. 7, 21 January 2010, Tallinn). Countries that joined the EU after 2004 preferred looser emission caps (The Economist, 28 Oct. 2009), i.e. possible increases in their permitted emissions, and backed their claim with the argument that further economic growth (and, consequently, access to more emission quotas) would be necessary in order to bridge the economic gap with the older member states (Vogel 2009:482, Parker and Karlsson 2010:934).

The issue of AAUs consolidated the new member states because they saw the possibility of buffering their emission target needs with the help of accumulated amounts of emissions. Under the first phase of the Kyoto Protocol, the new member states had accumulated AAUs and were eager to keep these units in the new agreement because of their monetary value. The Commission, supported by the forerunners, opposed this proposal, fearing that the increased supply of AAUs would undermine the targets of reducing emissions (European Voice, 29 Oct. 2009).

The policy preferences of the task-specific coalition on climate financing could be explained by the gap between the economic prosperity of countries in the coalition and that of the rich EU countries, and by the existing budgetary constraints due to the recession. Some of the countries that were hardly hit by the economic crisis (e.g. Hungary and Latvia) argued that *per capita* GDP in their countries was possibly not much higher than in countries that the EU was aiming to support financially within the framework of the climate change agreement. For example, comparing forecasts for *per capita* GDP, by 2012 less prosperous countries could be on the same level as potential recipients of climate financing, not to mention those developing countries that refused to take their share of the responsibility. The negotiation positions of these countries were largely framed under the constraints of domestic constituencies. The decision on climate financing was taken in autumn 2009, when the recession due to the economic crisis was at its worst. In Latvia, for example, GDP growth forecasts for the last quarter of 2009 dropped to -18 per cent, with slow recovery prospects. Having taken a loan from the IMF, the European Commission and other lenders in early 2009 (EUObserver, 3

July 2009) to ensure stability in the country's economy, Latvia was facing domestic constraints and looking for allies in the climate negotiations. Hungary faced similar problems of a domestic economic crisis as a result of the financial turmoil and in November 2008 received a loan from the IMF, World Bank and the European Commission (IMF, press release, 6 Nov. 2008). Besides, the new members had to deal with their commitments in emission reduction and to implement the existing EU legislation on climate change, which was costly.

The task-specific coalition of new member states comprised nine countries, namely Poland, Hungary, Slovakia, the Czech Republic, Slovenia, Lithuania, Latvia, Bulgaria and Romania. In October 2009, before the Environment Council and the ECOFIN meeting, Poland took over the role of lead country and invited Malta and Cyprus to join the group. Hence, the coalition of the new member states was known as *9+2*. The internal coordination mechanism within the group included several interaction channels, expert network among the capitals and in Brussels, COREPER ambassadors, the ministers, the prime ministers and also the territorial partnerships, for example Visegrad + Baltic consultations.

After the consolidated version of the draft Council Conclusions was distributed[34], the dossier was taken up by the COREPER in the first week of October. The involvement of the Permanent Representatives in the internal discussions added a diplomatic touch to the negotiations and additional channels for the informal exchange before the meetings. As one of the interviewees put it: "The real aggregation of like-minded actors started at the COREPER level" (interview no. 51, 3 March 2010, Tallinn). At this stage Poland, strongly supported by Hungary, took the initiative as a lead country in the coalition. Before the meeting at the COREPER level on 14 October, the 9+2 coalition organised an informal meeting in Brussels to frame the common wording on paragraph 25 of the Council Conclusions (on financial contributions). The coalition's main considerations were to stress the voluntary nature and fair share of the "fast-start" activities for the Annex II countries to the Kyoto Protocol. Furthermore, the group had similar preferences on financing aspects after 2012, meaning that the EU had to take into account the development prospects of the less prosperous countries in general and the impact of the economic recession in particular. The new member states with low emissions but facing strict budget deficit cuts due to international loans, backed the "ability to pay" criterion (European Voice, 29 Oct. 2009).

Informal exchange between the coalition members took place in advance of the COREPER meetings, as informal breakfasts or lunches. Finally, the commonly agreed text with the coalition's draft suggestions for paragraph 25 of the Council Conclusions was circulated for consideration to the EU-27

---

34 The Council Conclusions provided the basis for the EU position at COP15.

during the COREPER I meeting. The dossier was handled by the COREPER II, which took over from the ECOFIN counsellors. The coalition members framed a joint proposal on paragraph 25 of the Council Conclusions and offered their wording of the text for discussion on the ministers' level. The ECOFIN meeting on 20 October and the Environmental Council on 21 October tested the coalition's leverage.

Two distinct blocs had at this stage emerged with (1) eleven new member states representing concerns on the climate financing issue and AAU, and (2) the "forerunners" i.e. Nordic countries, the UK, the Netherlands, Germany, France and Portugal. Sweden and Denmark were ambitiously backed up by the United Kingdom, which was trying on the highest political level to "galvanise other governments into action" (Financial Times, 19 Oct. 2009 and 20 Oct 2009). British activity could be partly explained by political motives in the face of upcoming elections. The United Kingdom took upon the role of acting as external negotiator on behalf of the EU, encouraging the developed countries within the international political formats (G8, G20 etc.) to take up their responsibility. This also served also as supportive action for the Swedish Presidency in terms of resource capacity. France was sending "mixed messages" (interview no. 33, 15 January 2010, Stockholm), in spite of its ambitious commitments in the climate and energy package one year before. The Netherlands, a "green leader" since the first period of the Kyoto Protocol (Vogel 2009:473), remained proactive. Germany was an early proponent of the ambitious climate goals (Financial Times, 21 Sept. 2009) though the change in the German government and the nomination of a new federal environmental minister created some doubts as to Germany's position.

The ECOFIN meeting in October 2009 failed to agree on the text of the Council Conclusions on the financing issue, with disagreement on whether to name a concrete scale for public financing. (European Voice, 29 Oct. 2009). The Environmental Council of 21 October 2009 managed to agree on AAUs, finding a compromise that was acceptable to the 9+2 (interview no. 21, 11 December 2009, Riga). The hesitant countries managed to push for a favourable outcome, i.e. to keep the emission credits (with a monetary value) to buffer their emission records in the future. On this deal the 9+2 had to overcome the resistance of the forerunners (Denmark, the United Kingdom and Sweden), who considered that the AAU effects could negatively influence carbon market prices (European Voice, 30 Oct. 2009).

With a deadlock in both ECOFIN and the Environmental Council on the climate financing issue, the dossier was left to the heads of states to reach final agreement on. The Council outcome was reported by the media in the following way: "[...] divisions were exposed when a meeting of EU Finance Ministers broke up without agreement. Poland, supported by other Central and East European countries, insisted that the EU should work out how to spread the cost among its member states, before declaring to the world it is ready to pay" (European Voice, 29 Oct. 2009).

The European Council of 29/30 October finally agreed on the EU's negotiation position for the Copenhagen Conference, without specifying agreement on "how much its own contribution should be" (European Voice, 30 Oct. 2009). Under the pressure of the demands from the 9+2, the heads of states agreed to "return to the question of burden sharing at a future summit, expected to be after Copenhagen. A working party of officials should study the formulas on sharing the cost" (ibid.). Putting in the Council Conclusions a high political commitment towards external actors, the EU kept the option of "leaving the gate open" by adding the Annex to the official summit communiqué and stressing that the less prosperous member states would be taken into account. The 9+2 task-specific coalition had achieved its goals.

These findings convincingly support the hypothesis that institutionalised conditions enhance interaction among coalition members and thus give them a bargaining advantage by means of three mechanisms, namely exchange of information, expertise-pooling and rhetorical action. This case also illustrates the importance of policy preferences for goal-oriented action. Similar preferences on the EU mandate for COP15 and the high stakes the parties attached to these issues played the most important role for the group's operation. Interaction within the coalition took place both in the capitals and Brussels interaction channels and the institutionalised framework of existing geographical partnerships (Visegrad group, Baltic group). The involvement of the highest political level was a prerequisite for the increase in bargaining power. It has been acknowledged by scholars evaluating the work of the Presidency that the Swedish Presidency was not able to overlook the demands of the new member states during the European Council (Swedish Institute for European Policy Studies seminar, 10 Nov. 2009, Stockholm).

The outcome of the ministerial meetings demonstrated that the informal exchange and pre-meeting coordination resulted in an increase in the 9+2's bargaining power. The Presidency was put in a difficult position because failure to internally agree on the Commission's proposal would undermine the EU's global leadership in climate policy. Besides, Sweden had defined internal EU negotiations as one of the key priorities of its Presidency (Langdal and von Sydow 2009:9). Therefore, in its presidency's capacity Sweden took the initiative to hold bilateral talks with the reluctant governments in the hesitant group.

The Swedish Minister of Environment personally visited the capitals of the reluctant countries and together with his colleagues went through all sensitive aspects and concerns of each government trying to feel the possible scope of compromise. In Brussels the presidency organised the "bilaterals" on the COREPER level at an early stage – first asking them to fill in a questionnaire and to formulate the seven most urgent issues, then inviting each government to explain their positions. We also organised a tour de capital in the autumn and closer to the end of the Council negotiations with trips to the capitals of the lead countries in an attempt to convince them (interview no. 33, 15 January 2010, Stockholm).

The presidency could not override the claims of the coalition during the Environmental Council or at ECOFIN and unwillingly had to postpone the decision to the highest political level.

This case illustrates the hypothesis put forward in this study, demonstrating that the task-specific coalition jointly coordinated its positions by framing justified arguments that the presidency and the forerunners had to take into account. Firstly, the group pushed for the inclusion of the "capacity to pay" criterion when calculating climate financing by demonstrating each country's current economic growth record. Secondly, it convincingly insisted on competitiveness arguments, arguing that the whole idea of EU integration had been directed to balancing economic disparities in the EU. Consequently, the opponents were left without a choice in the face of these well-grounded arguments.

All in all, the task-specific coalition succeeded in pooling bargaining power and exerted an influence on the decision outcome. After the October European Council, six weeks before the start of COP15 in Copenhagen, in accordance with the promises made to the 9+2, a working group was established to address the remaining open questions on calculating burden-sharing. In December the Swedish Prime Minister started a round of bilateral discussions with the member states in order to seek promises for the "fast-start" payment (European Voice, 3 Dec. 2009); this issue was further taken up by COREPER ambassadors, who also prepared a draft of the December European Council communiqué. The idea was that this final document would shape the negotiation mandate for the Copenhagen Conference. Regarding the scale of the financial support from the EU, the draft contained a space for inserting a figure on finance for the period 2010–2012 (ibid.). The European Council meeting on 11/12 December took place when the Copenhagen Conference had already started. By that time the member states had taken their national decisions on the scale of contribution to "fast-start" activities.

Applying the theoretical framework of this study, the findings demonstrate that the task-specific coalition 9+2 was able to gain the bargaining advantage by applying institutionalised cooperation prior to the formal Council meetings. The overall outcome of the internal EU climate deal shifted closer to the 9+2's ideal point. The outcome should be regarded in the context of the recent EU commitment to become a global leader in climate change policy. Taking this normative background into account, the effect of the 9+2 interaction gains even more weight. The coalition members were able to rhetorically entrap their opponents by jointly presenting justified arguments. Figure 9 illustrates that in the internal EU climate deal the task-specific coalition succeeded in gaining more bargaining power than the committed countries. Their positions are indicated on the axis closer to the endpoint of position 0.

In its draft the Commission proposed further reducing emissions by 2020, aiming to move to 30 per cent target. Supported by the United Kingdom, the Netherlands, Denmark, France and Portugal, this served as an ambitions commitment by the EU. Some countries, for instance Sweden and Denmark individually considered even higher targets. The positions of the task-specific coalition 9+2 were closer to the 20 per cent target (see Fig. 9). The outcome of the December European Council was a compromise, namely a "wait and see" approach.

Partly due to the pressure from the 9+2, partly also because the reluctant developed countries (US, China, India) did not support the EU's ambitious climate change policy (Parker and Karlsson 2010:940), the final EU internal deal was weaker than initially envisaged by the Commission and the Presidency.

Figure 9: The effects of the institutionalised task-specific coalition on the bargaining power regarding the emission targets of the EU internal negotiations on the climate change

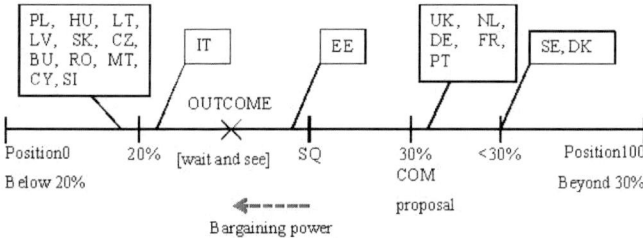

Source: Council Conclusions, 11 Dec. 2009, media reports.

Note: Fig. 9 does not intend to reflect the positions of all 27 member states.

The Council Conclusions set out the conditionality attached to funding pledged by the EU: "*if* other developed countries make comparable offers" (European Voice, 11 Dec. 2009), an approach that was proposed by the 9+2 in September when negotiations started. Also, the wording emission target was weaker in the final document than in the Commission proposal. The comparison below illustrates the shift in position towards the preferences of the task-specific coalition.

149

Table 10: Comparing the wording in the text of the proposal and the outcome

PROPOSAL Commission proposal 23 Jan. 2009	OUTCOME Council Conclusions, European Council 11 Dec. 2009
"The total effort [,,,] should amount to 30% below 1990 levels in 2020."	"[...] the EU reiterates its conditional offer to move to a 30% reduction by 2020 compared to 1990 levels, *provided* that other developed countries commit themselves to comparable emission reductions and that developing countries contribute adequately". (author's emphasis).

Source: Commission proposal 23 Jan. 2009, Council Conclusions 11 Dec 2009.

The coalition of new member states in climate negotiations represents an empirical example of a task-specific coalition based on the long-term common interests of the coalition parties and institutionalised cooperation.

Do the EU climate change negotiations before COP15 provide any evidence of a territorially constituted institutionalised coalition? Some elements of the activity of the territorial partnerships can be traced in the consultations of the Visegrad group on the burden-sharing issue. As the main empirical focus of this study is on Nordic-Baltic cooperation, the effects of the Nordic interaction prior to the negotiations in the Council will be briefly outlined in the following section.[35]

Sweden and Denmark, the former holding the EU Presidency and the latter hosting COP15 in Copenhagen, were among the "forerunners" (Financial Times, 22 Oct. 2009). Sweden is generally known as a country with high national commitments in regard to climate policy (interview no. 33, 15 January 2010, Stockholm). Similarly, Denmark has been a convinced forerunner in climate change policy, including the burden-sharing issue. In the October 2009 Environment Council, Connie Hedegaard, the Danish Climate and Energy Minister said: "Denmark would have liked to see finances formulated a very long time ago" (European Voice, 22 Oct. 2009). Finland supported its neighbours in general but was more cautions in entering into high individual commitments because of concerns expressed by industry that competitiveness would be impaired. In the situation when the NB6 could not agree on common ground, the group operated on the level of like-minded participants. Interviewees from the Nordic countries acknowledged that there was a separate Nordic partnership on the dossier. Exchange among the Nordic member states started before publication of the Commission Communication. Since the Nordic members shared common preferences, and since Denmark and Sweden were engaged in preparing COP15 on the level of international climate negotiations, the pre-meeting exchange took place within the well-established N5 framework, plus Iceland and Norway.

---

35   NB6 engaged in comparatively little activity on the climate change dossier, with the exception of the traditional prime ministers' breakfast meetings, which can be explained by the differences in policy prefereces, i.e. high degree of institutionalisation + low degree of preverence convergence.

"Nordic-5 in the environment and the COP framework is a concrete cooperation format. It has existed since 1996. Nordic ministers and experts exchange views on environment and climate policy. The format does not deal with the coordination of positions but rather focuses on the exchange of information and creating a common understanding. Iceland and Norway are also present" (interview no. 36, 15 January 2010, Stockholm).

The Nordic group was consolidated in its commitment to reach an ambitious climate deal at the Copenhagen Conference and supported the endeavours of the Swedish Presidency. In September 2009 climate negotiations featured in important meetings on the international negotiation circuit, namely at the UN General Assembly on 21–23 September in New York, at the start of the Bangkok climate change talks on 28 September and at the G20 summit in Pittsburgh on 24–26 September). It was relevant for the Nordic states to act jointly in the international negotiations on climate, since they all had high ambitions and a well-established cooperation network in the field of environmental policy.

Coalition theory postulates that coalitions are issue-specific, i.e. member states may not find common ground on one issue but frame coalitions on others (Blavoukos and Pagoulatos 2011:562). Following this reasoning, the climate change dossier provides an example of close NB6 cooperation, even though the group did not demonstrate coherence during the climate change negotiations on the policy domain level. This particular issue concerns the highly technical Land Use, Land-Use Change and Forestry (LULUCF) initiative. In this regard the climate dossier provides an example in which high institutionalisation is accompanied with converging preferences (high degree of institutionalisation + high preference convergence).

LULUCF is a potential market instrument for "maintaining forests to counteract emissions from deforestation" in the climate change context (Naturvårdsverket 2006). Since it is currently not included in the Emission Trading Scheme, LULUCF opened up future possibilities for reducing emissions by allowing compensation of credits from the land-use sector. In regard to the post-2012 climate change regime, the EU had to agree internally on how to deal with LULUCF credits.

The Nordic countries, especially Finland and Sweden, identified a strong common interest in the LULUCF dossier. The WPIEI/CC took over the issue from the WPIEI/CC subgroup on LULUCF at the beginning of October. The Presidency and the Commission called for immediate action and encouraged member states to deliver data on their forestry activities, since more clarity was necessary for the international negotiation framework in Bangkok. The draft Council Conclusions had to include a decision on how to take account of LULUCF in the context of the post-2012 climate agreement and the transmission of the AAUs to LULUCF. Analysis by the Commission proposed taking account of forestry activities when calculating the 30 per cent emission targets. The proposal was supported by countries rich in forests. On the expert group level the Baltic countries, large amounts of whose territory is covered by forests, identified similar interests as the Nordic member states although, having less expertise in this area they took advantage of the NB6 interaction:

"Initially our experts were uncertain about how to position themselves on the LULUCF issue, since we do not have much expertise in this field. Taking advantage of our regional cooperation framework we contacted Finnish experts and largely relied on their expertise" (interview no. 19, 18 January 2010, Riga).

The interview shows that those countries with fewer resources or less expertise on the issue exploit their territorial partnerships in sharing knowledge about specific technical issues. Relying on the expertise of the lead countries, the coalition members assumed the role of free riders and profited from the cooperation by enhancing their bargaining power. Accordingly, group coherence on the LULUCF issue was created through effective exchange on expertise-sharing. This observation is supported by a Nordic interviewee:

"At the beginning of the Presidency the Baltic States were not active on the LULUCF issue. When the issue was brought up in the Council they took the advantage of the Finnish leadership. Now we can say that there is a coherent regional group with some additional forest-rich member states sharing the same preferences" (interview no. 33, 15 January 2010, Stockholm).

After discussions at the working group level, a distinct coalition of like-minded countries was established, comprising Finland, Estonia, Latvia, Lithuania and a group of other countries (Austria, Portugal, Slovenia, the Czech Republic and Slovakia). The group agreed on common wording and submitted a statement to the October Environmental Council regarding paragraph 33 of the Council Conclusions (Council document 14777/09, 18 Nov. 2009). The joint statement, which was attached to the Council minutes, illustrates that the group interaction provided the coalition with bargaining power that began with territorial collaboration (knowledge sharing on the technicalities of the issue).

The theoretical design of this study also envisages a less frequent case when the preferences of the member states converge but the level of institutionalisation is kept low. Testing this case would imply the following configuration: low degree of institutionalisation + high preference convergence. The climate change dossier provides an example of such a case. Given high preference convergence, one could assume that the member states' incentives for engaging in institutionalised cooperation are rooted in their calculating that they can "take a share" of a collective advantage. If a member state does not join a coalition, there must be some reason for such behaviour. Provided that member states act rationally and calculate the costs and benefits of their actions, there have to be more benefits to joining a coalition than there are costs. Risk-averse member states deliberately refuse to join a coalition *if* joining makes them worse off than if they do not join. Motives for such calculations can, for example, be reputation costs.

The task-specific coalition on climate change has existed since 2008. During negotiations on the EU energy and climate package the group of new member states also included Estonia. Estonian policy preferences are rooted in its specific situation in regard to energy supply. The country is largely dependent on oil shale, a sedimentary rock used in electricity production of which there are large deposits in Estonia. Known for its high emission shares (Rudi 2009), this type of energy production certainly puts Estonia among the hesitant countries in terms of climate policy. Nevertheless, Estonia decided to leave the coalition of new member states when the most intensive internal coordination started. Shortly before the Council meeting, Estonia adopted its own position:

"We were not part of any of these coalitions but supported the Commission in trying to find a consensus between the two sides" (interview no. 51, 3 March 2010, Tallinn).

The reasons for this choice are provided by the following interviewee:

"The climate talks pitted East against West. Even if we were able to share the interests of this coalition in some respects, we said we would not join them [the East]. We cannot support the claim that the Eastern European countries are inefficient. We left. [...] If a group is negatively perceived by the decision-maker and you are a part of it, it becomes your reputation problem" (interview no. 7, 21 January, Tallinn).

The motives of the Estonian decision to stay outside the coalition may also be linked to the high reputation standards the Estonian government had set on the international stage when facing the important decision by Eurozone members to approve Estonian membership of the Eurozone. Besides, Estonia has repeatedly insisted on its close adherence to Scandinavia: "We should stop talking about the three Baltic States since only two are left. Estonia is no longer a Baltic country: it behaves like a Scandinavian country" (Baltic Business News, 26 Jan. 2011). Drawing on reputation considerations, Estonia "played a solo game" in the climate negotiations. With a coalition of eleven member states, Estonia was able to feel quite safe that the final deal would accommodate the interests of all the hesitant member states (inside and outside the coalition). Besides, by opting for a soft bargaining strategy, Estonia gained the reputation of being a cooperative player.

The case of a "solo game" is particularly interesting for this study because it reveals that a member state with similar outcome preferences may abstain from institutionalised cooperation on the basis of strategic considerations. This finding opens up further research possibilities, adding in additional variables to explain outcomes.

The value of the case of Estonia for the current research design is twofold. Firstly, this study hypothesises that the case of low institutionalisation + converging preferences represents a low level of bargaining power in the outcome. In the case of Estonia it is difficult to speculate whether the country would have been able to attain the outcome it favoured on its own. Secondly, the case demonstrates that the preference convergence carries more weight than the degree of institutionalisation. This assumption is based on a country's deliberate refusal to become part of a coalition whilst still sticking by its preferences.

Finally, the negotiation dossier on the intra-EU climate change agreement allows the alternative hypothesis to be tested, assuming that the conditions of institutionalisation within the group interactions increases the probability of persuasion and consequently leads to a shift in member states' preferences. This assumption would support sociological constructivist thinking, i.e. under institutional constraints actors adopt certain practices that change their identities and consequently lead to preference shifts. Under the climate change negotiations the actors used an institutionalised forum for socialisation, interaction based on trust and a cooperation framework that stems from a common regional heritage; nevertheless, they did not share preferences. The Nordic countries belonged to the forerunners in regard to climate policy commitments, whilst the Baltic countries shared more similarities with the new member states' positions. If the alternative hypothesis were true, the Baltic countries should have shifted their positions towards the more ambitious climate commitments, i.e. the Nordic group. The additional pressure here came from the normative constraints of the climate change dossier. Similarly, the Nordic countries should have lowered their ambitions in regard to climate change policy in solidarity with the less prosperous members of the NB6. Interview data do not support either of the two expected alternative scenarios. By means of institutionalised interaction, parties exchange information and share knowledge, but they do not engage in persuasive actions that would lead to preference shifts.

4.3 The Stockholm Programme

Informal preparatory work on the Stockholm Programme amongst neighbours started several months before the dossier formally appeared on the Council agenda. At Sweden's invitation, the NB6 ministers were invited to a high-level conference in Stockholm to identify possible common ground for a territorial coalition. Despite attempts to institutionalise the cooperation, a real coalition of Nordic-Baltic member states was never formed, illustrating the significance of the background condition, i.e. preference convergence, as suggested in the theoretical model applied in this study.

This section takes a closer look at deliberations on the Stockholm Programme in the Council, which were aimed at adopting a political agreement among the 27 member states for setting the EU agenda in the field of justice and home affairs (JHA) for the period 2010 to 2014. By providing empirical evidence of members states' interaction in the institutionalised territorial coalition NB6 and a task-specific coalition (Quadro group), this section tests the argument on the basis of a high degree of institutionalisation + low convergence of preferences. This section introduces the background of the Stockholm Programme and proceeds with the analysis of the effects and limitations of the institutionalised coalitions.

JHA is possibly the policy area that is most affected by EU treaty changes. The increasing "supranational dimension" of policy-making within the JHA has resulted in the need to establish common guidelines and "better planning across the EU in JHA matters" (Archer 2009). The Stockholm Programme is one of these responses that followed the Tampere Programme, which was adopted in 1999, and the Hague Programme, which was in force from 2004 to 2009. In terms of their legal nature these five-year programmes do not impose legally binding obligations on the member states (Euromove 2010). However, legislative acts that are based on multi-annual programmes are binding. Hence, the Stockholm Programme was an important dossier for the governments. Its importance can be seen both in the political sense and in terms of prospects for the future legislation in the field of JHA. Taking this into account, the adoption of the Stockholm Programme was defined as one of the priorities of the Swedish Presidency, leaving its real impacts to its "translation into practical measures" (Miles 2010:85).

The member states were aware of the increasing weight given to JHA policies under the provisions of the Lisbon Treaty. Having abolished the pillar system, the Treaty of Lisbon moved all JHA issues from the former first pillar and the third pillar under one Title (IV) and defined the goals to be achieved under the heading of the European Area of Freedom, Security and Justice (AFSJ) in greater detail. By extending more power to the EU and more strictly defining the distribution of competences, the AFSJ policies became more "common" and "uniform" (Peers 2008:234). With regard to immigration and asylum policies, the member states were now obliged to frame more ambitious policies. The second modification of the Lisbon Treaty that affected the behaviour of the member states relates to the changes to the voting regime. By applying QMV to most initiatives within the JHA (including the measures of legal migration that was previously decided by unanimity), the member states' chances of influencing the policy outcome were reduced. Finally, the increasing powers of the European Council under the Lisbon Treaty also increased the importance of the political decisions taken by the heads of states. To this end, the Stockholm Programme, which was being negotiated in 2009, was a political document with considerable future implications not only in terms of future legislation but also with an eye to the "new area" of decision-making on JHA policies.

The Council negotiations were based on the Commission Communication "An area of freedom, security and justice serving the citizen" (COM (2009)262 issued on 10 June 2009). The proposal contained several issues that were controversial and politically sensitive. Issues of migration and border control have traditionally been of great significance for domestic constituencies (Lindstrøm 2005:592). In order to find a balance when dealing with external pressure and normative concerns on the one hand, and the domestic commitments of maintaining high national social protection standards on the other, some countries have chosen to opt out of common JHA policies in the EU (Archer 2009, Ader-Nissen 2009).

One of the most controversial issues in the Stockholm Programme was that of immigration and asylum. Opening the internal borders under the Schengen agreement had enhanced internal movement of third-country nationals around the EU. Influx into the EU has also been fostered by increasing instability in several regions in the world. Existing EU law in the field of immigration and asylum can be characterised as agreement on the "lowest common denominator" (in Lindstrøm 2005: 589).

Facing the challenges posed by the ageing population,[36] the Stockholm Programme supports the global approach to migration issues, i.e. "well-managed, migration can benefit everyone" (debate in the European Parliament, 25 Nov. 2009). The central issue regarding asylum-seekers, however, related to solidarity and burden-sharing among the member states. Net migration in 2009 amounted to 900,000 people (EurActiv, 28 July 10). Solidarity on immigration and asylum policy is of particular interest for Mediterranean countries, including Greece, Italy and Malta, where asylum-seekers mainly arrive. In its draft of the Stockholm Programme, the Commission proposed equal rights for immigrants in all member states and the fair distribution of costs, responsibility and assets (boats, personnel, planes etc.) for asylum-seekers across all member states. Further, the proposal called for the role of the Frontex agency to be increased in regard to external border controls and implementation of tougher readmission policies. Immigration and asylum policy could be conceptualised as the "biggest political hot potato" in the EU negotiations on the Stockholm Programme (EurAciv, 14 Dec. 2009). The Mediterranean bloc had acted individually and jointly as a group in order to reduce immigration and push for solidarity and European cooperation in addressing the immigration problem. The efforts of Mediterranean countries seem to have paid off, since the number of migrants decreased in 2009 com-

---

36 Recent Eurostat data demonstrate negative population growth across the whole EU. High birth rates are registered only in the United Kingdom, France and Ireland, while most countries demonstrate low birth rates (in particular Germany, Austria, Portugal, Italy, Latvia, Lithuania, and Hungary). According to forecasts, by 2030 over a quarter of the EU's inhabitants will be over 65 years of age (EurActiv, 28 July 10). The economic crisis has contributed to the net outflows of populations from the member states, e.g. with 4.6 per cent recorded for Lithuania (Eurostat, 27 July 2010).

pared to 2008 (Oxford Analytica 2009). Italy, whose national Franco Frattini was Commissioner of JHA until 2009, exerted considerable pressure on stronger EU competences in the field of immigration (EurActiv 2009). Furthermore, the southern states have continuously called for the fair distribution of asylum-seekers across member states. This has been "fundamentally rejected" by the Nordic states, ranging from the UK and Denmark to Finland (Archer 2009). Hence, the issue of immigration and asylum was certainly a major concern of member states when negotiating the proposal of the Stockholm Programme (Leydon 2009).

Another issue that gained prominence in regard to the objectives defined by the Stockholm Programme was the compatibility of legal systems across the EU. Since the EU member states have different legal traditions, mutual trust and confidence in decisions made by other member states are essential. Since opening internal borders under the Schengen Agreement, mobility has increased and citizens can more easily travel and settle in other member states. Consequently, they become "subject" to the civil, criminal, commercial and family laws of the other state (Archer 2009). Given the variety of legal systems, cooperation in the field of cross-border crime prevention creates problems. These problems could be addressed in two ways: either by means of harmonisation or by mutual recognition, which would imply more trust and mutual respect for decisions made in another country.

Finally, the issue of balancing security and liberty was at the top of the Stockholm Programme agenda. This has been regarded by governments as the "main objective of the internal policies" in recent years (Öffentliche Sicherheit 2010). Since the 9/11 attacks, the fight against terrorism has gained a lot of attention in the JHA policy guidelines of the Hague Programme. Security effort have even overshadowed fundamental rights, personal freedoms and liberties. Some critics have referred to migration policy in the EU as creating the "fortress Europe" (debate in the European Parliament, 25 Nov. 2009), a phenomenon that has been criticised by civil liberty groups (Leydon 2009). Yet, extending personal freedom could also create security risks if abused. For example, enhanced information exchange, part of the political objectives of the Stockholm Programme, also raised some doubts about the information getting into the wrong hands (debate in the European Parliament, 25 Nov. 2009). Similarly, the proposed measure to bolster Frontex in strengthening external borders (EurActiv, 14 Dec. 2009) caused criticism among the human rights supporters, claiming that the human rights of undocumented migrants should be respected (Carrera and Merlino 2010).

In sum, though not directly designed as legally binding, the Commission proposal on the Stockholm Programme contained several issues that were controversial for the member states and that had to be negotiated by the Council before the Programme could be adopted in December. The biggest "hot potato" that split the governments of the EU states into the southern and northern blocs was the issue of the future shape of EU immigration and asylum policies, including sharing the burden among the member states. Further, the Stockholm Programme touched on an issue that has continuously given rise to controversy among the member states because of their different legal traditions, namely the issue of mutual recognition and trust. Finally, the Stockholm Programme addressed the politically complicated issue of striking a balance between increased security and the protection of individual human rights.

Given the controversies sparked off by the negotiation dossier, one might expect coalitions to have been formed across the preference dividing lines. This section illustrates coalitions in the Council negotiations of the Stockholm Programme focusing on the NB6 interaction. Furthermore, the study at hand identifies a task-specific coalition on immigration and asylum issues. It explains the reasons why these cooperation formats failed to deliver distinct bargaining power for its members.

The NB6 cooperation framework stretches across several policy fields. The JHA was a promising domain for the territorially constituted cooperation because of the intergovernmental decision-making mode. Indeed, interviewees assured me that the NB6 used to convene before the JHA Council meetings.[37] However, this trend has not proved to be consistent:

"As we became EU members in 2004, we gathered within the NB6 format before the JHA Council meetings. Yet, this tradition somehow expired. Probably we did not have enough in common on the issue level. I recall that we had a productive exchange on our policy priorities before upcoming Council presidencies. However, at the CATS and SCIFA working group level we could not find enough ground for common arguments" (interview no. 18, 19 February 2010, Riga).

One possible explanation is provided by the coalition formation models on political space, policy scope and the individual legislation level (Veen 2011). Institutional cooperation among the NB6 members within the regional framework of JHA policy successfully proceeds on a political level but demonstrates a lack of stability at the issue level. This pattern was confirmed by the empirical evidence on the Stockholm Programme. Given that the Swedish Presidency had defined the Stockholm Programme as one of its priorities, it apparently applied all existing procedural and structural tools at its disposal to ensuring that agreement was reached among the EU-27 in a highly sensitive migration policy field, and also to putting a "Swedish mark on it" (Miles 2010:85).

One of the measures taken by Sweden as the incoming Presidency was the initiative of the Swedish Minister of Justice, Beatrice Ask, and the Minister for Migration and Asylum Policy, Tobias Billström, to gather their NB6

---

37 This interview outlines interaction with the JHA. When it comes to home/internal affairs, the NB6 interaction is less institutionalised (if it is institutionalised at all).

colleagues in Stockholm. The aim of the informal regional meeting was to find common ground in preparations for the Stockholm Programme. The NB6 meeting was held three months before the start of the Swedish Presidency:

"The aim of this meeting was to reach some kind of Nordic-Baltic common ground on the Stockholm Programme. The target group was ministers dealing with JHA issues from the Nordic and the Baltic member states. I do not think that any of the Baltic countries have separate ministers for asylum and migration issues—they were invited to be represented by the minister in charge of the policies represented by the Stockholm Programme" (interview no. 29, 22 January 2010, Stockholm).

The ministerial meeting in the NB6 format was held on 22/23 April 2009 in Stockholm. The informal setting of the meeting and the small size of the group encouraged exchange between the participants on the priorities they were eager to include in the Stockholm Programme. Yet, given the sensitivity of JHA issues in the EU-27, the NB6 members attached varying importance to different issues. Sweden called for a strong and comprehensive Common Asylum System within the Stockholm Programme (EurActiv, 11 June 2009), whereas for Finland and Demark the idea of a quota system for distributing asylum-seekers across the EU member states went too far (Archer 2009:7). Instead, the Finnish delegation attached great importance to negotiations on the principle of mutual harmonisation of criminal law and found itself opposing the Swedish view of legal harmonisation. Denmark "by definition" held a different position in the field of the JHA policies. Following the Danish "no" on ratification of the Maastricht Treaty in 1992, Denmark had negotiated opt-outs in the field of JHA that provide the Danish delegation with the option of pulling out[38] of all JHA initiatives unless the decisions are taken by unanimous vote (interview no. 5, 26 January 2010, Copenhagen). Nevertheless, the Danish delegation indicated its preferences concerning the rights of free movement and family reunification. The Danish position is based on concerns about fraud and abuse that may lead to an uncontrolled influx of third-country nationals using arranged marriages as a means of settling in the EU. Having attracted wide public attention and having attached political significance to the "Metock Case"[39] (interview no. 5, 26 January 2010, Copenha-

---

38 Since immigration and asylum were shifted to the first pillar under the Maastricht Treaty and were thus subject to a supranational decision rule, Denmark has opted out of decisions on immigration and asylum. The Treaty of Lisbon, which abolishes the pillar system, has further implications for Denmark's positions, since most legislation in the JHA falls under the Danish opt-out (Adler-Nissen 2009:75).

39 The *Metock case* (C-127/08) was a controversial European Court of Justice case with major political significance for Ireland, the UK and Demark. The case ruled that Mr Metock, a non-Community citizen, was granted an entrance permit to the UK to accompany his spouse (an EU citizen). The ruling referred to Directive 2004/38/EC on the right of citizens of the Union and their family members to move and reside freely within the territory of the Member State.

gen), the issue regained political importance in relation to preparations for the Stockholm Programme. On the issue of family reunification, the Danish government had identified Ireland and the United Kingdom as like-minded partners. With similar domestic sensitivity for Ireland (after the failed referendum on the Lisbon Treaty), and the application of the opt-outs by the United Kingdom, the Danish government cooperated with the United Kingdom and Ireland in pushing for a reference to the above-mentioned problem in the EU policy documents. Having one of the "toughest stances" on immigration policy in Europe (Reuters, 18 Nov. 2010), Denmark was bound by its domestic consistencies (in particular due to the strong involvement of the Danish National Parliament in framing the Danish positions).

The Baltic member states shared a common understating of crimes committed by totalitarian regimes (the Estonian and Latvian position on the Stockholm Programme 2009). The initiative to insert a reference in the Stockholm Programme to totalitarian regimes is part of the heritage of the Baltic countries and the mass deportation of inhabitants of the Baltic States under communist rule (Strods and Kott 2002). The Baltic member states were "careful supporters" of immigration and asylum issues:

"We prefer to support the principle of voluntary engagement, i.e. we are open to examining each application from asylum-seekers, but we do not call for the resettlement approach. The principle of voluntary choice is a cornerstone of the Geneva Convention. Positioning on asylum issues is very much related to the economic prosperity, social standards and domestic acceptance of the country" (interview no. 50, 20 August 2010, Riga).

With respect to the different issues to which each of the NB6 members attached different importance, the NB6 cooperation did not develop into coordinated joint action on the Stockholm Programme dossier. Instead, the member states sought like-minded *ad hoc* peers outside the NB6.

The empirical evidence of NB6 interaction on the Stockholm Programme is particularly interesting with respect to the effects of the independent variable in the absence of the convergence of preferences, i.e. a high degree of institutionalisation + low convergence of preferences. Despite efforts by the lead country to organise high-level NB6 consultations, cooperation did not advance any further. This demonstrates that the condition of institutionalisation *alone* is not enough for providing the bargaining advantage.

The dossier on the Stockholm Programme provided a good opportunity to test the alternative hypothesis, since the member states' preferences differ. According to sociological constructivist theoretical assumptions, institutions have persuasive strength that shapes member states' preferences. Rather than striving for self-interest, the member states are supposed to adopt certain practices and that behaviour that is considered to be "appropriate". By sociological constructivist accounts, repeated interaction and socialisation would lead to shift in the actors' preferences due to "sincere persuasion" (Grobe 2010:9).

A qualitative analysis of the case study does not support this alternative theoretical assumption. On the contrary, the interviewees deny that they would have changed their positions after the informal ministerial conference in April, at which common ground was to be sought. Instead, each member state sought out like-minded peers outside the NB6 partnership. This demonstrates that utility-maximising behaviour prevails among the members.

As stated in the above, the Stockholm Programme is a suitable dossier for observing coalition-building because of its in-built controversies. This is particularly true in regard to immigration and asylum issues, where the positions of the member states are divided along the South-North axis. The southern group represents a typical example of a task-specific institutionalised coalition (for the theoretical background see 3.3.)

Initially formed as an *ad hoc* coalition comprising the southern EU member states, this like-minded group has become institutionalised by repeatedly convening on the immigration and asylum issue. Accordingly, this study defines it as a task-specific coalition. The origins of the group go back to September 2006. Sharing common concerns on the mass arrivals of migrants in southern Europe, the heads of states of Cyprus, France, Greece, Italy, Malta, Portugal, Slovenia and Spain signed an open letter calling for concerted action by the EU (Cassarino 2011:18). With increasing migration pressure resulting from the global recession in 2008, the southern countries, in particular those facing an increasing influx across the Mediterranean from North Africa, agreed on joint action. This was an opportune moment, since France (having participated in joint action in 2006) held the Council Presidency. In November 2008, on the initiative of the Maltese Justice and Home Affairs Minister Carmelo Mifsud Bonnici, the four southern member states that are most affected by an influx of illegal migrants and asylum-seekers established the so-called Quadro group.[40] The group comprises four member states: Malta, Greece, Cyprus and Italy (Spain had expressed an early interest in joining but then decided not to (CIBOD International Yearbook 2011)). One of the interviewees explained the reasons for Spain's reticence to join as follows:

"Sometimes people tend to think that Spain and Portugal are a part of the Quadro group. Spain has a quite different policy from the Quadro member Italy. My personal view is that Spain is much more solution-oriented and creative. They tried to solve the immigration problems bilaterally with the immigrants' countries of origin without passing the solutions to the EU. Spain has a more hands-on policy, and they have also been open to labour migration. In this regard Sweden holds similar positions to Spain" (interview no. 29, 22 January 2010, Stockholm).

The objective of the group was to "ensure that the momentum gained during the past French EU presidency, in addressing the major southern European

---

40 The name of the group stems from the number of participating countries.

illegal migration issue, is kept up during the Czech and upcoming Swedish EU presidencies" (Times of Malta, 13 Jan. 2009). The institutional structure of the group was set up on the political and expert level. After the first informal meeting of ministers, inter-group cooperation was transferred to the "technocrat level", and the technocrats were invited to draft a paper to be presented to EU-27 ministers (ibid.). Since 2008 the task-specific coalition of four member states has cooperated in the shadow of formal decision-making. Technical expert groups regularly met to fine-tune proposals that were then further presented on behalf of the group in Council meetings (Independent, 21 Dec. 2008).

The Quadro group focused on four issues: calling for solidarity, solutions regarding readmission of migrants, strengthening the border agency Frontex, and calling for a European Asylum Support Office. The call for solidarity and burden-sharing refers to the current regulation (Dublin II system), which sets out that the state in the EU that an asylum-seeker first arrives is responsible for processing the request for asylum (CIBOD International Yearbook 2011). Calling for the reform of the Dublin II system and pushing for realisation of the principle of burden-sharing (Times of Malta, 13 Jan. 2009), the Quadro group has since 2008 issued several joint initiatives addressing the EU-27 and the Commission. For instance, the group invited the Commission to take up readmission negotiations with the third countries and to allocate more funding for border control. Strengthening the Frontex includes more financial resources and operational resources for the border control of illegal immigration. Finally, the Quadro group called for the establishment of the European Asylum Support Office, which would assist with practical operational needs and the over-burdened national administrations, to be speeded up (ibid.). During the Czech Presidency the Quadro group delivered a joint document on 13 January 2009 "pressing for the Council Conclusions and effective implementation of readmission agreements" (Cassarino 2011:18).

Negotiations on the Stockholm Programme provided the task-specific coalition with the opportunity to re-engage in its activity. The Stockholm Programme approaches the immigration and asylum problems differently than the previous Hague Programme. Instead of harmonising immigration and asylum policies, the Stockholm Programme focuses on practical provisions, taking account of the needs of the European labour market and linking immigration to other policy fields, for instance external relations. This perspective is characterised as the "global approach to migration" (CIBOD International Yearbook 2011). Though coordinating their positions internally, the group did not succeed in gaining a bargaining advantage while negotiating for the Stockholm Programme in Council. The Presidency's view on why that was the case was:

"We expected them [the Quadro group] to increase their voice during the negotiations under the Swedish Presidency, but it seems that they did not get along very well internally.

They share a common goal, but also have competing interests: Malta and Italy often hold very diverging positions. France has been a partial external supporter of this group, but never joined it. It will be interesting to see what happens" (interview no. 29, 22 January 2010, Stockholm).

Council negotiations on the Stockholm Programme proceeded relatively smoothly, in spite of expected controversies. The majority of the open questions were settled on the level of COREPER before the JHA Council. In regard to the issues that were close to the heart of the Quadro group, no significant breakthrough has been reached.

"The Stockholm Programme could serve as a policy development under the resettlement issue. The outcome, however, was closer to a status quo. One could see some efforts from the member states to move the policy forward. There was a paper issued by Malta on the burden-sharing issue and on mandatory financial support for solving problems related to immigration. But in practical terms agreement on the Stockholm Programme did not contain any revolutionary changes in the field of immigration and asylum policy" (interview no. 50, 20 August 2010, Riga).

The empirical interview data are supported by analytical reviews that evaluate the Stockholm Programme as "rather vague" in comparison to preceding multi-annual programmes (CIBOD International Yearbook 2011). The same criticism was expressed by the European Parliament (EurActiv, 14 Dec. 2009).

On the asylum issue, the Commission's proposal of 10 June 2009 appears to be very close to the Council's negotiation outcome (*"Sharing of responsibilities and solidarity between the Member States"*, heading 6.2.2 of the Council Conclusions, 2 Dec. 2009). Thus, the task-specific coalition did not manage to shift the outcome towards its preferences. The draft Council Conclusions were passed formally through the GAERC meeting on 7 December 2009 without any debate(interview no. 29, 22 January 2010, Stockholm), and adopted by the heads of state during the European Council on 10 December. Figure 10 shows that the Quadro group did not succeed in pushing the outcome away from the SQ. The positions of the member states were distributed along the axis, with three groups of states: the first consisting of hesitant countries (Finland, Estonia, Latvia, Lithuania) closer to the endpoint of position 0, the second – sharing concerns of family reunification regulation and the third – the Quadro group, urging for more ambitions immigration policy in the EU. Nevertheless, the Quadro group failed to demonstrate bargaining power.

Figure 10: Effects of Quadro group cooperation on bargaining power

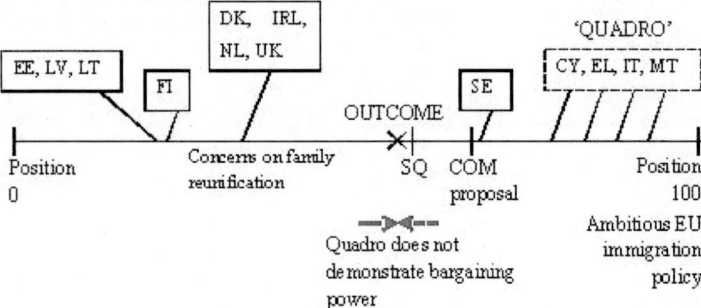

Source: Commission proposal 10 June 2009; Council Conclusions 2 Dec. 2009, media reports.

Note: Fig.10 does not intend to reflect the positions of all 27 member states.

The major reason for this failure was the heterogeneity of preferences within the group on the narrow issue level. Though on the policy domain level the coalition is stable and consistent, the analysis on the narrow issue level reveals the differences in actors' preferences. Since this study did not carry out any field work on interview selection among the southern members of the group, the nuances of the controversies within the group remain hidden. Based on the interviews with the Presidency, this case demonstrates that the task-specific coalition did not yield any bargaining power for its members during the Stockholm Programme negotiations in Council.

CONCLUSIONS

One of the interviewees describes the essence of institutionalised coalitions, putting the argument of this book in a nutshell:

"Actors in each policy field create the cooperation constellations that they consider purposeful. We have fruitful discussions in the NB6 institutionalised framework on those issues where we identify common interests" (interview no. 28, 22 January 2010, Stockholm).

The aim of this book was to shed light on a category of coalitions in the context of the EU Council that has so far been explored less frequently, namely institutionalised territorially constituted coalitions and task-specific groups. Decision-making in the Council is characterised by informal interaction between governments, largely with reference to negotiation outcomes. The member states' behaviour and strategic choices are restricted by formal and informal institutions representing "humanly devised constraints that structure political, economic and social interaction" (North 1991:97). Institutionalised coalitions can be distinguished from *ad hoc* coalitions on account of their lasting stability. Institutionalised interaction does not follow voting power considerations alone. The asymmetrical distribution of information and the transaction-cost perspective explain why member states are willing to engage in interaction in sub-groups and to coordinate positions prior to formal negotiations. By drawing on examples of the territorially constituted and task-specific institutionalised coalitions, this book explored the effects of such institutionalised coalitions on member states' bargaining power in Council negotiations. By proposing a theory of the causal mechanisms of institutionalised inter-state cooperation in coordinating positions and exchanging views prior to formal decision-making, this study fills the gap in EU bargaining literature by explaining the effects with the help of rational choice theoretical accounts.

Previous academic studies acknowledge the existence of stable alignments of member states compared to *ad hoc* coalitions. The assumption that day-to-day interaction among the member states follows the strategic logic of selecting cooperation partners for power-pooling reasons on the basis of geographical proximity and preference proximity served as the point of departure for this study. Moreover, the informal cooperation has gained in prominence since the adoption of the Lisbon Treaty, which, by extending the QMV rule to more areas, has enhanced the coalitional behaviour of member states in Council negotiations.

The basic research question of this study was: To what extent and under what conditions can institutionalised coalitions that do not constitute a blocking minority increase member states' bargaining power? In answering this question the study developed a theory and offered an explanatory chain of causality. The main focus in the theoretical model was on the degree of institutionalisation of inter-state cooperation. Drawing on rational choice institutionalism, the study argued that the degree of institutionalisation matters. Apart from unstable and unpredictable *ad hoc* coalition patterns, it distinguishes between two types of more stable institutionalised coalition patterns: territorially constituted and task-specific coalitions. The logic of coordinating positions in order to reach collectively agreed goals (Elgström et al. 2001) differs from *ad hoc* coalition-building behaviour. In their search to increase their power, the members of institutionalised coalitions cannot always rely on blocking the decision at the end-game because their combined votes often do not achieve the necessary voting thresholds. Hence, this study hypothesised that the institutional setting provides actors with power resources beyond their voting power. The argument was that the bargaining power of institutionalised coalitions stems from three mechanisms: (1) the exchange of information that counterbalances the asymmetries in information distribution in the pre-negotiation stage; (2) the pooling of expertise that allows the member states to share resources and provide a common line of argument for their positions; and (3) rhetorical action, which strengthens justifications that may lead to the normative entrapment of member states outside the coalition. This argument was tested with the help of qualitative research methods by drawing on primary data gained from semi-structured elite interviews and the process of tracing three negotiation dossiers along their decision-making path. All three dossiers, namely the Baltic Sea Strategy, the Stockholm Programme and the climate change agreement before COP15, were negotiated in the Council in the autumn of 2009 under the Swedish Council Presidency.

The evidence gained through the elite interviews with government officials in the Nordic-Baltic group (NB6) and the Benelux group, lends support to the theoretical assumptions that the high degree of institutionalisation cements interaction within the sub-group and provides the conditions for the more effective information exchange and expertise-pooling. The degree of institutionalisation varies across different territorially constituted coalitions. The Benelux group is more advanced in terms of the formalisation of cooperation on account of a trilateral treaty. Allthough the aim of the study was not to focus on the Benelux group, it served as a valuable example of institutionalized cooperation and helped to generalised the findings, which were obtained in the NB6. Elite interviews with capital-based and Brussels-based Benelux interviewees supported the hypothesis that the institutionalised set-up increases the power-pooling potential during the pre-negotiation stage. In contrast to some scholarly assumptions about the erosion of the Benelux partnership (Hosli 1996:259), the testimonies of this study backed the idea of coherence within the group. The tactics of inter-group coordination and common memoranda ensure that the Benelux group is perceived by other negotiating parties as a well-organised group with deep-rooted interaction procedures. The unity of the group is, however, challenged by preference divergence across several issues.

Compared to the Benelux group, the Nordic-Baltic (NB6) cooperation framework has a lower degree of institutionalisation in terms of formal agreements. Historically, the NB6 stems from the regional cooperation framework that initially started with Nordic institutional structures, for example the Nordic Council and the Nordic Council of Ministers. After enlargement the sub-group was extended to the Baltic Sea region by encompassing Latvia, Lithuania and Estonia. A broader regional institutional framework in the region, NB8, also includes Norway and Iceland, whereas in the EU policy context the interaction is reduced to three Nordic and three Baltic countries. The most common and coherent interaction format involving the governments of the NB6 are the informal breakfast meetings involving the NB6 ministers and prime ministers in advance of Council meetings in Brussels. The in-depth interviews and testimonies of the Nordic and the Baltic member states reveal interesting data about routine interaction between NB6 members. These data are valuable in two respects: First, they capture information that is impossible to obtain from document analysis by process tracing or when viewing the coalition-building at the end-game of the Council's decision-making. Second, they offer different country perspectives that allow the findings to be generalised.

Pre-meeting collaboration amongst the members of the territorial coalitions occurs along several interaction channels. This study attributed significance to the pre-negotiation phase in contrast to the common tradition in coalition research of approaching the end-game. Focusing empirically on the Nordic-Baltic cooperation within the three selected dossiers, it traced governmental interaction at different stages of the negotiations; starting with early consultations with the Commission at the outset of the drafting phase and further observing the intergovernmental contacts in sub-groups in the Council working groups, at the COREPER and at the political level. Interaction includes capital-to-capital or Brussels communication channels. The interview evidence shows that the most common NB6 exchange formats are EU directors' meetings before the presidency term, issue-specific networks of experts, the network of political advisors to the prime ministers, and consultation practice on the highest political level.

According to the institutional logic, institutions are stable if they fulfil the tasks they are assigned and if the costs of keeping them functioning are not too high. The stability of territorial coalitions has changed over the time. Member states calculate the institutional efficiency and the pay-offs, in particular when resources are scarce or when the benefits of interaction do not fulfil their expectations. The most coherent interaction format for the NB6 is informal exchange prior to Council meetings. Similarly, the ministers of foreign affairs meet monthly before the GAERC[41] meetings in Brussels. Other ministers, for example the ministers of justice and ministers of the environment, meet from time to time, but this trend is decreasing. In some policy fields the NB6 members used to hold capital-format consultations on a rotating basis. These findings are consistent with the findings in the literature that coalition behaviour varies across different policy fields and decision-making modes (Veen 2011:65).

The frequency of interaction matters; the more frequent the meetings, the more institutionalised the cooperation framework becomes. This applies in particular to ministers of foreign affairs, who meet monthly and have established a more consistent interaction network than other Council formations with a meeting frequency of two meetings per presidency term. The pre-meeting exchange before Council meetings and European summits is highly informal. Institutionally, the setting is limited to ministers or prime ministers only, with possibly one senior servant from each member state participating. This in-camera setting facilitates the conditions for mutual trust and, accordingly, more open exchange of (even sensitive) information. Under repeated interaction, the "shadow of the future" is long and the prospects of future cooperation cement the coalition. In general, member states are reluctant to broaden the scope of institutionalised cooperation to include a larger number of members, provided that the effectiveness of institutions depends upon the number of participants. Yet, acting rationally, the coalition members may extend the interaction format to include additional "useful" participants by inviting the Council Presidency or other influential member states. The choice of additional peers largely depends on the issue at hand. Under incomplete information, a "cooperation framework-plus" format helps actors deal with the transaction costs problems.

Under what conditions and how do institutionalised coalitions give their members a bargaining advantage? To answer this research question, the study introduced an additional independent variable, namely policy preferences. Consequently, the research design contained three constellations of the independent variables: a high degree of institutionalisation and a high convergence of preferences; a high degree of institutionalisation and a low convergence of preferences; and a low degree of institutionalisation combined with a high convergence of preferences. A qualitative analysis of three negotiation dossiers under the Swedish Council Presidency allows conclusions to be drawn on the effects of each independent variable.

The first option (highly institutionalised interaction), which is supported by convergent underlying preferences, is most evident in the dossier of the Baltic Sea Strategy. The creation of a new macro-regional strategy was a common interest of the Baltic Sea littoral states. Intergovernmental coopera-

---

41 The study was carried out before the Lisbon Treaty, which introduced GAC and FAC instead of GAERC.

tion amongst the "insiders" of the territorially constituted coalition (NB6+2) took place from the early stages of the draft proposal. The findings support the research hypothesis, demonstrating that institutionalised cooperation provides a bonus in terms of bargaining power. Due to the exchange of information and joint action at different levels of decision-making throughout the dossier, the members of the sub-group are better positioned than other countries outside the institutionalised coalition. Taking advantage of the existing regional structural framework, and additionally supporting it with a newly established network of contact points, the NB6+2 coalition in fact framed a pre-agreement that granted its members a considerable advantage before the issue was discussed among the EU-27. Acting (and being perceived) as a group, the NB6+2 moved the negotiation outcome as close as possible to its own ideal point. Exploiting the institutional interaction environment, coalition members formulated credible justifications of their arguments and, through rhetorical action, convinced "outsiders" to accept their text proposals. The efficiency of this tactic can be seen in the group's success in convincing reluctant countries about the relevance of the concept of "macro-regional cooperation" in EU governance.

Another case in which the strength of institutionalised coalitions appears convincing is the intra-EU negotiations on climate change before the international climate change conference in Copenhagen. This dossier permits process tracing on two institutionalised coalitions, namely the NB6 and a task-specific coalition called "9+2". The latter emerged in 2008 during negotiations on the EU energy and climate package, i.e. one year before preparations for the Copenhagen conference started. Based on preference configurations, the member states on the climate policy issue were divided across new-old member state cleavages, whereas, on separate issues, the members of the NB6 exploited the institutional cooperation advantage and good relationship with neighbouring countries to generate knowledge and pool expertise on a highly technical issue (LULUCF). The Baltic countries, a large share of whose territory is covered by forests but which have less expertise on how to link forestry issues and emissions, acted as "free riders" by relying on the Nordic (Finnish in particular) expertise to their advantage. Consequently, the coalition agreed on a common statement that was attached to the minutes of the meeting of the Environmental Council. These results imply that institutionalised cooperation facilitates the pooling of expertise and generation of knowledge, which, by reducing the uncertainty of actors, serve as important determinants of bargaining power.

The empirical analysis focused on the case where the degree of institutionalisation was still high but the underlying policy preferences among the group members diverged. Since homogeneity of preferences is rare in EU decision-making, this constellation of independent variables is highly realistic in Council negotiations. In general terms, one can observe that institutionalised interaction, once initiated, becomes a habit. Even if preferences diverge, the member states come together to exchange information about their positions following a routine, since abolishing an institution implies costs. Yet, negotiations on the Stockholm Programme show that institutionalised conditions alone do not ensure further steps are taken in terms of joint action if the parties do not share common preferences in regard to the outcome. It may, therefore, be helpful to refer to the analytical three-level approach by identifying common interests on political space, political domain and issue level. The NB6 cooperation is most persistent on the political space level (e.g. identifying common ground for the Stockholm Programme on the ministerial level). Yet, on the issue level the NB6 interaction becomes fragmented and the governments, instead, search for like-minded *ad hoc* peers to respond to the commitments of their domestic constituencies. This is an important finding in terms of an explanatory theoretical framework for the study. Apparently, preference convergence is a necessary pre-requisite for power-pooling mechanisms through institutionalised cooperation.

The study draws on theoretical explanations of rational choice institutionalism and hypothesises that the institutional conditions support and enhance the interactions of single actors who aim to gain from exchanges without compromising their own domestic preferences. States deliberately cooperate in informal networks with their neighbours because they realise that by doing so they can improve their bargaining situation. Where informal interaction before negotiations starts to play an increasingly important role, institutionalised coalitions offer gains from cooperation. It has to be noted that preference convergence is a necessary condition for increasing bargaining power by framing a common position or undertaking another joint group activity.

Finally, the empirical analysis focused on a less probable, but theoretically plausible, case where preferences converge but member states refuse to engage in coalitional behaviour based on tactical considerations. One of the most striking findings in terms of coalition behaviour is that a member state may abstain from joining a coalition because of strategic considerations. Negotiations on the climate change dossier provide an example where a single member state (in spite of converging preferences) stayed outside the coalition because of the high reputation costs. In this particular case it is difficult to measure the actual bargaining power of the "solo player", since it shares the gains in terms of the preferred outcomes by relying on the efforts of a coalition. In the absence of a coalition, there would be no bargaining power gains for an individual player.

Coalition formation is more likely to occur at the early decision-making stage. With a large share of issues being agreed upon even without involving ministers, this is highly relevant. The empirical analysis of the climate change dossier shows that coalition behaviour culminates at the COREPER level. Several interviewees acknowledged that alliances are best exposed on the diplomatic level. However, that does not mean that coalitions are formed only when the dossier reaches discussions amongst COREPER ambassadors. Quite the contrary, the case of the Baltic Sea Strategy demonstrates that coalition-formation started before the proposal had even been issued by the Commission. In other words, the earlier the better. Once the coalition is formed, it "follows the dossier" through the different levels and Council configurations of decision-making. Often the working group is the most appropriate level for exerting bargaining power because the majority of dossiers are resolved without engaging the COREPER level. It is essential to get the higher political level involved on highly controversial issues, which explains the high level of institutionalisation of the prime ministers' interaction. Furthermore, the study finds support for the theoretical assumption that institutionalised territorially constituted coalitions are most stable on the "policy space level" Veen (2011), i.e. when drawing on broad socio-economic preferences, in contrast to narrow issue-specific negotiations. The well-connected framework on the political level gives "approval" to interactions on all other networks within the sub-group. Hence, by engaging political elites, the cooperation framework is given more credibility, both internally and externally. Coalition members may even draw gains from the perception of power, since external actors expect them to behave as a group. This grants the territorial partnership the aura that it is "acting as a group" that each member can use to its advantage.

By trying to open a "black box" of unexplored informal pre-meeting interaction amongst the member states, the study has provided evidence of the existence of more persistent and stable preference-based coalitions in Council negotiations. The aim has been to map the possibly numerous like-minded persistent and more stable coalitions across different policy fields, applying the same theoretical framework as to territorially constituted coalitions. The significance here was attributed mainly to the preference variable, labelling these country alignments as task-specific coalitions. More concretely, the study describes the Aachen group, Salzburg group, Quadro group, net contributors group, Copenhagen group, the like-minded groups (on trade and agriculture) and the G6. The logic of collective *durable* action within institutionalised coalitions is to increase bargaining power by exchanging information, generating common knowledge and expertise, and presenting jointly justified arguments for positions. The list of task-specific coalitions provided in this study is not exhaustive; there may be more similar country constellations across different policy fields.

There are, however, some remarkable tendencies of task-specific coalitions that allow us to approach them in the same vein as territorial coalitions. They usually consist of between four and eight member states (maintaining the efficiency of institutionalised interaction); they act as "open-systems", i.e.

may be reduced or extended according to the changes in preferences of specific countries; they use different interaction channels, i.e. capital-to-capital and the Brussels route; and they "share responsibilities", counterbalancing their structural shortcomings by rotating meetings among the partners. In general, the operation of task-specific coalitions in terms of procedures, rules, structures and frequency is very similar to interactions amongst territorially constituted coalitions. Given the institutionalised setting of task-specific coalitions, they follow a similar causality mechanism of power-pooling mechanisms.

Drawing on rational choice institutionalism, the study hypothesised that the behaviour of the members of institutionalised coalitions is utility-driven. The main argument was that institutions offer the preconditions for an individual actor to solve collective action dilemmas and encourages it to take a collectively superior course of action. Member states' behaviour is driven by strategic calculus on how to draw gains from interactions in terms of information sharing and knowledge generation in order to reach an agreement as close to the actors' ideal preferences as possible. Thus, the main differences between rational choice and sociological institutionalism theoretical approaches are in regard to explanations, namely what kind of behaviour on the part of political actors they cause. Applying the rationalist theoretical framework, institutions are created for a functional purpose because they offer more benefits than costs. Sociological institutionalism, on the contrary, assumes that, because of interaction, the actors adjust their behaviour (and consequently also their preferences) to the common good. Their behaviour follows the logic of the "right thing to do", not the striving for self-interest.

The empirical evidence does not support the alternative hypothesis, i.e. that institutionalised conditions of cooperation contribute to a shift of preferences as a consequence of the persuasion process. In particular, two dossiers were relevant when it came to testing the alternative hypothesis: the Stockholm Programme and the climate change negotiations. Neither of these provided any evidence of any preference shifts, yet the institutionalised interaction contributes to the "understanding of divergences".

The title of this book – *(Why) Do Neighbours Cooperate?* – challenged the existing assumption in the literature that territorial partnerships in the EU have exhausted their potential. By developing a theory that draws on rational choice theoretical accounts, the study offered a causality mechanism to explain the bargaining power of coalition members in EU Council negotiations apart from voting power considerations (alone). The best effects of this mechanism (information exchange, expertise-pooling and rhetorical action) are observed where policy preferences are homogeneous. However, one has to admit that interests rarely converge in the EU. The empirical findings demonstrated that, on the issue level in particular, cooperation in territorial partnerships is hindered by the heterogeneity of preferences. However, when viewed on the political space level (i.e. in terms of broader socio-economic preferences and normative standards), the potential for framing common ground is still present. Having often experienced the divergence of policy preferences on the issue level, governments' eagerness to cooperate on the political space level may fade. In other words, not being able to pool power at the issue level, members of the institutionalised coalitions may abstain from any cooperation at all.

This study demonstrated theoretically and empirically the potential and limitations of institutionalised coalitions. If member states aim to proactively frame common policies (rather than focusing on disparities on the issue level), they should be aware of the existing potential of institutionalised conditions of cooperation and, by indicating convergent preferences, drive forward EU policy-making together.

REFERENCES

Achen, Christopher, H. (2006) 'Institutional Realism and Bargaining Models', in Thomson Robert, Stokman, Frans N,, Aachen, Christofer H and König, Thomas (eds), *The EU Decides*, Cambridge University Press.
Ader-Nissen, Rebecca (2009) 'Behind the Scenes of Differentiated Integration: Circumventing National Opt-Outs in Justice and Home Affairs', *Journal of European Public Policy*, Vol. 16, No. 1, pp. 62–80.
Altes, Korthals (2007) 'The Benelux: The Benefits and Necessity of Enhanced Cooperation', Paper No. 53, Advisory Council of International Affairs.
Andrén, Nils (1984) 'Nordic Integration and Cooperation – Illusion and Reality', *Cooperation and Conflict*, Vol. 19, No. 4, pp. 251–262.
Antola, Esko (2009) 'EU Baltic Sea Strategy', Report by the Konrad Adenauer Stiftung, London office.
Archer, Toby (2009) 'The Stockholm Programme. Europe's Next Step on Its Quest to be an "Area of Freedom, Security and Justice"', Briefing Paper No. 49, The Finnish Institute of International Affairs.
Arregui, Javier (2008) 'Shifting Policy Positions in the European Union', *European Journal of Political Research*, Vol. 47, No. 6, pp. 852–875.
Arregui, Javier and Thomson, Robert (2009) 'States' Bargaining Success in the European Union', *Journal of European Public Policy*, Vol. 16, No. 5, pp. 655–676.
Aspinwall, Mark D. and Schneider, Gerald (2000) 'Same Menu, Separate Tables: The Institutionalist Turn in Political Science and the Study of European Integration', *European Journal of Political Research*, Vol. 38, No. 1, pp. 1–36.
Baeten, Rita (2007) 'Health and Social Services in the Internal Market', in Degryse, Christophe and Pochet, Philippe (eds), *Social Developments in the European Union 2006*, pp. 161–185, Brussels: ETUI-REHS, OSE and Saltsa.
Bailer, Stefanie (2003) 'Bargaining Success in the European Union: The Impact of Exogenous and Endogenous Power Resources', ECPR Conference Paper, Marburg, Germany, 18–21 September.
Bailer, Stefanie (2004) 'Bargaining Success in the European Union', *Comparative European Politics*, Vol. 4, No. 4, pp. 355–378.
Bailer, Stefanie (2005) 'Where do Preferences Come from? Determinants of Positions in EU Negotiations', Paper Presented at the Annual Meeting of the American Political Science Association, 30 August–3 September.
Bailer, Stefanie and Schneider, Gerald (2006) 'Nash versus Schelling? The Importance of Constraints in Legislative Bargaining', in Thomson, Robert; Stokman, Frans, N.; Achen, Christopher H. and König, Thomas (eds), *The European Union Decides*, Cambridge: Cambridge University Press.
Bailer, Stefanie (2010) 'What Factors Determine Bargaining Power and Success in EU Negotiations?' *Journal of European Public Policy*, Vol. 17, No. 5, pp. 743–757.
Bal, Leendert J. (2004) 'Member States Operating in the EU Council of Ministers: Inside Impressions', in Meerts, Paul and Cede, Franz (eds), *Negotiating European Union*, pp. 127–143, New York: Palgrave Macmillan.
Baldwin, A.David (1989*) Paradoxes of Power*, Basil Blackwell.

Barnett, Michael and Finnmore, Martha (1999) 'The Politics, Power and Pathologies of International Organizations', *International Organization*, Vol. 53, No. 4, pp. 699–732.

Barry, Brian (1980) 'Is it Better to be Powerful or Lucky', Part 2, Political Studies, Vol. 28, No. 3, pp. 338–352.

Bearce, David; Floros, Katharine and McKibben, Heather (2009) 'The Shadow of the Future and International Bargaining: The Occurrence of Bargaining in a Three-Phase Cooperation Framework', *The Journal of Politics*, Vol. 7, No. 2, pp. 719–732.

Bellamy, Richard and Palumbo, Antonino (eds) (2010) *Political Accountability*, Rarnham: Ashgate.

Bengtsson, Rikard (2009) 'An EU Strategy for the Baltic Sea Region: Good Intentions Meet Complex Challenges, Working Paper Nr. 9, Swedish Institute of European Policy Studies, SIEPS.

Bergmann, Annika (2006) 'Adjacent Internationalism. The Concept of Solidarity and Post-Cold War Nordic-Baltic Relations', *Cooperation and Conflict*, Vol. 41, pp. 73–97.

Beyers, Jan and Dierickx, Guido (1998) 'The Working Groups of the Council of the European Union: Supranational or Intergovernmental Negotiations', *Journal of Common Market Studies*, Vol. 36, No. 3, pp. 289–317.

Beyers, Jan and Trondal, Jarle (2004) 'How Nation States 'Hit, Europe: Ambiguity and Representation in the European Union', *West European Politics*, Vol. 27, No. 5, pp. 919–942.

Beyers, Jan (2005) 'Multiple Embeddedness and Socialization in Europe: The Case of Council Officials', *International Organization*, Vol. 59, No. 4, pp. 899–936.

Birkavs, Valdis and Gade, Søren (2010) 'NB8 Wise Men Report', Nordic Council of Ministers.

Bjurulf, Bo and Elgström, Ole (2004) 'Negotiating Transparency: The Role of Institutions', *Journal of Common Market Studies*, Vol. 42, No. 2, pp. 249–269.

Blavoukos, Spyros (2008) 'Negotiating in Stages: National Positions and the Reform of the Stability and Growth Pact', *European Journal of Political Research*, Vol. 47, No. 2, pp. 247–267.

Blavoukos, Spyros and Pagoulatos, George (2009) 'Is there a 'South Bloc' in the EU Economic Governance Negotiations?' University of Athens, Conference Paper for the Workshop at Robert Schuman Centre for Advanced Studies, 25–28 March.

Blavoukos, Spyros; Pagoulatos, George (2011) 'Accounting for Coalition-Building in the European Union: Budget Negotiations and South', *European Journal of Political Research*, Vol. 50, No. 4, pp. 559–581.

Bostok, David (2002) 'COREPER Revisited', *Journal of Common Market Studies*, Vol. 40, No. 2, pp. 215–234.

Broman, Matilda (2009) 'Taking Advantage of Institutional Possibilities and Network Opportunities: Analyzing Swedish Strategic Action in EU Negotiations', PhD Thesis, Lund University.

Browning, Christopher (2007) 'Branding Nordicity: Models, Identity and the Decline of Exceptionalism', *Cooperation and Conflict*, Vol. 42, No. 1, pp. 27–51.

Börzel, Tanja (2010) 'European Governance: Negotiation and Competition in the Shadow of Hierarchy', *Journal of Common Market Studies*, Vol. 48, No. 2, pp. 191–219.

Cameron, Fraser (2005) 'The EU and International Organizations: Partners in Crisis Management', EPC Issue Paper No. 41, Brussels, European Policy Centre.

Carrera, Sergio and Merlino, Massimo (2010) 'Assessing EU Policy on Irregular Immigration under the Stockholm Programme', CEPS Papers on Liberty and Security.

Cassarino, Jean-Pierre (2011) 'Beyond Asymmetries: Cooperation on Readmission in the EU Neighborhood', Conference Paper, EUSA, Boston, 3–5 March.

Checkel, Jeffrey T. (2001) 'Why Comply? Social Learning and European Identity Change', *International Organization*, Vol. 55, No. 3, pp. 553–588.

Checkel, Jeffrey T. (2002) 'Persuasion in International Institutions, ARNENA Working Papers WP 02-14, http://www.arena.uio.no/publications/wp02_14.htm, accessed 30 October 2010.

Checkel, Jeffrey T. (2005) 'International Institutions and Socialization in Europe: Introduction and Framework', *International Organization*, Vol. 59, No. 4, pp. 801–826.

Cede, Franz (2004) 'The EU as the Epitome of a Negotiation Process', in Meerts, Paul and Cede, Franz (eds), *Negotiating European Union*, Gordonsville: Palgrave Macmillan.

Cini, Michelle (2011) 'European Governance and the Democratic Deficit: Where does Power Lie in the EU', *Political Insight, Political Studies Association*, No. 4, pp. 13–15.

Clark, William R.; Duchesne, Erick and Meunier, Sophie (2000) 'Domestic and International Asymmetries in United States-European Trade Negotiations', *International Negotiation*, Vol. 5, No. 1, pp. 69–95.

Costa, Oriol (2008) 'Is Climate change changing the EU? The Second Image Reversed in Climate Politics', *Cambridge Review of International Affairs*, Vol. 21, No. 4, pp. 527–544.

Craig, P. (2010) The Lisbon Treaty. Law, Politics, and Treaty Reform, Oxford University Press.

Degrand-Guillaud, Anne (2009) 'Actors and Mechanisms of EU Coordination at the UN', *European Foreign Affairs Review*, Vol. 14, No. 3, pp. 405–430.

Delreux, Tom (2009a) 'The EU Negotiates Multilateral Environmental Agreements: Explaining the Agents' Discretion', *Journal of European Public Policy*, Vol. 16, No. 5, pp. 719–737.

Delreux, Tom (2009b) 'Cooperation and Control in the European Union', *Cooperation and Conflict*, Vol. 44, No. 2, pp. 189–208.

Dudley, Geoffrey; Richardson, Jeremy (1999) 'Competing Advocacy Coalitions and the Process of 'Frame Reflection': A Longitudinal Analysis of EU Steel Policy', *Journal of European Public Policy'*, Vol. 6, No. 2, pp. 225–248.

Dluhosch, Barbara and Ziegler, Nikolai (2008) 'The Paradox of Weakness in International Trade Negotiations',at http://www.wu.ac.at/europainstitut/noeg/dluhosch_ziegler_s2.3-4, accessed 13 March 2010.

Dupont, Christophe (1994) 'Coalition Theory: Using Power to Build Cooperation', in Zartman, William (ed), *International Multilateral Negotiations. Approaches to the Management Complexity*, Chapter 7, San Francisco: Jossey-Bass.

Dür, Andreas (2008) 'Bargaining Power and Trade Liberalization: European External Trade Policies in 1960s', *European Journal of International Relations*, Vol. 14, No. 4, pp. 645–669.

Dür, Andreas and Mateo, Gemma (2004) 'Treaty-Making in the European Union: Bargaining, Issue Linkage, and Efficiency', *European Integration online Paper*, Vol. 8, No. 18, pp. 1–18, http://eiop.or.at/eiop/pdf/2004-018.pdf, accessed 13 October 2009.

Dür, Andreas and Mateo, Gemma (2010a) 'Bargaining Power and Negotiation Tactics: Negotiations on the EU´s Financial Perspective, 2007–2013', *Journal of Common Market Studies*, Vol. 48, No. 3, pp. 557–578.

Dür, Andreas and Mateo, Gemma (2010b) 'Choosing a Bargaining Strategy in EU Negotiations: Power, Preferences and Culture', *Journal of European Public Policy*, Vol. 17, No. 5, pp. 680–693.

Dür, Andreas; Mateo, Gemma and Thomas, Daniel (2010c) 'Negotiation Theory and the EU: The State of Art', *Journal of European Public Policy*, Vol. 17, No. 5, pp. 613–618.

Elgström, Ole and Jönsson, Christer (2000) 'Negotiation in the European Union: Bargaining or Problem Solving?' *Journal of European Politics*, Vol. 7, No. 5, pp. 684–704.

Elgström, Ole; Bjuruf, Bo; Johansson, Jonas and Sannerstedt, Anders (2001) 'Coalitions in European Union Negotiations'. *Scandinavian Political Studies*, Vol. 24, No. 2, pp. 111–128.

Elgström, Ole and Jönsson, Christer (2004) *European Union Negotiations: Processes, Networks and Institutions*, UK: Stratford Books.

Elster, Jon (1998) *Deliberative Democracy*, Cambridge: Cambridge University Press.

Emmanouilidis, Janis (2007) 'A Differentiated Europe – 12 Thesis', Discussion Paper, The Center for Applied Policy Research, Munich.

Faure, Guy Olivier (2002) 'International Negotiation: the Cultural Dimension', in Kremenyuk, Victor A. (ed), *International Negotiation: Analysis, Approaches, Issues*, 2nd ed., pp. 392–415, San Francisco: Jossey–Bass.

Fearon, James (1995) 'Rationalist Explanations for War', *International Organization*, Vol. 49, No. 3, pp. 379–414.

Fearon, James (1998) 'Bargaining, Enforcement and International Cooperation', *International Organization*, Vol 52, No. 2, pp. 269–305.

Filzmoser, Michael and Vetschera, Rudolf (2008) 'A Classification of Bargaining Steps and Their Impact on Negotiation Outcomes', *Group Decision and Negotiation*, Vol. 17, No. 5, pp. 421–443, http://www.springerlink.com/content/y473m69037735658/fulltext.pdf, accessed 27 October 2010.

Finke, Daniel (2009) 'Challenges to Intergovernmentalism: An Empirical Analysis of EU Treaty Negotiations since Maastricht', *West European Politics*, Vol. 32, No. 3, pp. 466–495.

Fisher, Roger and Ury, William (1981) *Getting to Yes: Negotiating Agreement without Giving In*, London: Hutchinson Business.

Fouilleux, Eves; Maillard de Jacques and Smith, Andy (2005) 'Technical or Political? The Working Groups of the EU Council of Ministers', *Journal of European Public Policy*, Vol. 12, No. 4, pp. 609–623.

Gehring, Thomas and Oberthür, Sebastian (2009) 'The Causal Mechanisms of Interaction between International Institutions', *European Journal of International Relations*, Vol. 15, No. 1, pp. 125–156.

Goldmann, Kjell and Sjöstedt, Gunnar (1979) Power, Capabilities, Interdependence. Problems in the Studies of International Influence, London and Beverly Hills: SAGE.

Golub, Jonathan (1999) 'In the Shadow of the Vote? Decision-Making in the European Community', *International Organization*, Vol. 53, No. 4, pp. 733–766.

Golub, Jonathan (2012) 'Cheal Dates and the Delusion of Gratification: Are Votes Sold or Traded in the EU Council of Ministers?, *Journal of European Public Policy*, Vol.19, No.2, pp. 141–160.

Grobe, Christian (2010) 'The Power of Words: Argumentative Persuasion in International Relations', *European Journal of International Relations*, Vol. 16, No. 1, pp. 5–29.

Habeeb, William Mark (1988) Power and Tactic in International Negotiations: How Weak Nations Bargain with Strong Nations, Baltimore: Johns Hopkins University Press.

Hagemann, Sara and Hoyland, Bjorn (2008) 'Parties in the Council', *Journal of European Public Policy*, Vol. 15, No. 8, pp. 1205–1221.

Hall, Peter and Taylor, Rosemary (1996) 'Political Science and the Three New Institutionalisms', *Political Studies*, XLIV, pp. 936–957.

Haug, Constance and Bergkhout, Frans (2010) 'Learning the Hard Way. European Climate Policy after Copenhagen', *Environment Magazine*, Vol. 52, No. 3, pp. 21–27.

Hayes-Renshaw, Fiona and Wallace, Helen (2006) *The Council of Ministers*, 2nd ed., Basingstoke: Palgrave Macmillan.

Heisenberg, Dorothee (2005) 'The Institution of Consensus in the European Union: Formal Versus Informal Decision-Making in the Council', *European Journal of Political Research*, Vol. 44, No. 1, pp. 65–90.

Heisenberg, Dorothee (2008) 'How should We Best Study the Council of Ministers?' in Naurin, Daniel and Wallace, Helen (eds), *'Unveiling the Council of the European Union. Games Governments Play in Brussels'*, pp. 261–276, New York: Palgrave Macmillan.

Hix, Simon (1999) 'Dimensions and Alignments in European Union Politics: Cognitive Constraints and Partisan Responses', *European Journal of Political Research*, Vol. 35, No. 1, pp. 69–106.

Hix Simon (2005) *The Political System of the European Union,* Basingstoke: Palgrave Macmillan.

Hix, Simon (2008) *What's Wrong with the European Union and How to Fix It?* Cambridge and Malden, MA: Polity Press.

Hofmann, Herwig (2009) 'Legislation, Delegation and Implementation under the Treaty of Lisbon: Typology Meets Reality', *European Law Journal*, Vol.15, No. 4, pp. 482–505.

Hopmann, P. Terrence (1996) *The Negotiation Process and the Resolution of International Conflicts*, Columbia: University Press of South Carolina.

Hosli, Madeleine (1996) 'Coalitions and Power: Effects of Qualified Majority Voting on the Council of the European Union', *Journal of Common Market Studies*, Vol. 3, No. 2, pp. 255–273.

Hosli, Madeleine (1999) 'Power, Connected Coalitions, and Efficiency: Challenges to the Council of the European Union', *International Political Science Review*, Vol. 20, No. 4, pp. 371–391.

Hosli, Madeleine and Arnold, Christine (2007) 'The Importance of Actor Cleavages in Negotiating the European Constitutional Treaty', European Governance Papers, No. C-07-03.

Hosli, Madeleine; Mattila, Mikko and Uriot, Mark (2009) 'Voting Behaviour in the Council of the European Union After the 2004 Enlargement', EUSA, Conference Paper, Los Angelos 23–25 April.

Hug, Simon and König, Thomas (2002) 'In View of Ratification: Governmental Preferences and Domestic Constrains at the Amsterdam Intergovernmental Conference', *International Organization,* Vol. 56, No. 2, pp. 447–476.

Jobse, Johanna (2010) 'The Benelux Union and the Visegrad Group Inside the European Union: Dealing with Environment and Climate Change', Master Thesis, Central European University, Budapest.

Joenniemi, Pertti (2009) 'The EU Strategy for the Baltic Sea Region: A Catalyst for What?' Danish Institute for International Studies, Brief.

Jönsson, Christer (2002) 'Diplomacy, Bargaining and Negotiation', in Carlsnaes, Walter; Risse, Thomas and Simmons, Beth A. (eds), *Handbook of International Relations*, pp. 212–234, London: SAGE.

Jönsson, Christer and Strömvik, Maria (2004) 'Negotiation in Networks', in Elgström, Ole and Jönsson, Christer (eds), *European Union Negotiations: Processes, Networks and Institutions,* pp. 117–129, London: Routledge.

Juknys, Romualdas; Miskins, Vaclovas and Dagiliute, Renata (2005) 'New Eastern EU Member States: Decpupling of Environmental Impact from Fast Economy Growth', *Environment Research, Engineering and Management,* Vol. 34, No. 4, pp. 68–76.

Kaeding, Michael and Selck, Torsten (2005) 'Mapping Out Political Europe: Coalition Patterns in EU Decision-Making', *International Political Science Review*, Vol. 26, No. 3, pp. 271–290.

Kapstein, Ethan Barnaby (1992) 'Between Power and Purpose: Central Bankers and the Politics of Regulatory Convergence', *International Organization*, Vol. 46, No. 1, pp. 265–288.

Kassim, Hussein (2001) The National Coordination of EU Policy: The European Level, Oxford: Oxford University Press

Keohane, Robert (1971) 'The Big Influence of Small Allies', *Foreign Policy*, Vol. 1, No. 2, pp. 161–182.

Keohane, Robert (1989) 'Power and Interdependence'. (2nd ed) Harvard University.

Keohane, Robert and Nye, Joseph (1989) *Power and Interdependence: World Politics in Transition*, 2nd ed., Boston: Little Brown.

Klemenčič, Manja (2005) 'EU Governments' Collective Strategies in 2002–2004 Institutional Reform Negotiations', Paper delivered at the Graduate Workshop on The Constitutional Treaty: Anatomy, Analysis and Assessment, Institut d'Etudes Politiques de Paris, 7–8 July.

Klemenčič, Manja (2011) 'Formal Intergovernental Alliances in the European Union: Dissapearing or Still Alive?', Conference paper, EUSA, 3–4 March.

König, Thomas and Bräuninger, Thomas (1998) 'The Formation of Policy Networks: Preferences, Institutions, and Actors' Choice of Information and Exchange Relations', *Journal of Theoretical Politics,* Vol. 10, No. 4, pp. 445–471.

Laatikainen, Katie Verlin (2003) 'Norden's Eclipse. The Impact of the European Union's Common Foreign and Security Policy on the Nordic Group in the United Nations', *Cooperation and Conflict,* Vol. 38, No. 4, pp. 409–441.

Lehtonen, Tiia (2009) 'Small Sates – Big Negotiations. Decision-Making Rules and Small State Influence in EU Treaty Negotiations', PhD Thesis, European University Institute.

Leydon, Kevin (2009) 'The Swedish Presidency and the Stockholm Programme', Comment in the www.iiea.com (16.07.2009), accessed 10 May 2011.

Lewis, Jeffrey (2000) 'The Methods of Community in EU Decision-Making and Administrative Rivalry in the Councils Infrastructure', *Journal of European Public Policy,* Vol. 7, No. 2, pp. 261–289.

Lewis, Jeffrey (2003) 'Informal Integration and the Supranational Construction of the Council', *Journal of European Public Policy,* Vol. 10, No. 6, pp. 996–1019.

Lewis, Jeffrey (2005) 'The Janus Face of Brussels: Socialization and Everyday Decision Making in the European Union', *International Organization,* Vol. 59, No. 4, pp. 937–971.

Lewis, Jeffrey (2010) 'How Institutional Environments Facilitate Cooperative Negotiation Styles in EU Decision-Making', *Journal of European Policy,* Vol. 17, No. 5, pp. 648–664.

Limonard, Bastiaan and Piepenbrink-Lagerwaard, Mirjam (2010) 'Policy Review on Strengthening European Cooperation and the Position of the Netherlands', IOB, (forthcoming).

Lindstrøm, Channe (2005) 'European Union Policy on Asylum and Immigration. Addressing the Root Causes of Foreign Migration: A Justice and Home Affairs Policy of Freedom, Security and Justice?' *Social Policy and Administration,* Vol. 39, No. 6, pp. 587–605.

Lukes, Steven (1974) *Power: A Radical View,* London, Basingstoke: Macmillan Press.

Majone, Giandomenico (2009) *Europe as the Would-Be World Power,* Cambridge: Cambridge University Press.

Manners, Ian (2002) 'Normative Power Europe: A Contradiction in Terms?' *Journal of Common Market Studies,* Vol. 40, No. 2, pp. 235–258.

March, James G. and Olsen, Johan P. (1998) 'The Institutional Dynamics of International Political Orders', *International Organization,* Vol. 52, No. 4, pp. 943–969.

March, James G. and Olsen, Johan P. (2009) 'The Logic of Appropriateness', ARENA Working Papers, 04/09, University of Oslo.

Mattila, Mikko; Lane, Jan-Erik (2001) 'Why Unanimity in the Council? A Roll-Call Analysis of Council Voting', *European Union Politics,* Vol. 2, No. 1, pp. 31–52.

Mattila, Mikko (2004) 'Contested Decisions: Empirical Analysis of Voting in the European Union Council of Ministers', *European Journal of Political Research,* Vol. 43, No. 1, pp. 29–50.

Mattila, Mikko (2009) 'Roll Call Analysis of Voting in the EU Council of Ministers after the 2004 Enlargement', *European Journal of Political Research,* Vol. 48, No. 6, pp. 840–857.

McKibben, Heather Elko (2010) 'Issue Characteristics, Issue Linkages, and States' Choice of Bargaining Strategies in the European Union', *Journal of European Public Policy*, Vol. 17, No. 5, pp. 694–707.

Meerts, Paul and Cede, Franz (eds) (2004) *Negotiating European Union*, Houndsmills: Palgrave Macmillan.

Meunier, Sophie (2000) 'What Single Voice? European Institutions and EU-US Trade Negotiations', *International Organization*, Vol. 54, No. 1, pp. 103–135.

Miles, Lee (2010) 'The Swedish Presidency', *Journal of Common Market Studies*, Vol. 48, No. s1, pp. 81–93.

Milner, Helene (1992) 'International Theories of Cooperation among Nations: Strengths and Weakness', *World Poltics*, Vol. 44, No. 3, pp. 466–496.

Moravcsik, Andrew (1993) 'Preferences and Power in the European Community: A Liberal Intergovernmental Approach', *Journal of Common Market Studies*, Vol. 31, No. 4, pp. 474–513.

Moravcsik, Andrew (1997) 'Taking Preferences Seriously: A Liberal Theory of International Politics', *International Organization*, Vol. 51, No. 4, pp. 513–553.

Moravcsik, Andrew (1998) The Choice for Europe: Social Purpose and State Power from Messina to Maastricht, Ithaca, NY: Cornell University Press.

Moravcsik, Andrew (1999) 'Theory and Method in the Study of International Negotiation: A Rejoinder to Oran Young', *International Organization*, Vol. 53, No. 4, pp. 811–814.

Moravcsik, Andrew and Nikolaïdis, Kalypso (1999) 'Explaining the Treaty of Amsterdam: Interests, Influence, Institutions', *Journal of Common Market Studies*, Vol. 37, pp. 59–85.

Moravcsik, Andrew (2010) 'Liberal Theories of International Relations: A Primer' (unpublished), http://www.princeton.edu/~amoravcs/, accessed 20 May 2010.

Moravcik, Andrew and Schimmelfennig, Frank (2009) 'Liberal Intergovernmentalism', in Diez, Thomas and Wiener, Antje (eds) *'European Integration Theory'*, Oxford: Oxford University Press.

Morin, Jean-Frederic; Gold, Richard, E. (2010) 'Consensus-Seeking, Distrust and Rhetorical Entrapment: The WTO Decision on Access to Medicines', *European Journal of International Relations,* No.16, pp. 563–587.

Mouritzen, Hans (1995) 'The Nordic Model as a Foreign Policy Instrument: Its Rise and Fall', *Journal of Peace Research*, Vol. 32, No. 1, pp. 9–21.

Musial, Kazimierz (2009) 'Reconstructing Nordic Significance in Europe on the Threshold of the 21st Century', *Scandinavian Journal of History*, Vol. 34, No. 3, pp. 286–306.

Naturvårdsverket (2006) 'The Integration of LULUCF in the EU's Emission Trading Scheme', Report 5625. http://www.naturvardsverket.se, accessed 15.02.2011.

Naurin, Daniel (2008) 'Coalition-Building in International Multilateral Negotiations. Party Ideology, National Interests and In-Group Bias in the Council of the European Union', Working Paper, Department of Political Sciences, Gothenburg University.

Naurin, Daniel and Lindahl, Rutger (2007) 'Network Capital and Cooperation Patterns in the Working Groups of the Council of the EU', EUI Working Paper, RSCAS 2007/14.

Naurin, Daniel and Lindahl, Rutger (2008) 'East-North-South: Coalition Building in the Council before and after Enlargement', in Naurin, Daniel and Wallace, Helen (eds) *Unveiling the Council of the European Union: Games Governments Play in Brussels*, pp. 66–78, Basingstock: Palgrave Macmillan.

Naurin, Daniel and Wallace, Helen (2008) Unveiling the Council of the European Union. Games Governments Play in Brussels, New York: Palgrave Studies.

Nedergaard, Peter (2007) 'Blocking Minorities: Networks and Meaning in the Opposition Against the Proposal for a Directive on Temporary Work in the Council of Ministers of the European Union', *Journal of Common Market Studies*, Vol. 45, No. 3, pp. 695–717.

Nedergaard, Peter (2008) 'Coordination Process in International Organizations: The EU at the International Labour Conference in 2005', *European Integration online Paper*, Vol. 12, No. 3, pp. 2–19.

Nedergaard, Peter (2009) 'Policy Learning Processes in International Committees. The Case of the Civil Servant Committees of the Nordic Council of Ministers', *Public Management Review*, Vol. 11, No. 1, pp. 23–37.

Niemann, Arne and Mak, Jeannette (2010) '(How) do Norms guide Presidency Behavior in EU Negotiations?' *Journal of European Public Policy*, Vol. 17, No. 5, pp. 727–742.

North, Douglass (1990) *Institutions, Institutional Change and Economic Performance*, Cambridge: Cambridge University Press

North, Douglas C. 1991. Institutions, *Journal of Economic Perspectives* 5(1): 97–112.

Novak, Stéphanie (2010) 'Decision Rules, Social Norms and the Expression of Disagreement: The Case of Qualified Majority Voting in the Council of the European Union', *Social Science Information*, Vol. 49, No. 1, pp. 83–97.

Odell, John (2000) *Negotiating the World Economy*, Ithaca, NY: Cornell University Press.

Odell, John (2010) 'Three Islands of Knowledge about Negotiation in International Organizations', *Journal of European Policy*, Vol. 17, No. 5, pp. 619–632.

Panke, Diana (2010) '*Small States in the European Union. Coping with Structural Disadvantages*', Ashgate, 2010.

Parker, Charles and Karlsson, Christer (2010) 'Climate Change and the European Union's Leadership Moment: An Inconvenient Truth?' *Journal of Common Market Studies*, Vol. 48, No. 4, pp. 923–943.

Peers, Steve (2008) 'Legislative Update: EU Immigration and Asylum Competence and Decision-Making in the Treaty of Lisbon', *European Journal of Migration Law*, Vol. 10, Nr. 2, pp. 219–247.

Ploeg, Carin (2008) 'The Distribution of Power in the Council of the European Union', Working Paper, University of Amsterdam.

Pollack, Mark (2006) 'Rational Choice and EU Politics', Working Paper No. 12, ARENA, http://www.ar ena.uio.no, accessed 5.11.2010.

Powell, Robert (1999) In the Shadow of Power: States and Strategies in International Politics, Princeton, NJ: Princeton University Press.

Putnam, Robert (1988) 'Diplomacy and Domestic Politics: The Logic of Two-Level Game', *International Organization*, Vol. 42, No. 3, pp. 427–460.

Quaglia, Lucia (2008) 'Completing the Single Market in Financial services: An Advocacy Coalition Framwork', SEI Working Paper Nr.102.
Raunio, Tapio and Wiberg, Matti (1998), 'Winners, Losers in the Council: Voting Power Consequences of EU Enlargement', *Journal of Common Market Studies*, Vol. 36, No. 4, pp. 549–562.
Reynaud, Julien; Lange, Fabien; Gatarek, Lukasz and Thimann, Christian (2008) 'Proximity in Coalition Building'. EconPapers, 24 June.
Risse, Thomas (2000) 'Let's Argue! Communicative Action in World Politics', *International Organization*, Vol. 54, No. 1, pp. 1–39.
Risse, Thomas (2005) 'Social Constructivism and European Integration', in Wiener, Antje and Diez, Thomas (eds), *European Integration Theory*, pp. 159–175, Oxford: Oxford University Press.
Risse, Thomas and Kleine, Mareike (2010) 'Deliberation in negotiations', *Journal of European Public Policy,* Vol. 17, No. 5, pp. 708–726.
Rood, J.Q.T (1997) 'Benelux: The Benefits and Necessity of Enhanced Cooperation', Advisory Council of International Affairs, Report No. 53.
Roozendaal, Peter; Hosli, Madeleine and Heetman, Caspar (2008) 'Coalitions in the Council of the European Union'. Workshop Paper, Leiden University, 25 January.
Rudi, Ülo (2009) 'The EU Energy and Climate Policy Impacts the Future Energy Mix in Estonia', *Estonian Academy Publishers*, Vol. 26, No. 3, pp. 185–188.
Saam, Nicole and Sumpter, David (2009) 'Peer Selection in EU Intergovernmental Negotiations', *Journal of European Public Policy*, Vol. 16, No. 3, pp. 356–377.
Schelling, Thomas (1960) *The Strategy of Conflict*, Cambridge, MA: Harvard University Press.
Schiff, Amira (2007) 'Pre-Negotiation and its Limits in Ethno-National Conflicts: A Systematic Analysis of Process and Outcomes in the Cyprus Negotiations', *International Negotiation*, Vol. 13, No. 3, pp. 387–412.
Schild, Joachim (2010) 'Mission Impossible? The Potential for Franc-German Leadership in the Enlarged EU', *Journal of Common Market Studies*, Vol. 48, No. 5, pp. 1367–1390.
Schimmelfennig, Frank (2000) 'International Socialization in the New Europe: Rational Action in an Institutional Environment', *European Journal of International Relations*, Vol. 6, No. 1, pp. 109–139.
Schimmelfennig, Frank (2001) 'The Community Trap: Liberal Norms, Rhetorical Action, and the Eastern Enlargement of the European Union'*, International Organization*, Vol. 55, No. 1, pp. 47–80.
Schimmelfenning, Frank (2005 a) 'Liberal Intergovernmentalism', in Wiener, Antje and Diez Thomas (eds), *European Integration Theory,* pp. 75–94, Oxford and New York: Oxford University Press.
Schimmelfennig, Frank (2005 b). 'Strategic Calculation and International Socialization: Membership Incentives, Party Constellations, and Sustained Compliance in Central and Eastern Europe', *International Organization*, Vol. 59, No. 4, pp. 827–860.
Schimmelfennig, Frank and Thomas, Daniel (2009) 'Normative Institutionalism and EU Foreign Policy in Comparative Perspective', International Politics, Vol. 46, No. 4, pp. 491–504.

Schneider, Christina J. (2011) 'Weak States and Institutionalized Bargaining Power in International Organizations', *International Studies Quarterly*, No. 55, pp. 1–25.

Schneider, Gerald; Finke, Daniel and Bailer, Stefanie (2010) 'Bargaining Power in the European Union: An Evaluation of Competing Game-Theoretical Models', *Political Studies*, Vol. 58, No. 1, pp. 85–103.

Schure, Paul and Verdun Amy (2008) 'Legislative Bargaining in the European Union: The Divide between Large and Small Member States', *European Union Politics*, Vol. 9, No. 4, pp. 459–486.

Schymik, Carsten and Krumrey, Peer (2009) 'EU Strategy for the Baltic Sea Region. Core Europe in the Northern Periphery?' Working Paper FG 1/08, April, SWP Berlin.

Shell, Richard (1999) Bargaining for Advantage: Negotiation Strategies for Reasonable People, 2nd ed., New York: Penguin Books.

Selck, Torsten J. and Kuipers, Sanneke (2005) 'Shared Hesitance, Joint Success: Denmark, Finland, and Sweden in European Union Policy Process', *Journal of European Public Policy*, Vol. 12, No. 1, pp. 157–176.

Selck, Torsten J. (2006) Preferences and Procedures: European Union Legislative Decision-Making, New York: Springer.

Slapin, Jonathan (2006) 'Who is Powerful? Examining Preferences, Testing Sources of Bargaining Strength at European Intergovernmental Conferences', *European Union Politics*, Vol. 7, No. 1, pp. 51–76.

Smith, Michael E. (2004) Europe's Foreign Security Policy. The Institutionalization of Cooperation, Cambridge : Cambridge University Press.

Smith, Karen E. (2006) 'Speaking with One Voice? European Union Co-ordination on Human Rights Issues at the United Nations', *Journal of Common Market Studies*, Vol. 44, No. 1, pp. 113–137.

Spencer, Thomas; Tangen, Kristian and Korppoo, Anna (2010) 'The EU and the Global Climate Regime: Getting Back in the Game', Briefing Paper No. 55, The Finnish Institute of International Affairs, 25 February, 2010.

Stacey, Jeffrey and Rittberger, Berthold (2003) 'Dynamics of Formal and Informal Institutional Change in the EU', *Journal of European Public Policy*, Vol. 10, No. 6, pp. 858–883.

Starkey, Brigid; Boyer, Mark A. and Wilkenfeld, Jonathan (1999) *Negotiating a Complex World: An Introduction to International Negotiation*, Lanham, MD: Rowman & Littlefield.

Stein, Janice Gross (1989) *Getting to the Table: Process of International Prenegotiation*, Baltimore: Johns Hopkins University Press.

Strods, Heinrihs and Matthew Kott (2002) 'The File on Operation ‚Priboi': A Reassessment of the Mass Deportations of 1949', *Journal of Baltic Studies*, Vol. 33, No. 1 pp. 1–36, http://www.mfa.gov.lv/en/latvia/history/briefing-papers/briefing-paper4, accessed 2.04.2011.

Sundelius, Bengt (1977) 'Trans-Governmental Interactions in the Nordic Region', *Cooperation and Conflict*, Vol. XII, pp. 63–85.

Tallberg, Jonas (2003) European Governance and Supranational Institutions: Making States Comply, London: Routledge.

Tallberg, Jonas (2004) 'The Power of the Presidency: Brokerage, Efficiency, and Distribution in EU Negotiations', *Journal of Common Market Studies*, Vol. 42, No. 5, pp. 999–1022.

Tallberg, Jonas (2006), 'Formal Leadership in Multilateral Negotiations: A Rational Institutionalist Theory', *The Hague Journal of Diplomacy*, Vol. 1, No. 2, pp. 117–141.

Tallberg, Jonas (2007) 'Bargaining Power in the European Council', SIEPS Working Paper 2007:1.

Tallberg, Jonas (2008) 'Bargaining Power in the European Council', *Journal of Common Market Studies*, Vol. 46, No. 3, pp. 685–708.

Tallberg, Jonas and Johansson, Magnus (2008) 'Party Politics in the European Council', *Journal of European Public Policy*, Vol. 15, No. 8, pp. 1222–1242.

Tallberg, Jonas (2010a) 'The Power of the Chair: Formal Leadership in International Cooperation', *International Studies Quarterly*, Vol. 54, No. 1, pp. 241–265.

Tallberg, Jonas (2010b) 'Explaining the Institutional Foundations of European Union Negotiations', *Journal of Common Market Studies*, Vol. 17, No. 5, pp. 633–647.

Tatham, Michael (2010) 'You do What You have to Do? Preference Intensity and Territorial Interest Representation in EU Environmental Affairs', Conference paper, PSA conference, Edinburgh, UK.

Teply, Larry L. (2005) *Legal Negotiations in a Nutshell*, 2nd ed., St. Paul, MN: Thomson West.

Terk, Erik (2010) 'A Completely Different EU Animal in our Backyard', Paper of the Estonian Institute for Future Studies, http://www.tlu.ee/?LangID=5&CatID=3918&ArtID=7808&action=article, accessed 23 February 2011.

Thomas, Daniel C. (2009) 'Explaining the Negotiation of EU Foreign Policy: Normative Institutionalism and Alternative Approaches', *International Politics*, Vol. 46, No. 4, pp. 339–357.

Thomson, Robert and Hosli, Madeleine (2006) 'Who Has Power in the EU? The Commission, Council , Parliament in Legislative Decision-Making', *Journal of Common Market Studies*, Vol. 44, No. 2, pp. 391–417.

Thomson, Robert; Stokman, Frans N.; Achen, Christopher H. and König, Thomas (eds) (2006), *The European Union Decides*, Cambridge: Cambridge University Press.

Thomson, Robert (2009) 'Actor Alignments in the European Union Before and After Enlargement', *European Journal of Political Research*, Vol. 48, No. 6, pp. 756–781.

Thomson, Robert, Resolving Controversies in the European Union: Inputs, Processes and Outputs in Legislative Decision-Making Before and After Enlargement, 2011, Cambridge University Press, 290 p.

Thomson, Robert (2012) 'A New Dataset on Decision-Making in the European Union Before and After the 2004 and 2007 Enlargements (DEUII), Journal of European Public Policy, No.19, Vol.4, pp. 604–622.

Tsebelis, George (1990) *Nested Games: Rational Choice in Comparative Politics*, Berkeley: University of California Press.

United Nations Framework Convention on Climate Change, Article 2. http://unfccc.int/essential_background/convention/background/items/1353.php, accessed 7 March 2010.

Ury, William; Brett, Jeanne M. and Goldberg, Stephen B. (1988) 'Negotiation Fundamentals: Three Approaches to Resolve Disputes. Interests, Rights, and Power', in Ury, William; Brett, Jeanne M. and Goldberg, Stephen B. (eds), *Getting Disputes Resolved,* San Francisco: Jossey-Bass.

Veen, Tim, The Political Economy of Collective Decision-Making, Springer Verlag Berlin Heidelberg, 2011.

Vogler, John (2009) 'Climate Change and EU Foreign Policy: The Negotiation of Burden-Sharing', *International Politics*, Vol. 46, No. 4, pp. 469–490.

Wallace, Helen (2010) 'An Institutional Anatomy and Five Policy Modes', in Wallace, Helen; Pollack, Mark A. and Young, Alasdair R. (eds), *Policy-Making in the European Union,* 6th ed., Chapter 4, Oxford: Oxford University Press.

Wallace, William and Giegerich, Bastian (2010) 'Foreign and Security Policy: Civilian Power Europe and American Leadership', in Wallace, Helen; Pollack, Mark A. and Young, Alasdair R. (eds), *Policy-Making in the European Union,* 6th ed., Chapter 18, Oxford: Oxford University Press.

Warntjen, Andreas (2010) 'Between Bargaining and Deliberation: Decision-Making in the Council of the European Union', *Journal of European Policy*, Vol. 17, No. 5, pp. 665–679.

Wendt, Alexander (1994) 'Collective Identities Formation and the International State', *American Political Science Review*, Vol. 88, No. 2, pp. 384–396.

Wetterberg, Gunnar (2010) 'Förbundstaten Norden', TemaNord:528, Nordiska Ministerrådet.

Widgrén, Mika (2009) 'The Impact of Council Voting Rules on the EU Decision-Making', *CESifo Economic Studies*, Vol. 55, No. 1, pp. 30–56.

Winkler, Michael (1998) 'Coalition-Sensitive Voting Power in the Council of Ministers: The Case of Eastern Enlargement', *Journal of Common Market Studies*, Vol. 36, No. 3, pp. 391–404.

Wolfe, Rebecca and McGinn, Kathleen (2005) 'Perceived Relative Power and Its Influence on Negotiations', *Group Decisions and Negotiations*, Vol. 14, No. 1, pp. 3–20.

Wouters, Jan and Vidal, Maarten (2008) 'Towards a Rebirth of Benelux?' Working Paper No. 2, Leuven Centre for Global Governance Studies.

Zartman, William (1977) 'Negotiation as a Joint Decision-Making Process', *The Journal of Conflic Resolution,* Vol. 21, No. 4, pp. 619–638.

Zartman, William and Berman, Maureen (1982) *The Practical Negotiator*, New Haven: Yale University Press.

Zimmer, Christina; Schneider, Gerald and Dobbins, Michael (2005) 'The Contested Council: Conflict Dimensions of an Intergovernmental EU Institution', *Political Studies*, Vol. 53, No. 2, pp. 403–422.

Policy documents

CIBOD International Yearbook 2011, The European Union's Priorities for the Area of Migration and Asylum, Produced by CIBOD.

Commission Communication of 10.06.2009, COM (2009) 248 'Concerning the European Union Strategy for the Baltic Sea Region', Info-Europa, No. 179.

Commission Communication 10.06.09, COM (2009) 262 'An Area of Freedom, Security and Justice Serving the Citizen', Info-Europa, No. 179.

Commission Publication (2010) 'Climate Change', available at http://ec.europa.eu/clima/publications/docs/factsheet-climate-change_en.pdf, accessed 22 November 2011.

Debate at the European Parliament, 25.11.09, 'Debate in Strasbourg on the Stockholm Programme', Swedish EU Presidency, available at http://www.se2009.eu/en/meetings_news/2009/11/25/debate_in_strasbourg_on_t he_stockholm_programme.html, accessed 11 May 2011.

Directive 2006/123/EC, 'Directive 2006/123/EC of the European Parliament and of the Council of 12 December 2006 on Services in the Internal Market', Official Journal of the European Union, L 376/36.

Estonian Non-paper, January 2009. The Baltic Sea Strategy project.

Estonian position on the Stockholm Programme 2009.

EP Motion for a Resolution, 6.10.200, available at http://www.statewatch.org/stockholm-programme.htm, accessed 13 May 2011.

European Parliament Resolution on a Baltic Sea Region Strategy for the Northern Dimension, 2006/2171(INI), available at http://www.europarl.europa.eu/sides/getDoc.do?type=TA&language=EN&refere nce=P6-TA-2006-0494, accessed 22 March 11.

Ideas for the Baltic Sea strategy, Estonia, July 2008, available at http://www.euroregionbaltic.eu/downloads/file116.pdf, accessed 10 March 2011.

Joint Declaration on the implementation of the EU Strategy for *the Baltic Sea Region, SES2008/141/SES-09, available at http://www.interact-eu.net/downloads/1730/Stockholm_Declaration_regarding_EUSBSR.pdf, accessed 20 September 2009.*

Latvian position on the Stockholm Programme 2009.

Memorandum by the Swedish government, *Regeringens skrivelse* 2009/10:159, available at http://www.sida.se/PageFiles/2323/Regeringens%20skrivelse%20t%20Riksdage n%20EUSBSR.pdf, accessed 30 March 2011.

Metock case (2008) C-127/08, available at http://eur-lex.europa.eu/LexUriServ/LexUriServ.do?uri=CELEX:62008J0127:EN:HTML, accessed 16 May 2011.

Regeringskansliets faktapromemoria (Swedish position) 2008-09:FPM151 EU:s strategi för Östersjöområdet, Regeringskansliet, available at http://www.riksdagen.se/webbnav/index.aspx?nid=251&dok_id=GW06FPM151, accessed 21 March 2011.

Text of the Treaty of Benelux Union (revising the Treaty of BEU from 1958), available at http://www.benelux.int/pdf/pdf_en/act/20080617_nieuwVerdrag_en.pdf, accessed 4 February 2011.

TFEU: Consolidated Reader-Friendly Edition *of the* Treaty on European Union (TEU) *and the* Treaty on the Functioning of the European Union (TFEU) *as amended by the* Treaty of Lisbon (2007), available at http://www.eudemocrats.org/fileadmin/user_upload/Documents/D-Reader_friendly_latest%20version.pdf, accessed 12 February 2009.

Programme developing a Europe that Protects. A Europe based on Responsibility and Solidarity in Immigration and Asylum Matters, Statewatch Observatory, available http://www.statewatch.org/stockholm-programme.htm, accessed 8 May 2011.

Work Programme for the Swedish Presidency of the EU (June 23, 2009) available at www.se2009.eu, accessed 5 July 2011.

Council documents

Council Conclusions 14 December 2007, No. 16616/1/07, available at European Council website http://www.european-council.europa.eu/council-meetings/conclusions.aspx, accessed 21 March 2011.

Council Conclusions 3 February 2009, Annex to No. 7065/09, 'Contribution to the Spring European Council (19–20 March 2009): Further Development of the EU Position on a Comprehensive Post-2012 Climate Agreement', available at http://register.consilium.europa.eu/pdf/en/09/st07/st07065.en09.pdf, accessed 3 March 2011.

Council Conclusions 9 June 2009, Annex to No. 10827, 'Council Conclusions on International Financing for Climate Action', available at http://register.consilium.europa.eu/pdf/en/09/st10/st10827.en09.pdf, accessed 20 January 2011.

Council Conclusions 30 October 2009, No. 15265/1/09 REV1, available at European Council website http://www.european-council.europa.eu/council-meetings/conclusions.aspx, accessed 2 February 2011.

Council Document 18 November 2009, No. 14777/09, available at http://register.consilium.europa.eu/pdf/en/09/st14/st14777.en09.pdf, accessed 5 June 2010.

Council Document 25 November 2009, http://register.consilium.europa.eu/pdf/en/09/cm05/cm05013.en09.pdf , accessed 14 April 2011.

Council Document 23 November 2009, No. 16484/1/09 REV1, Swedish Presidency, available at http://www.se2009.eu/polopoly_fs/1.25686!menu/standard/file/Draft%203%20Rev%20Add%20Stockholm%20Programme%2030%20Novermber%202009.pdf, accessed 8 May 2011.

Council Conclusions 2 December 2009, Annex to No. 17024/09, 'The Stockholm Programme – An Open and Secure Europe Serving and Protecting the Citizens', available at http://register.consilium.europa.eu/pdf/en/09/st17/st17024.en09.pdf, accessed 4 April 2011.

Council Document 10 May 2010, Nr. 9442/10, 'Standing Committee on Operational Cooperation on Internal Security (COSI)', available at http://register.consilium.europa.eu/pdf/en/10/st09/st09442.en10.pdf, accessed 14 January 2011.

Presidency Conclusions, 10 July 2009, Brussels European Council, 18/19 June 2009.

Working Documents for Informal JHA, 15–17 July 2009 (meeting No. 421), 'Preparing the Stockholm Programme: Developing a Europe that Protects', available at http://www.statewatch.org/news/2009/jul/eu-jha-informal-stockholm-wd-1-a-europe-that-protects.pdf, accessed 2 February 2011.

Media and internet sources

Aftenposten, 27 October 2009: *'EU splittet foran det store klimatoppmøtet'*, www.aftenposten.no, accessed 28 October 2009.
Baltic Business News, 26 January 2011, *'Estonia has Behaved Like a Scandinavian Country'*, http://www.balticbusinessnews.com/article/2011/1/26/estonia-has-behaved-like-a-scandinavian-country, accessed 21 February 2010.
Baltic Review, 25 September 2009, *'The EU Gathers Around the Baltic Sea'*, http://baltic-review.com/2009/09/25/the-eu-gathers-around-the-baltic-sea/, accessed 2 February 2011.
BNS, 9.11.2009. *Baltijas regiona konkuretspeja.*
Dagens Industri, 12 December 2010, *'Debatt: Nordiska ministrar – nu går vi före resten av EU'*
Dagens Nyheter, 9 February 2012, *'Möte med risker'*.
Inclusion, 10 July 2005, *'Tiny Estonia Exports e-Government Worldwide'*, http://einclusion.hu/2010-07-05/tiny-estonia-exports-e-government-worldwide/, accessed 1 May 2011.
Euractiv, 14 February 2001, *'Austria Proposes Benelux-Like Alliance for CEECs'*, http://www.euractiv.com/en/enlargement/austria-proposes-benelux-alliance-ceecs/article-110693, accessed 20 January 2011.
EurActiv, 19 May 2005, *'Hague Programme – JHA programme 2005–10'*, http://www.euractiv.com/de/sicherheit/hague-programme-jha-programme-2005-10/article-130657, accessed 8 May 2011.
EurActiv, 5 July 2005, *"Großen Fünf' wollen stärker gegen Einwanderung vorgehen,* http://www.euractiv.com/de/sicherheit/groen-fnf-wollen-strker-gegen-einwanderung-vorgehen/article-141988, accessed 4 Februaty 2011.
EurActiv, 4 November 2008, *'EU mulls Sustainable Baltic Sea Strategy'*, http://www.euractiv.com/en/climate-environment/eu-mulls-sustainable-baltic-sea-strategy/article-176904, accessed 23 March 2011.
EurActiv, 11 Juny 2009, *'Commission Tables Baltic Region Blueprint'*, http://www.euractiv.com/en/climate-environment/commission-tables-baltic-region-blueprint/article-183073, accessed 23 March 2011.
EurActiv, 1 September 2009, *'EU Mulls Immigration Burden-Sharing'*, http://www.euractiv.com/en/mobility/eu-mulls-immigration-burden-sharing/article-184983, accessed 11 May 2011.
EurActiv, 10 September 2009, *'Miliband Calls for EU „Environmental Union" on Climate'*, http://www.euractiv.com/en/climate-change/miliband-calls-eu-environmental-union-climate/article-185312, accessed 17 February 2011.
EurActiv, 29 September 2009, *'Baltic Sea Strategy Seen as Model for Danube, Adriatic'*, http://www.euractiv.com/en/climate-environment/baltic-sea-strategy-seen-model-danube-adriatic/article-185597, accessed 12 March 2011.
EurActiv, 5 October 2009, *'Commission Tables Baltic Region Blueprint'*, http://www.euractiv.com/en/climate-environment/commission-tables-baltic-region-blueprint/article-183073, accessed 11 November 2009.
EurActiv, 27 October 2006, *'Call for G6 to Unite Against Terror'*, http://www.euractiv.com/en/security/call-g6-unite-terror/article-159136, accessed 5 Februaty 2011.

EurAciv, 14 December 2009, *'SwedenRrevives EU Homeland Security Plans'*, http://www.curactiv.com/en/justice/sweden-revives-eu-homeland-security-plans/article-188280, accessed 11 May 2011.

EurActiv, 29 January 2010, *'Germany and Sweden Largest Net Contributors to EU Budget'*, http://www.euractiv.com/en/enlargement/germany-sweden-largest-net-contributors-eu-budget/article-116165, accessed 1 February 2011.

EurActiv, 28 July 2010, *'Einwanderung treibt EU-Bevölkerung über 500 Millionen'*, http://www.euractiv.com/en/node/496723, accessed 5 May 2011.

EUObserver, 13 April 2010, *'Cross Border Macro-Regions Unlikely to Gain Own Funding'*, http://euobserver.com/?aid=29852, accessed 30 March 2011.

EUObserver, 3 July 2009, *'Commission Approves Second Slice of Latvian Loan'*, http://euobserver.com/9/28409, accessed 20 September 2009.

EUObserver, 6 December 2010, *'Nordic Countries Huddle Together as World Gets Bigger'*, http://euobserver.com/886/31329, accessed 12 December 2010.

EU-27watch, July 2010, *'The Netherlands: Firm but Fair Ttowards New EU Member States'*, http://www.eu-27watch.org/?q=system/files/EU-27%20Watch%20No.%209%20-%20Netherlands_Q2.pdf, accessed 2 February 2011.

Euromove, 2010, *'Justice and Home Affairs – the Stockholm Programme'*, http://www.euromove.org.uk/index.php?id=10333, accessed 10 May 2011.

European Parliament, 19 November 2009, *'Article'*, http://www.europarl.europa.eu/sides/getDoc.do?language=en&type=IM-PRESS&reference=20091113STO64424, accessed 12 May 2011.

European Voice, 10 September 2009, *'Europe's Poor Must Not be Forgotten'*, http://www.europeanvoice.com/article/imported/europe-s-poor-must-not-be-forgotten-/65823.aspx, accessed 15 March 2011.

European Voice, 22 October 2009, *'Denmark Urges EU to Maintain Climate-Change Ambition'*, http://www.europeanvoice.com/article/2009/10/denmark-urges-eu-to-maintain-climate-change-ambition/66241.aspx, accessed 10 January 2011.

European Voice, 29 October 2009, *'In the Green Corner,... EU to Finalize Climate Change Position'*,http://w ww.europeanvoice.com/article/imported/in-the-green-corner-/66268.aspx, accessed 14 March 2011.

European Voice, 30 October 2009, *'Carbon credit Compromise Stuck'*, http://topics.europeanvoice.com/topic/about/Global+warming/about/Post-Kyoto+Protocol+negotiations+on+greenhouse+gas+emissions, accessed 15 April 2011.

European Voice, 30 October 2009, *'European Council Settles on Climate Change Figures'*, http://www.europeanvoice.com/article/2009/10/european-council-settles-on-climate-change-figures/66309.aspx, accessed 3 May 2011.

European Voice, 3 December 2009, *'Sweden Calls for Climate Finance Pledge'*, http://www.europeanvoice.c om/article/imported/sweden-calls-for-climate-finance-pledge/66574.aspx, accessed 15 April 2011.

Financial Times, 23 January 2008, *'EU Commission President's Climate Change Speech'*.

Financial Times, 20 July 2009, Stern, Nicholas *'EU Power Struggle Threatens Climate Change Agreement'*,http://www.ft.com/cms/s/0/d84e3c2a-74c3-11de-8ad5-0014 4feabdc0.html, accessed 30 November 2010.

Financial Times, 21 September 2009, Jose Manuel Barroso: *'EU Still Clings to Its Climate Leadership'* http://www.ft.com/cms/s/0/cac5c574-a6b8-11de-bd14-00144feabdc0.html, accessed on 30 November 2010.

Financial Times, 19 October 2009, Harvei, Fiona *'Concession Rises Hopes for Climate Deal'* http://www.ft.com/intl/cms/s/0/45450bde-bcd5-11de-a7ec-00144feab49a.html, accessed 15 October 2010.

Financial Times, 20 October 2009, *'Brown Calls for Steeper Emission Cuts'*, http://www.ft.com/intl/cms/s/0/4207eaf0-bc9d-11de-a7ec-00144feab49a.html, accessed 20 October 2010.

Financial Times, 22 October 2009, *'EU Eyes Ships and Aircraft Climate Deal*' http://www.ft.com/cms/s/0/239abe18-be72-11de-b4ab-00144feab49a.html, accessed 15 December 2010.

Folketinget, 2 October 2009, Letter of Anne-Marie Meldgaard, Parliament of Denmark, to the Chairman of EP Committee on Civil Liberties, Justice and Home Affairs, accessed through Statewatch observatory 9 May 2010.

Hedetoft, Ulf (2006) 'Denmark: Integrating Immigrants into a Homogenous Welfare State', *Migration Information Source MPI*, http://www.migrationinformation.org/Profiles/display.cfm?ID=485, accessed 16 May 2011.

Helsingin Sanomat, 17 September 2009, *'Commission Steps Back from EU Baltic Sea Strategy'*, http://www.hs.fi/english/article/Commission+steps+back+from+EU+Baltic+Sea+strategy/1135249394396, accessed 15 September 2010.

IMF Press Release, 15 December 2008, *'IMF Set to Lend $2.4 Billion to Latvia'*, http://www.imf.org/external/pubs/ft/survey/so/2008/car121908a.htm, accessed 23 February 2011.

IMF Press release, 6 November 2008, *'IMF Agrees $15.7 Billion Loan to Bolster Hungary's Finances'*, http://www.imf.org/external/pubs/ft/survey/so/2008/car110608a.htm, accessed 23 February 2011.

Independent, 21 December 2008, *'Quadro Group Technical Experts Meet in Nicosia'*, http://www.independent.com.mt/news.asp?newsitemid=80388, accessed 17 May 2011.

Interact-eu, (2009),*'EU Macro-Regional Strategies'*, http://www.interact-eu.net/macro_regional_strategies/macro_regional_strategies/283/3921, accessed 21 March 2011.

Justitiedepartament, 2009, Ministry of Justice, http://www.sweden.gov.se/sb/d/1476 accessed 14 June, 2011.

Montroy, Matthias, 15 April 2009, *'Kritik am Stockholm Programm'*, http://www.heise.de/tp/artikel/30/30127/1.html, accessed 8 May 2011.

Norden. News and Events, 10 June 2009, *'Nordic Stamp on EU Baltic Sea Strategy'*, http://www.norden.org/en/news-and-events/news/nordic-stamp-on-eu-baltic-sea-strategy, accessed 2 December 2010.

Öffentliche Sicherheit, 2010, No. 3-4 (BM.I), *'Das Stockholm Programm'*, http://www.bmi.gv.at/cms/BMI_OeffentlicheSicherheit/2010/03_04/start.aspx, accessed 15 March 2011.

Oxford Analytica 31 August 2009 (Forbes), 'E.U. Struggles With Migration Issues', http://www.forbes.com/2009/08/28/eu-migration-mediterranean-business-oxford.html, accessed 5 May 2011.

Press Release, Ministry of Administration and Interior of Romania, 'The Representatives of the Member States of the Salzburg Forum Reiterated the Decision to Support Romania and Bulgaria in View of Joining the Schengen Area', http://www.mai.gov.ro/engleza/index10.htm, accessed 10 March 2011.

Press Release, Ministry of Interior of Czech Republic, 'The Ministerial Meeting of the Salzburg Forum', http://www.mvcr.cz/mvcren/photogallery/the-ministerial-meeting-of-the-salzburg-forum.aspx, accessed 3 April 2011.

Press Release by the European Commission, 28 January 2009, 'Climate Change: Commission Sets out Proposals for Global Pact on Climate Change at Copenhagen', http://europa.eu/rapid/pressReleasesAction.do?reference=IP/09/141&format=HTML&aged=0&language=EN&guiLanguage=en, accessed 11 February 2011.

Press Release by the European Commission, 10 June 09, 'European Commission Outlines its Vision for the Area of Freedom, Security and Justice in the Next Five Years', http://europa.eu/rapid/pressReleasesAction.do?reference=IP/09/894, accessed 14 April 2011.

Press Release, 10 juni 2009, Regeringskansliet, 'Östersjön ska pekas ut som pilotprojekt för EU:s havsmiljöåtgärder', http://www.regeringen.se/sb/d/11983/a/128094, accessed 13 July 2009.

Press Release, 10 juni 2009, Regeringskansliet, 'Cecilia Malmström välkomnar EU:s Östersjöstrategi', http://www.regeringen.se/sb/d/11980/a/128067, accessed on 14 April 2011.

Press Release, 23July 2009, Regeringskansliet, 'Informal Environmental Council', http://www.regeringen.se/sb/d/12063/a/129915, accessed 10 December 2010.

Press Release by the European Commission, 30 September 2008, 'Commissioner Danuta Hübner and Swedish Prime Minister Fredrik Reinfeldt launch debate on EU strategy for Baltic Sea Region', http://europa.eu/rapid/pressReleasesAction.do?reference=IP/08/1430, accessed 22 March 2011.

Press Release, General Affairs Council, 26 October 2009, http://www.consilium.europa.eu/uedocs/cms_data/docs/pressdata/en/gena/110776.pdf, accessed 5 January 2011.

Press Release, 19 January 2011, 'UK Nordic-Baltic summit', http://ukinlatvia.fco.gov.uk/en/news/?view=News&id=537516982, accessed 25 January 2011.

Publication of the UK Parliament, 2009, 'The Stockholm Programme: Home Affairs – European Union Committee', http://www.publications.parliament.uk/pa/ld200809/ldselect/ldeucom/175/17503.htm, accessed 10 May 2011.

Report of the Future Group, June 2008, 'Freedom Security, Privacy – European Home Affairs in an Open World', http://www.bmi.bund.de/cae/servlet/contentblob/128608/publicationFile/8341/European_home_Affairs_executive_summary_en.pdf, accessed 12 May 2011.

Seminar at SIEPS, 10 November 2009, *'The Swedish Presidency: European Perspectives'*, Stockholm, Medelhavsmuseet, http://www.sieps.se/en/publikationer/the-swedish-presidency-european-perspectives- 20093op, participated at the seminar.
Spotlight Europe, No. 2009/08, September 2009, 'Europe Begins at Home. The Ruling in Karlsruhe – Criticism and Praise',http://www.bertelsmann-stiftung.de/cps/rde/xbcr/bst/spotlight%20europe%20-%20 Europe%20begins%20at%20home.pdf, accessed 23 March 2011.
Salzburg Forum, available at: http://www.salzburgforum.org, accessed February 12, 2011.
Swedish government website: www.sweden.gov.se, accessed May 5, 2011.
The Economist, 15 October 2009, *'Bangkok blues'*, http://www.robertlanegreene.com/?p=1 62, accessed 18 November 2009.
The Economist, 20 January 2011, *'David Cameron, Policy Wonk'*, http://www.economist.com/blogs/bagehot/2011/01/britain_and_nordic_world, accessed 20 February 2011.
The Economist, 15 October 2011, *'The Driver and the Passenger. How a Skewed Franco-German Partnership Upsets the Euro'*.
The Economist, 10 December 2011, *'Beware the Merkozy Receipe'*.
Times of Malta, 13 January 2009, *'Quadro Group Report Stresses Solidarity and Burden Sharing'*, http://www.timesofmalta.com/articles/view/20090113/local/quadro-group-report-stresses-solidarity-and-burden-sharing.240515, accessed 17 May 2011.

Speeches

Swedish Minister of EU Affairs Malmström, Cecilia, 12 December 2007, Speech: *'An EU strategy for the Baltic Sea region'*, Starsbourg, http://www.regeringen.se/sb/d/3211/a/94598, accessed on 3 March 2011.
Commissioner Danuta, Hübner, 30 September 2008, Speech: *'EU Strategy for the Baltic Sea Region'*, Stakeholders Conference, Stockholm, http://europa.eu/rapid/pressReleasesAction.do?reference=SPEECH/08/474&format=HTML&aged=0&language=EN&guiLanguage=en, accessed 28 March 2011.
Commissioner Danuta, Hübner, 5 February 2009, Speech: *'The Sea of Opportunity, EU Strategy for the Baltic Sea Region'*, Rostock, http://www.danuta-hubner.pl/komisja/Hubner/ec.europa.eu/commission_barroso/hubner/speeches/pdf/2009/0205_rostock.pdf, accessed 5 December 2010.
Minister Cecilia Malmström, 23 June 2009, Speech: *'On the Baltic Sea Strategy'*, Stockholm, http://www.se2009.eu/en/meetings_news/2009/6/23/speech_by_minister_cecilia_malmstrom_on_the_eu_baltic_sea_strategy.html, accessed 2 March 2011.
Diana Wallis, 18 September 2009, Speech at Stockholm Ministerial Conference, *'On the Baltic Sea Strategy'*, Stockholm, http://dianawallismep.org.uk/en/article/2009/064171/keynote-address-on-the-baltic-sea-strategy, accessed 2 February 2011.

ANNEX

List of interviews

NUMBER	TIME AND PLACE
1	July 6, 2009, Brussels (phone)
2	January 25, 2010, Copenhagen (face-to-face)*
3	January 25, 2010, Copenhagen
4	January 25, 2010, Copenhagen
5	January 26, 2010, Copenhagen
6	January 26, 2010, Copenhagen
7	January 21, 2010, Tallinn
8	January 21, 2010, Tallinn
9	February 15, 2010, Tallinn (written answer)
10	February 15, 2010, Tallinn (written answer)
11	January 21, 2010, Tallinn
12	January 21, 2010, Tallinn
13	January 12, 2010, Helsinki
14	January 12, 2010, Helsinki
15	January 12, 2010, Helsinki
16	January 12, 2010, Helsinki
17	January 12, 2010, Helsinki
18	February 19, 2010, Riga
19	February 18, 2010, Riga
20	November 19, 2009, Riga (by phone)
21	December 11, 2009, Riga
22	December 11, 2009, Riga
23	February 18, 2010, Riga
24	August 19, 2010, Luxembourg (by phone)
25	July 2, 2010, the Hague (by phone)
26	July 2, 2010, the Hague (by phone)
27	November 19, 2009, Stockholm
28	January 22, 2010, Stockholm
29	January 22, 2010, Stockholm
30	December 16, 2009, Stockholm
31	October 23, 2009, Stockholm
32	October 16, 2009, Stockholm
33	January 15, 2010, Stockholm
34	October 23, 2010, Stockholm
35	June 11, 2010, Stockholm
36	January 15, 2010, Stockholm

37	May 31, 2010, Stockholm
38	June 1, 2010, Stockholm
39	June 1, 2010, Stockholm
40	June 7, 2010, Stockholm
41	June 2, 2010, Stockholm
42	June 2, 2010, Stockholm
43	June 8, 2010, Stockholm
44	June 7, 2010, Stockholm
45	June 10, 2010, Stockholm
46	June 16, 2010, Stockholm
47	June 16, 2010, Stockholm
48	June 3, 2010, Stockholm
49	June 17, 2010, Stockholm
50	August 20, 2010, Riga
51	March 3, 2010, Tallinn (by mail)

*All following interviews conducted by face-to-face mode, unless indicated differently.

ANNEX

List of interviews

NUMBER	TIME AND PLACE
1	July 6, 2009, Brussels (phone)
2	January 25, 2010, Copenhagen (face-to-face)*
3	January 25, 2010, Copenhagen
4	January 25, 2010, Copenhagen
5	January 26, 2010, Copenhagen
6	January 26, 2010, Copenhagen
7	January 21, 2010, Tallinn
8	January 21, 2010, Tallinn
9	February 15, 2010, Tallinn (written answer)
10	February 15, 2010, Tallinn (written answer)
11	January 21, 2010, Tallinn
12	January 21, 2010, Tallinn
13	January 12, 2010, Helsinki
14	January 12, 2010, Helsinki
15	January 12, 2010, Helsinki
16	January 12, 2010, Helsinki
17	January 12, 2010, Helsinki
18	February 19, 2010, Riga
19	February 18, 2010, Riga
20	November 19, 2009, Riga (by phone)
21	December 11, 2009, Riga
22	December 11, 2009, Riga
23	February 18, 2010, Riga
24	August 19, 2010, Luxembourg (by phone)
25	July 2, 2010, the Hague (by phone)
26	July 2, 2010, the Hague (by phone)
27	November 19, 2009, Stockholm
28	January 22, 2010, Stockholm
29	January 22, 2010, Stockholm
30	December 16, 2009, Stockholm
31	October 23, 2009, Stockholm
32	October 16, 2009, Stockholm
33	January 15, 2010, Stockholm
34	October 23, 2010, Stockholm
35	June 11, 2010, Stockholm
36	January 15, 2010, Stockholm

37	May 31, 2010, Stockholm
38	June 1, 2010, Stockholm
39	June 1, 2010, Stockholm
40	June 7, 2010, Stockholm
41	June 2, 2010, Stockholm
42	June 2, 2010, Stockholm
43	June 8, 2010, Stockholm
44	June 7, 2010, Stockholm
45	June 10, 2010, Stockholm
46	June 16, 2010, Stockholm
47	June 16, 2010, Stockholm
48	June 3, 2010, Stockholm
49	June 17, 2010, Stockholm
50	August 20, 2010, Riga
51	March 3, 2010, Tallinn (by mail)

*All following interviews conducted by face-to-face mode, unless indicated differently.